TRUE TO LIFE

ENGLISH FOR ADULT LEARNERS

UPPER-INTERMEDIATE

Ruth Gairns
Stuart Redman

TEACHER'S BOOK

CAMBRIDGE
UNIVERSITY PRESS

PUBLISHED BY THE PRESS SYNDICATE OF THE UNIVERSITY OF CAMBRIDGE
The Pitt Building, Trumpington Street, Cambridge, United Kingdom

CAMBRIDGE UNIVERSITY PRESS
The Edinburgh Building, Cambridge CB2 2RU, UK
40 West 20th Street, New York, NY 10011–4211, USA
477 Williamstown Road, Port Melbourne, VIC 3207, Australia
Ruiz de Alarcón 13, 28014 Madrid, Spain
Dock House, The Waterfront, Cape Town 8001, South Africa

http://www.cambridge.org

First published 1998
Fifth printing 2005

Printed in the United Kingdom at the University Press, Cambridge

ISBN 0 521 57481 1 Teacher's Book
ISBN 0 521 57483 8 Class Book
ISBN 0 521 57482 X Personal Study Workbook
ISBN 0 521 57480 3 Class Cassette Set
ISBN 0 521 57479 X Personal Study Workbook Cassette
ISBN 0 521 58943 6 Personal Study Workbook Audio CD

CONTENTS

INTRODUCTION   iv

1 WHAT HAVE WE GOT IN COMMON?   1
2 SLEEPING IT OFF   6
3 HOW DO WE BEHAVE?   11
4 GETTING YOUR MESSAGE ACROSS   17
5 BUILDINGS   24
   PROJECT: WRITING BIOGRAPHIES   30
6 TRAVELLING CAN BE HARD WORK   31
7 HOW DOES IT LOOK?   37
8 ADDRESSING THE ISSUES   43
9 MAKING THE MOST OF YOUR TIME   49
10 TELLING STORIES IN ENGLISH   54
   PROJECT: GROUP MAGAZINE   60
11 EATING OUT   61
12 THEATRICAL INTERLUDE   67
13 ON THE JOB   75
14 ACCIDENTS WILL HAPPEN   81
15 WAYS OF BEING BETTER OFF   87
   PROJECT: EDUCATION IN THE ADULT WORLD   94
16 THAT'S A MATTER OF OPINION   96
17 MANNERS   102
18 WHAT ARE THE ODDS?   109

WORKSHEETS   114
TESTS   130
TEST ANSWER KEYS   140
ACKNOWLEDGEMENTS   143

INTRODUCTION

Who this course is for

True to Life is a five level course designed to take learners from beginner to upper-intermediate level.

The course is specifically designed for adult learners. Topics have been chosen for their interest and relevance to adults around the world, and activities have been designed to provide adults with the opportunity to talk about their experiences, express opinions, use their knowledge and imagination to solve problems and exchange ideas so as to learn from one another.

True to Life Upper-intermediate is for learners who have covered a basic course such as *True to Life Elementary*, *Pre-intermediate* and *Intermediate*. It provides between 60 and 80 hours upwards of classroom activity, depending on the time available and the options used.

Key features

True to Life incorporates the best of current classroom methodology by providing teaching materials to meet the needs of different learners and learning styles, but particular attention has been paid to the following:

1 Learner engagement and personalisation

We believe that learning is more effective when learners are actively engaged in tasks which they find motivating and challenging. Moreover, it is essential for learners to have opportunities to see the relevance of new language to their own personal circumstances. We have, therefore, provided a very large number of open-ended and interactive tasks which allow learners to draw on their knowledge of the world *and* to be creative. These tasks are used not just for fluency work but also in quite controlled tasks designed to activate specific language areas (vocabulary, grammar and functions).

2 Speaking and listening

It has been our experience that adult learners lay great emphasis on oral/aural practice in the classroom, often because it is their only opportunity to obtain such practice. We have, therefore, decided to limit the amount of reading material in the Class Book (but increase it in the Personal Study Workbook) so that we can devote more time and space to speaking and listening. Users should find that opportunities for speaking practice are present in most stages of the lessons.

3 Recycling

We have decided to employ the 'little and often' approach to revision. Instead of sporadic chunks, we have devoted one lesson in every unit to revision. This section is called *Review and development*; it gives learners a chance to review material while it is still relatively fresh

in their minds, and ensures that material from every unit is formally recycled on two separate occasions, excluding the tests in the Teacher's Book. For example:

Unit 10

Lesson 1	*Lesson 2*	*Lesson 3*	*Lesson 4*
input	input	input	Review and development of Units 8 and 9

Unit 11

Lesson 1	*Lesson 2*	*Lesson 3*	*Lesson 4*
input	input	input	Review and development of Units 9 and 10

4 Flexibility

It is important that learners know what they are learning and can see a clear path through the material. It is also important, though, that teachers can adapt material to suit the needs of their particular class. We have provided for this with the inclusion of further activities in the Teacher's Book (called *Options*), and worksheets in the Teacher's Book which may be photocopied. This, then, gives teachers a clear framework in the Class Book, but with additional resources to draw upon in the Teacher's Book for extra flexibility.

5 Vocabulary

In *True to Life*, vocabulary is not treated as a separate section because it forms an intrinsic and fundamental part of every unit, and a wide range of vocabulary activities is included throughout the five levels. Moreover, great importance is attached in these activities to spoken practice of newly presented lexical items, so learners have the opportunity to use new words and phrases in utterances of their own creation.

In the Class Book and, even more so, in the Personal Study Workbook, vocabulary learning skills are introduced and developed, as are activities which make learners more aware of important aspects of word grammar. These include lexical storage and record keeping, contextual guesswork, wordbuilding, collocation and so on.

6 The Personal Study Workbook

This aims to be as engaging on an individual basis as the Class Book is on a group basis. Personalisation is, therefore, carried through to the Personal Study Workbook, which provides a range of activities, both structured and open-ended, designed to motivate learners to continue their learning outside the classroom. *Speaking partners:* The single thing most learners want to practise outside the classroom is speaking; unfortunately, it is often the most difficult to organise. We have, therefore, continued the concept of 'speaking partners' throughout the Personal Study Workbook as in the two previous levels. *Speaking partners* invites learners to find a partner who they meet (or phone) on a regular basis outside the classroom, and practise speaking English with, using ideas and activities suggested in the Workbook.

Components and course organisation

At each level, the course consists of the following:
Class Book and Class Cassette Set
Personal Study Workbook and Personal Study Cassette or Audio CD
Teacher's Book

The Class Book

The Class Book contains 18 units and three projects. Each unit provides three to four hours of classroom activities and is divided into four lessons, with each lesson designed to take approximately one hour, although some may last significantly longer if freer activities are allowed to run their course. Teachers are, of course, free to explore the material in different ways (indeed we have indicated ways of doing this in the following teacher's notes), but each lesson has been designed as a self-contained, logical sequence of varied activities, which can be used as they stand.

The first three lessons contain the main language input. This consists of:
– a clear grammatical syllabus
– an emphasis on lexical development
– key functional exponents
– listening and reading practice
– speaking and writing activities

The final section of each unit provides review and development activities based on the two previous units; e.g. the final section of Unit 4 revises Units 2 and 3; the final section of Unit 5 revises Units 3 and 4.

The Class Book contains three projects, spaced at regular intervals, although they can be used at any time. Each project gives learners the opportunity to practise a range of skills extended over a period longer than a normal lesson. Two of the projects (Writing biographies and Group magazine) involve a number of collaborative tasks, leading to a piece of writing. The third exposes learners to different types of public English exams, which in our experience are of interest at this level.

At the back of the Class Book there is:
– a Language Reference section
– additional material for some of the activities
– the tapescript of the recordings for the Class Book
– a list of irregular verbs
– the phonetic alphabet

The Class Cassette Set

The listening material on the Class Cassette Set is very varied – scripted, semi-scripted and unscripted – and a particular feature is the regular inclusion of dual-level listening texts. These provide two versions of a listening passage, one longer and more challenging than the other.

This feature allows teachers to select the listening material that best meets the needs of their particular learners, but also gives more scope for exploitation. In some cases, the content of the listening in each version is different, so teachers may start with the easier listening and then move on to the more difficult one; in other cases where the content is the same but more challenging, the teacher could (if facilities permit) split the group and give a different listening to different learners. And there is nothing to stop a teacher doing version 1 at one point in the course, and then returning to do version 2 days, weeks or even months later.

The Personal Study Workbook

The Personal Study Workbook runs parallel to the Class Book, providing 18 units which contain further practice and consolidation of the material in the Class Book.

The exercises at the beginning of each unit concentrate on consolidating grammar and vocabulary; later exercises focus on skills development, with a space at the end of each unit for learners to record their problems and progress in English.

The Personal Study Cassette or Audio CD

The Personal Study Cassette or Audio CD provides further material for listening practice, and there is a tapescript at the back of the Workbook along with an answer key for most of the exercises.

The Teacher's Book

This offers teachers a way through the activities presented, but also provides a wide range of ideas that will enable them to approach and extend the activities in different ways. Some of these include worksheets which may be photocopied and distributed in class.

In addition, the Teacher's Book provides:
– guidance on potential language difficulties
– a complete answer key to the exercises in the Class Book
– four photocopiable tests, each test covering a section of the Class Book
– tapescripts of the Class Book recordings

WHAT HAVE WE GOT IN COMMON?

CONTENTS

Language focus: determiners (*both, neither,* etc.)
expressing connections and relationships
expressing worries/concerns
compound adjectives
describing appearance
vocabulary: social issues
ellipsis

Skills: Speaking: finding things in common with other learners
social issues in your country
attitudes to clothes, fashion, etc.
problems when listening to spoken English
Listening: a game – people ask questions to discover
what others have in common
a dictogloss
Reading: European survey of attitudes
Writing: a dictogloss

COMMON FEATURES

Introduction

This first lesson gives learners an opportunity to find out about other members of the group through a variety of activities which require the manipulation of different determiners. This gives you a chance to listen to the group and assess their ability (if this is also your first lesson with the class). An added language focus is a range of ways of expressing connections and relationships, e.g. *Is it anything to do with ...?*. This language is highlighted in a listening passage and then practised in a personalised speaking activity.

Suggested steps

1

Put the learners into pairs, then write the example sentence on the board. Ask the group if they can correct the grammatical error. When you have elicited the sentence *Both of us are very keen on sport,* ask the pairs to decide if this is true of them. If not, how could they change the sentence to make it true? This should produce various permutations (as in the examples in the Class Book), and you could also point out at this early stage that after *neither,* the verb can be singular or plural in informal spoken English, but a singular verb is preferred in written English. The group should then be able to carry on in pairs with the rest of the activity.

Check the grammar mistakes with the group and conduct a short feedback on some of their answers. You may at this point wish to elicit rules about

singular/plural verbs and word order, and put them on the board or refer learners to the Language Reference on page 141.

Answer key

(The facts will depend on your learners.)
Neither of us has ever done anything illegal. (correct)
We both come from a village. OR Both of us come from a village.
Both of us have a lot of spare time. (correct)
We both have to work for a living. OR Both of us have to work.
Both my partner and I can change ... OR My partner and I can both change ...
Neither my partner nor I know(s) anything ... OR Neither of us know(s) ...
Neither one of us is ... (correct, if a little unusual) or Neither of us ...

Option

If you already know the group and, more important, they already know each other, you could adapt the sentences in the Class Book but practise the same language using sentences of your own based on your knowledge of the group. (This could even be sentences based on a previous course with these learners.)

2

Create new groups of four (or three or five, if it is more convenient), and explain the second activity. Impress on them that they should try to find an unusual/interesting fact which is true about all of them.

3 🔊

Play the recording and ask each member of the group to write down the answer. At the end, see which answer is most common. If there is significant disagreement, you may wish to play the recording a second time, but note that they will be listening to the recording again to complete the next exercise, and interest in a listening text can wane if played too many times.

Answer key

Both men have been hospitalised as a result of a football injury.

Tapescript

A: OK, yeah, yeah, we've thought of, we've got something, yeah.

B: Ah, right then. Um, I've got a bit of a feeling actually about this.

C: Have you?

B: Yeah. Does it have anything to do with sport?

A: Yes.

C: Is it, er, in any way connected to the team that you support?

A and D: No.

B: Ah, that's that theory, then.

D: Stumped. That's two questions.

B: That's two questions.

C: Was that a clue? Is it anything to do with cricket?

A: No, that's three questions.

B: Is it anything to do with football?

D: It is, yeah.

B: So, it's to do with football, so, and it's not connected with the team that you support. Is it, erm, to do with the fact that you both play?

D: Sort of ...

A: Yeah, sort of.

C: Is it to do with an injury that may have occurred during playing?

A: Yes, yes, you're on the right track.

B: Is it that you've both broken your leg playing football?

A: No. But you're quite warm.

C: Has it got anything to do with the fact that you have broken a bone of any sort during football?

D: Very very close.

A: So close it's unbelievable, but no.

D: But no.

B: Is it ... is it that while playing football you've each been injured in some way that you couldn't play for a long time, so you might've broken something or sprained something – you've been laid off?

A: Yes.

C: Is that it?

A: Well done. Eight, wasn't it, eight questions?

D: Yes, we've both been hospitalised with football injuries.

B and C: Ahh.

4 🔊

Give learners time to read through the sentence beginnings and ask you questions, then follow the instructions in the Class Book. Learners can check their answers by consulting the tapescript on page 159.

5

If you want the group to complete this activity without referring to the sentence beginnings on the page, drill them, or allow them two or three minutes to repeat and memorise the different patterns. You can then complete Exercise 5. Monitor the games quite carefully to ensure they are reasonably fluent in manipulating the different constructions. Give some feedback at the end. This can include error correction, but remember to give positive feedback as well, and try to concentrate on any additional language items that learners needed but didn't know. These are more likely to be remembered and learners can make use of them at a later date.

6

The lesson has already given you a chance to see how the class operates in pairs and small groups; this final activity is an opportunity to see how they work as a whole class.

To ensure the activity doesn't lose momentum, give the learners a few minutes to prepare sentences, then you can select learners at random to shout out suggestions. Any member of the class who disagrees can challenge the sentence with their reason for doing so. If you wish, you can highlight the singular/plural forms on the board.

Personal Study Workbook

4: Different cultures, common themes: determiners and physical descriptions
7: You are my soul-mate: writing

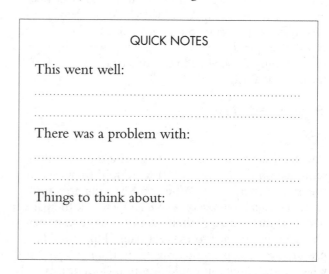

QUICK NOTES

This went well:

....
....

There was a problem with:

....
....

Things to think about:

....
....

Introduction

The text at the centre of this lesson is based on research carried out in Europe. If you work predominantly with learners from different parts of the world, you may feel that the subject matter will not be sufficiently relevant. However, the lesson does introduce and provide opportunities to practise a wide range of common lexical chunks, e.g. *by far the most; ... affects me to some extent; are increasingly worried about ...,* etc.

Suggested steps

1

It is important that learners understand the items in the box as they all appear later in the text. You could work with the whole class and elicit answers from different learners, checking pronunciation along the way.

Before the personalised speaking activity, highlight the target language (*affects me very directly,* etc.) which learners can activate immediately, but also make it very clear that if anyone feels uncomfortable talking about a particular issue, they should say so using the expression given to them, i.e. *I'd rather not discuss that.* Equally, if you as a teacher feel uneasy with any of these topics, move straight to Exercise 2.

2

Work through the sentences, paying special attention to the language in italics, which again represents high-frequency ways of expressing concern. It would be asking a lot for learners to incorporate this language immediately into their spoken English, so this time they only have to complete the gaps and then use the target language in a more controlled way. Don't worry if this seems like an overload of new language at the beginning of the lesson – almost all of it is recycled in the text they are about to read, and post-text activities will provide further opportunities to use some of it.

3

It is important that learners are clear about the source of the opinions expressed in the text, and that is why we have asked them to read the first paragraph and digest it before moving on.

4

The task is just a way to get learners to scan the text in their initial reading and not get too involved in all the details. When the four minutes are up (shorten or lengthen the time if you feel it is necessary or desirable), let the pairs exchange answers while you monitor to see if they have got a good grasp of the information.

5

You could see if learners can answer the questions without referring to the text, and then just scan the text a second time to find the relevant information. Conduct a brief feedback.

Answer key

1. false   2. true   3. true   4. false   5. true

6

This is an opportunity for a general reaction to the text, but you may like to give learners two or three minutes to ask further questions about new language, e.g. *give something a high priority, a lack of (something),* etc.

Personal Study Workbook

6: Does it affect them?: listening

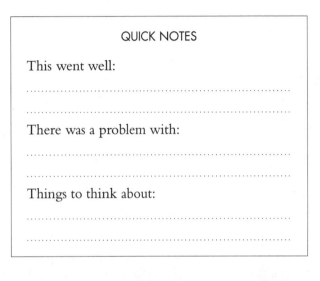

QUICK NOTES

This went well:

....

....

There was a problem with:

....

....

Things to think about:

....

....

SIMILAR BUT QUITE DIFFERENT!

Introduction

The lesson looks at similarities and differences again, but this time the focus is on appearance. A wide range of vocabulary used to describe clothes and appearance is included (the assumption is that learners will already know some / quite a lot of it), and this is then practised in an activity which also draws learners' attention to a common example of ellipsis, before finishing with a personalised exchange of opinion about a range of issues connected with clothes, fashion and appearance.

Suggested steps

1

Learners will be interested to discover who you look like in your family, so you could talk about yourself to start the lesson. If necessary, highlight the phrase *look like (look a bit / quite / just like).* Then put the class into small groups to do the same thing.

Option

You could bring in photos of members of your family if you have them available; and ask learners the day before to bring in photos of their families.

2

Some of the vocabulary will already be known, so you could begin by eliciting the five categories with examples before learners complete the task in pairs. Monitor the activity while they work and in feedback, and help with meaning and/or pronunciation where necessary. Check the validity of their own examples at the end, adding them to the board if you wish.

Answer key

1. Appearance	2. Skin	3. Hair	4. Build	5. Clothes
presentable	clean-shaven	shoulder-length	slim	short-sleeved
well-dressed	wrinkles	straight	average build	polo-neck
scruffy	sun-tanned	curly	well-built	tight-fitting
casual	dark-skinned	wavy	overweight	high-heeled
smart(ish)	freckles	balding	skinny	baggy

3

Ellipsis is extremely common but many learners seem largely unaware of it. This activity draws attention to two forms of ellipsis (see the Language Reference on page 141 of the Class Book if you want a more detailed description), and you may need to highlight them quite carefully and elicit further examples using the pictures. Learners can then put these forms to use in their description of the people in the photographs. At the end, elicit some more examples from the group to assess how they are using the target vocabulary and the forms of ellipsis.

> *Language Point*
> You will need to point out the different stress patterns in these forms. For example:
> so am I   so have I   which I never do
> which I'm not

4

This is quite a long list and many groups will not have time to talk about all of them. You could, therefore, start by asking learners to read through the questions and mark the statements where they have a clear opinion they would like to express. You could then form groups based on their responses and allow them to discuss the statements of their choice. You could monitor the groupwork to collect examples of correct and incorrect language for feedback.

5

This would be very suitable for homework if you are short of time.

Personal Study Workbook

1: Spot the mistake: vocabulary and expressions
2: How do you look?: compound adjectives

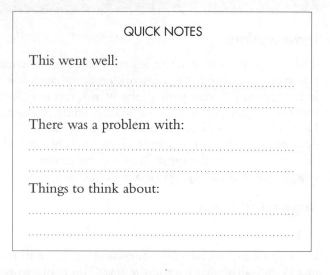

QUICK NOTES

This went well:

....

....

There was a problem with:

....

....

Things to think about:

....

....

DICTOGLOSS

Introduction

The aim of the lesson is to raise awareness about listening in a foreign language: Why is listening difficult? What problems do learners have? What can they do about them? Some of the ideas are incorporated in the tapescript of the dictogloss, others emerge when learners actually do the dictogloss. The final reconstruction of the text is also a very exacting and challenging collaborative writing task.

Suggested steps

1

You could start the list as a whole class and then divide learners up into smaller groups to continue it. At the end, collect all the ideas together, and make a note of the types of listening which are the most difficult.

2

You could ask your learners to read through the different stages of the dictogloss, or you could take the stages one at a time and explain it yourself. Either way, it is vital that the learners are clear about the procedure and don't start complaining when they don't have time to write down everything they hear (as they would in a normal dictation).

3

Follow the different stages set out in Exercise 2. If you sense that the dictogloss is a bit hard, you can obviously pause the cassette a little to allow more time for writing. If it's too easy, try constructing your own dictogloss to take account of the level of the class.

At the end you will have to adjudicate on whether their own versions are in correct or acceptable English and close enough to the original version.

Tapescript

When you are listening to a foreign language, you probably won't worry if there are a *few* new words, but a *lot* of new vocabulary will almost certainly be a major problem. Sometimes though, a speaker may use familiar words and you still don't understand. This may be because they are speaking quickly, or they have an unfamiliar accent. It's also true that it's harder to understand two or three people than just one person, mainly because there are lots of interruptions and people speak over each other. Finally, if you don't know much about the topic of conversation, it's more difficult to follow.

4

Learners will have identified with some of the problems mentioned in the dictogloss, but this is an opportunity for them to elaborate. Monitor their conversation and add the ideas to the board or OHT where everyone can see them.

5 ▭

Play the recording and check the answers. At the same time, try to elicit any particular problems learners had in understanding the speakers. Write them on the board. Are there many differences between the problems mentioned on the recording and those discussed by the class? If so, can you account for this?

No one should expect any simple answers to the questions posed in this lesson, but developing a more acute awareness of some of the problems is an important step forward.

Tapescript

JACQUI: I don't know about you two, but I find it almost impossible, when I'm speaking on my mobile phone, to understand what the other person is saying to me if they're speaking a foreign language. For instance, I live in France, and when I'm phoning someone to ask for the train times or if I'm anywhere but in a room on my own, so if I'm in a café, if I'm on the street, I just can't understand, I can't understand what they're saying, it's so difficult.

LINFORD: Yeah, I know what you mean. I mean, I find it really difficult to understand people on the phone because you can't see their movements, their gestures or their expressions, so if you're not quite sure of what they're saying, it's just that much harder to, to take on board, because you can't see anything. (Hm ... very difficult) But, erm, yeah, it's ... but ... and also speakers that don't speak clearly – you know, mumble or just speak very quietly. It's so frustrating because you want to ask them to speak up.

KATHERINE: Yes, and they have to repeat it so many times ... and I have a problem, when someone's telling a story, but they don't start at the beginning and go on to the end, they keep going backwards and forwards. (Yeah) That's very difficult.

JACQUI: Yes, so you don't know whether they're saying it *has* happened, it *might* happen, it

will happen. (Hmm) And also when people, when someone's telling you a story, and you're really interested, and then suddenly, they go off the point and they start talking about something else, and you think, 'Is it me? You know, have I misunderstood?' I think when you're having to concentrate like that, it's very, very difficult when they start talking about something else.

KATHERINE: I think it's difficult to concentrate for a long time. I can only really manage a short burst of listening, and then my mind wanders. (Yeah)

JACQUI: Yes, I think it's very tiring listening to a foreign language for a long time. (Yeah)

6

We have given one or two ideas to start the discussion, but you can take it much further, i.e. not just different forms of listening, but also strategies learners might use with these forms. For example, in face-to-face situations, encourage learners to ask for repetition or clarification if they don't understand. Common sentences include:
Could you repeat that, please?
Sorry, I'm not quite with you.
Could you explain that again, please?
I'm sorry, I didn't quite follow that.
etc.
When using tapes, make use of transcripts to help to identify problems, but not until learners have listened without the aid of a transcript; etc.

Option

If you would like to incorporate dictogloss into your teaching, you should refer to *Grammar Dictation* by Ruth Wajnryb (OUP), for a wealth of texts and ideas at different levels.

Personal Study Workbook

5: Our common insults: reading
8: Speaking partners

If you would like to follow up with more work on learner training, you could do Worksheet 1 on page 114, which gives learners a chance to talk about dictionary use.

QUICK NOTES

This went well:

....

....

There was a problem with:

....

....

Things to think about:

....

....

2

SLEEPING IT OFF

```
                            CONTENTS
Language focus:   connectors: concession
                  participle clauses
                  present perfect simple vs. continuous
                  sleep vocabulary
                  ailments and body problems

        Skills:   Speaking:  discussing an unusual exhibition
                             sleep quiz
                             ailments within and beyond our control
                  Listening: reactions to an art exhibition
                             people talking about common ailments/illnesses
                  Reading:   a text with answers to sleep quiz
                             summary of art exhibition
                  Writing:   a paragraph describing an ailment/illness
```

A GOOD NIGHT'S SLEEP

Introduction

The first part of the lesson introduces and practises a range of lexical items connected with sleep. In the next stage, learners have an extended speaking activity with a quiz on sleep, and then they find out the answers in a text. The final part of the lesson highlights a number of connectors contained in the text, and after some contrastive analysis of these connectors, learners have an opportunity to use some of them in a guided activity.

Suggested steps

1

It is probably a good idea to start by telling the group how you slept on the previous night. If possible, try to weave in several of the items from the next exercise in a natural way. You can obviously cut down the time on this activity by asking learners to do it in pairs rather than ask five different people. Feed in new language if the need arises.

2

You could follow the instructions in the Class Book and allow learners to find the meaning in pairs with the use of dictionaries, or try the *Option* below. There are one or two words and phrases that might be confused with words not included, and also one or two phrases that might need further clarification. Some of these potential problems are explained in the following Language Point.

Language Point

1. *Sleepy* is the feeling you experience when you are tired and would like to go to bed. *Drowsy* also means tired, but it tends to be used when the tiredness is brought on by alcohol, drugs, heat or a large meal, and it may be a feeling we don't want to have.

2. Learners sometimes see a familiar word and assume they know it. You may need to point out that *still* in the phrase *lie still* means to lie down without moving, and not to remain in a position of lying down. Similarly *fast asleep* means deeply sleep, and not to go to sleep quickly, as many learners assume.

Option

If you are working with a multilingual group from different language learning backgrounds (and different knowledge of English), it may be more fruitful to do this as a class mingling activity, i.e. allow learners to move around the class and talk to different people in order to find the meaning of any new words and phrases. At the end, conduct a brief feedback to check a few concepts and add further explanations of your own if you feel it is necessary.

With a monolingual group, you could do the activity in pairs, then conduct a feedback by asking learners to see if they agree on the best L1 translation for each word or phrase. Comparisons of this type are often a good way to illustrate the value, and also the limitations, of translation. If the learners are using bilingual dictionaries, it may also show up the strengths and weaknesses of their dictionaries.

With monolingual or multilingual groups, it is important in the practice activity to get the learners to cross off words and phrases as they use them in their sentences, and to impress on them they have to use all of the items before they finish. This makes the activity more challenging and also more fun. As a class you can listen to some of the sentences.

3

This can be done in pairs or small groups. When they have finished, elicit a few answers from different groups, then direct them to the answers and accompanying text on page 153. This may promote further brief discussion.

4

You could ask learners to try the whole exercise first before referring to the Language Reference. Alternatively, ask them just to answer the first question, then discuss it as a whole class. If they have a reasonable grasp of the material, they can then carry on with the rest of the exercise, with or without the help of the Language Reference. Clarify any problems at the end.

Answer key

Answer 1: *Nevertheless* but not *although*.
Answer 3: Both are possible.
Answer 7: *Even though* but not *in spite of*.
Answer 9: *Despite the fact that* but not *despite*.

5

When the learners have finished, let them compare and discuss their answers in groups.

Answer key

Possible answers:
1. I like a soft one.
2. the noise of the storm.
3. Hay fever is a nightmare for many in summer.
4. I slept like a log.
5. I don't really like them.
6. my sleep has improved considerably this year.

Personal Study Workbook

1: Sleep: vocabulary
4: Remedies: pronunciation
6: Wake up; you're having a nightmare!: listening

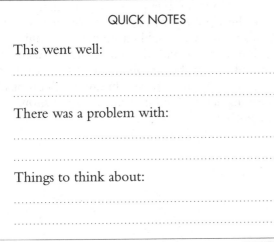

QUICK NOTES

This went well:

....

....

There was a problem with:

....

....

Things to think about:

....

....

SLEEPING BEAUTY

Introduction

The whole lesson is based around a most unusual exhibit that appeared in an art exhibition in London (a woman sleeping in a glass case). A reading text provides information about the exhibit, and a listening text gives people's reactions to the exhibit. The learners have an opportunity to give their own reaction to the exhibit as well as practising participle clauses in several guided activities.

Suggested steps

1

You don't want to give the game away by allowing the learners to see the picture of the exhibit in their books, so start by writing the words in the pink box on the board and explain the meaning where necessary. Then put the learners into small groups for the task.

2

Now the group can look at the picture in the Class Book. Elicit a few quick responses and impressions. Then, after they have read the text, check understanding briefly by asking one or two learners to summarise a part of the text. The discussion can take place in small groups, or you may wish to conduct it with the whole class.

3 ▭

Before you play the recording let the group read through the actions and reactions in the list, and check understanding, e.g. *stare* and *take no notice*. Play the recording and conduct feedback. If there is much disagreement, play a second time.

Option

If you think your group have different levels of listening ability, you could split the class: the stronger learners have to write down the actions and reactions while listening; the rest follow the task in the Class Book. You can then mix the learners to compare answers.

Answer key

– staring at her
– laughing
– crying
– watching her move and turn over
– watching other people's reactions
– following her round as she turned over

Tapescript

KAREN: What I really liked, I don't know if it happened to you, was when, when she actually sort of moved and turned over ...
NIGEL: Yes ...
KAREN: All the group of people went round to the other side so they could be where her face was, so ... that was actually what they were interested in, not the whole thing ... they were sort of moving

like a, like an audience ... it was odd ...

NIGEL: Weird ...

KAREN: Strange ...

NIGEL: I saw someone come in and just burst out laughing ...

KAREN: Yeah, well ...

NIGEL: They did, they just burst out laughing, and I thought she was going to laugh as well, actually.

KAREN: Yeah ...

NIGEL: I'm sure her face twitched.

KAREN: Yeah?

NIGEL: I'm sure she couldn't have been taking it seriously.

KAREN: Yeah, and the children, I thought the children's reactions were, were funny as well. There, there were a couple of little ones there and they just burst out crying ...

NIGEL: I know. I saw them; they were very upset – they didn't know if she was alive or dead, did they?

KAREN: No – just wanted to get out.

NIGEL: It's an extraordinary thing to take children to see, anyway, really, isn't it? Extraordinary thing for *us* to go and see!

KAREN: Did you see those people as well that were just sort of waiting, waiting ... 'She's not going to move, she's not going to move ... yes, she is, no, she's not ...' Of course she's going to move! sort of ... almost scoring the number of times she twitched.

NIGEL: I know. And one chap was just staring at her for about half an hour; I mean, why?

KAREN: Yes, I saw him – I avoided him! Yeah – do you think people go day after day?

NIGEL: Well, a huge amount of people did go.

KAREN: Yeah, and you'd sort of hear people ... I was just amazed that it would attract so many people, yet they were so sort of sceptical about it – but they'd gone.

NIGEL: Yes. It was funny seeing people's reactions though, I mean a few people were just like us – they just actually went, the main reason they went was to see what other people's reactions would be.

KAREN: Yeah, well, yeah, I agree with you, I mean, that was really interesting actually watching them ...

4

After you have been through the examples, let learners complete the task individually, but point out to them that they have to provide a suitable verb in each case. At the end they can compare with a partner before a group feedback.

Answer key

the remains of a cigar smoked by Winston Churchill
a cheque written by the writer Virginia Woolf to Quentin Bell
a watercolour paint box used by the artist, Turner
part of a plane flown by the American aviator, Charles Lindbergh

a manuscript written by the poet, Wilfred Owen
a cushion used/sat on by the psychoanalyst, Sigmund Freud

5

Encourage light-hearted examples here, and elicit one or two from the group before they work in pairs. Monitor their efforts and select some of the best to be read out at the end.

Personal Study Workbook

5. Hiccup madness: reading

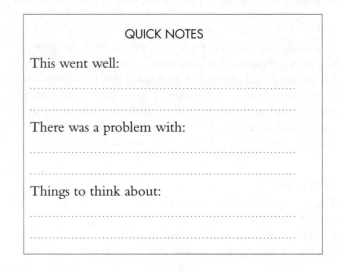

QUICK NOTES

This went well:

....

....

There was a problem with:

....

....

Things to think about:

....

....

SLEEP AND OTHER PROBLEMS

Introduction

The main language focus here is a contrast between the present perfect simple and continuous. Learners have to choose the correct form from a listening text (and recognise that the two forms are interchangeable in some contexts), and then consolidate their understanding before moving on to a writing activity in which there are opportunities for them to use both forms. The context is common ailments, e.g. jet lag, insomnia and hiccups; and the different things people have done to cure them or overcome them.

Suggested steps

1

As there are potential problems with pronunciation here, e.g. asthma (the silent *th*), hiccups (stress on first syllable), ulcers /ˈʌlsəz/, etc., you could check meaning and pronunciation together with the whole group. Elicit one or two examples of problems which are self-inflicted or beyond one's control, then put them into small groups for the speaking activity and monitor the discussion. Conduct feedback at the end.

You could ask your learners if they know of any difference in meaning between these items and/or their collocational restrictions.

As a singular noun, *ache* indicates a continuous dull pain and is usually restricted to compounds associated with these parts of the body: *toothache*, *headache*, *backache*, *earache*, and *stomach-ache* (also written as one word). As a plural noun it can be used more generally:

I've got aches and pains all over my body after that fall.

It is also used as a verb:

My feet ache after all that walking.

Pain (n) describes a wide range of physical suffering and discomfort, and can be slight or acute. It can follow the part of the body it refers to, e.g. *back pain* or *chest pain*, but usually it precedes the part of the body it refers to:

I've got a terrible pain in my leg.

She's had this pain in her arm for weeks.

2 ▢▢

Play the recording, let learners compare answers, and then play it a second time if they are having difficulty.

Answer key

1. back pain	osteopath, exercises
2. insomnia	waking up at five, exhausted
3. mouth ulcers	avoid certain types of food; ointment
4. asthma	living in a city makes it worse; inhaler
5. sunburn	ruined my holiday; sit in the shade; lotions and creams

Tapescript

1. ... for ages now, so I thought I'd just have to live with it, but recently I've been going to an osteopath, and the sessions with her, along with the exercises she gets me to do on my own, really seem to be helping. Of course, it could be ...

2. ... and it can take quite a while. At the moment, I mean, it's a real nuisance, because for the last few days I've been waking up at five in the morning and then of course, by the afternoon I'm exhausted, but I've forced myself to stay awake and I'm just starting to get used to the change ...

3. Well, I used to get them a lot, so whenever I did, I avoided certain types of food and just put up with them, but I've just discovered this fantastic ointment which clears them up in no time. I wish someone had told me about it ten years ago ...

4. Almost everyone I know has been to all sorts of different doctors. Me, I've seen three specialists, and all of them have said that living in a big city is making it worse. I just have to make do with my inhaler and get on with it ...

5. ... three or four hours. I should have known better, but you just forget, you know, and it's really ruined my holiday because since the second day, I've been sitting in the shade all the time and I've spent at least £30 on lotions and creams to relieve the pain, not to mention making Paul's life a misery ...

3

Direct learners to the tapescript on page 153 and explain the activity. Tell them to write in both forms if both are possible, and do the first one with the class if you wish.

Option

In this level of the course we have included a number of activities in which learners work on the tapescript. Learners often enjoy looking through tapescripts to uncover new lexis, and can also benefit from listening to a passage with the aid of a tapescript – it can help them to identify a listening problem by seeing how certain phrases sound in natural speech. If you have time, we think it is worth spending a few minutes of class time in this way. While learners work on the text, you can move round and offer help where necessary.

Answer key

1. I've been going
2. I've been waking up (Both are possible, but the present perfect continuous is more likely to emphasise the fact that it is a continuing problem.)
3. I've just discovered
4. I've seen
5. I've been sitting (much more likely, but the present perfect simple is just possible); have spent

4

Follow the instructions in the Class Book. You could set a time limit to encourage more urgency and make it more competitive if you feel your group responds well to this type of challenge.

Answer key

1. I have tried everything and I have even been seeing a sleep specialist.
2. How long have you been having problems getting to sleep?
3. She has got a hangover this morning because she has been drinking all weekend.
4. I have been using a new medicated shampoo because I have had dandruff for months.
5. He has been working for the airline for over ten years and has flown millions of miles.

5

If necessary, learners can refer back to the tapescript for guidance, both before and during this final task. If you are short of time, you could give this as homework.

You could finish with Worksheet 2 on page 115 of this Teacher's Book as it practises and recycles a range of new lexis from the unit in the Class Book.

Personal Study Workbook

2: It's a hard life: vocabulary
3: I've been working: present perfect simple vs continuous
7: Any tips?: writing letters of advice
8: Speaking partners

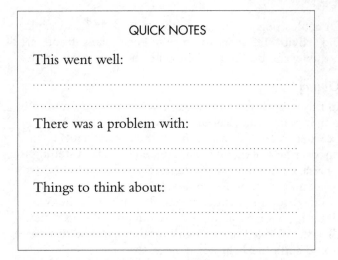

QUICK NOTES

This went well:

....

....

There was a problem with:

....

....

Things to think about:

....

....

REVIEW AND DEVELOPMENT

REVIEW OF UNIT 1

1

Games of this sort are best explained by a dry run. Ask a learner to think of a job and you can then ask suitable questions from the list in the Class Book. Afterwards, think of a job yourself and ask the group to come up with a few suitable questions. Remind everyone that they must be *yes/no* questions. Finally, put them into groups to play the game. At the end, you may wish to discuss any new or interesting question forms that learners either used or clearly wanted to use (but didn't know).

2

Give learners a few minutes to label the pictures and then check the answers with the class before you move on to the speaking activity.

Answer key

a short-sleeved shirt; a sun-tanned body; shoulder-length curly hair; a polo-neck sweater; a wrinkled face; someone with freckles/a freckly face; a bald head; tight jeans/tight-fitting jeans

For the speaking activity, draw the learners' attention to the phrase *reminds me of ...*, then let them work in pairs or small groups.

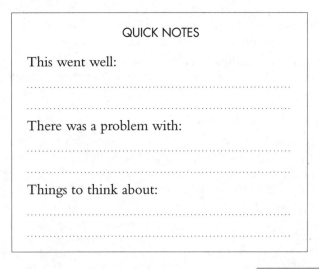

QUICK NOTES

This went well:

....

....

There was a problem with:

....

....

Things to think about:

....

....

HOW DO WE BEHAVE?

CONTENTS

Language focus:		*wish* and *if only* + past perfect
		expressing thanks and pleasure
		so vs. *such* (*a*)
		verbs of social communication, e.g. interrupt, threaten
		focusing adverbs
Skills:	Speaking:	how people react in difficult situations
		discussing the letters you write and receive
		embarrassing anecdotes
	Listening:	people talking about their jobs
		letters of thanks (for completion)
		embarrassing stories
	Reading:	professional people discussing the merits of job applicants
	Writing:	a letter of thanks

DON'T JUST SIT THERE – DO SOMETHING!

Introduction

The lesson is based round an experiment to find out how people would react in an underground train if they saw a strange man pestering a woman on the train. The lesson incorporates a number of verbs and phrases relevant to the topic, and there are several speaking activities in which learners give their own response to the situation and use the target language. A reading text giving the result of the experiment brings the lesson to an end.

Suggested steps

1

At this stage, don't give any background to the lesson, just elicit responses to the picture and write them on the board. If you are working with a monolingual group and they can only express their response in the L1, write that down as well (the listening in Exercise 2 may give them the L2 equivalents they are looking for).

2 🎧

Play the recording and check their answers. Direct learners to the tapescript on page 160, give them two or three minutes to work on their own, then elicit words and phrases they have noted down and check/clarify the meaning. Among the items they should have recorded are *pester, threaten, annoy* (*someone*) and *chat someone up*. Learners will later have an opportunity to use these items (they will almost certainly need them), so make sure they understand them.

Tapescript

WILLIE: I think they probably know each other, because although he's giving her a bit of a hard time (at least it looks that way), I've just got this feeling they might be brother and sister, 'cos they look quite like each other.

NICK: I don't agree, actually …

WILLIE: No?

NICK: No, I think, I think he's drunk or something, and, er, being quite threatening. I mean, he's pestering her, definitely, and she's just decided, 'Look, the way out of this is just to ignore him,' you know …

WILLIE: You don't think she's just seen something out the window?

NICK: No, no, I don't.

CECILIA: No … I actually think that she's had enough of him annoying her, and she's got up, and she's about to leave, and he's trying to …

WILLIE: Oh, really?

CECILIA: Yeah, and he's trying to say a final word to make her stay. I think that he's noticed her and he's been chatting her up for ages, and she's had enough, and she's about to leave, and he's having a last …

WILLIE: So they didn't know each other before, you think?

CECILIA: No.

NICK: No, not at all, no, I think she was standing there, and he's actually, he's maybe been talking to other people, and they've all been ignoring him, and then he's come down to try his luck with her, and she's just, you know, praying for the next station to come up.

CECILIA: Mm.

WILLIE: Mm.

3

These verbs are more difficult than they look as there are several overlapping concepts, e.g. *protect oneself/someone* vs. *stick up for oneself/someone*, and *interfere* vs. *intervene* vs. *interrupt*. Dictionary definitions are unlikely to give more help with the definitions than the ones already given, but they may provide examples that will help, so encourage your learners to look at them closely. If necessary, clarify with more examples at the end. There will be opportunities for learners to use these verbs in the later speaking activities, and most of them appear in the text in Exercise 6, so they are key items in the lesson. Check that learners can pronounce them correctly before moving on.

Answer key

1. interrupt   2. interfere   3. threaten   4. warn
5. protect   6. stick up for someone or oneself
7. intervene   8. ignore

4

Get the group to read the three scenes first, and clarify any new vocabulary. Then put them in groups for the discussion. With multilingual groups it is obviously a good idea to mix the nationalities as much as possible. With monolingual groups, you could ask the group if scenes like these might be more common in one part of the country than another. We have found, in fact, that learners from the same country can disagree quite strongly on the frequency of these situations in their own country.

Move round the groups discreetly during the discussion and – when you sense it has run its course – give them some feedback on their English. In particular, try to help them with concepts they were unable to express to their satisfaction because they lacked the necessary language.

Option

You could put the class in groups of three and get them to read one scene each, and then explain it to others in the group before moving on to the discussion.

5

Follow the instructions in the Class Book. You can monitor the learners' English while they talk, and you may also decide, after five or ten minutes, to open up the discussion to include the whole class rather than restrict it to small groups. Give more language feedback at the end.

6

You can now explain the photo at the beginning of the lesson and the experiment that took place. Learners are usually very motivated by now to read the text. At the end, elicit reactions from the group.

Personal Study Workbook.

2: Could you explain that?: vocabulary
6: When should we intervene?: reading

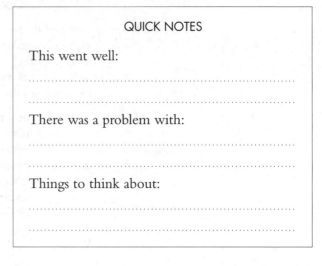

QUICK NOTES

This went well:

....

....

There was a problem with:

....

....

Things to think about:

....

....

....

THANKS FOR EVERYTHING

Introduction

This lesson gives practice in expressing thanks and pleasure in formal and informal letters, and introduces a number of common written conventions, e.g. *I'm just writing to …*, *I look forward to …*, etc. For this reason, the lesson may be particularly useful for learners going on to do public exams such as FCE and CAE. However, much of the target language in the lesson is equally common in spoken English, e.g. *so* and *such (a)*, and focusing adverbs, and there are several opportunities for extensive spoken interaction during the lesson, as well as model letters to read and an intensive listening task.

Suggested steps

1

Check that your group understand the items in the list (especially *condolence*), then put them in small groups for the discussion, which could last five minutes or fifteen minutes depending on the group. With a multilingual group, cross-cultural differences can be particularly interesting.

2

Some learners seem to assume that a gap has to be filled with a single word, so remind the class that they can use phrases as well. Move round and monitor their answers but don't give any correct answers away at this stage.

Play the recording and ask learners to write in the answers on the cassette. They can compare them with their own and you can discuss any differences.

Answer key and tapescript

1.

Dear Auntie Carole and Uncle Charles,
I'm writing to thank you very much for the generous cheque you sent me for my birthday. As you know, I have been hoping to get a car for ages as it would *simply* be so much more convenient, and now I'll be able to afford one. When I've bought it, I'll come and visit you. I hope you're both well and have a lovely holiday in France.
Love,
David

2.

Thanks *for* a lovely evening on Saturday. The meal was wonderful and it was great to see you both in *such* good form. We *particularly* enjoyed meeting your crazy neighbours and look *forward* to seeing you here after we get back from our holidays.
Best wishes,
Jan and Terry

3.

Dear Dieter,
This is *just* to thank you for looking after me *so* well last week. I really *appreciated* the help you gave me; without it, the trip wouldn't have been *such a* great success.
It was very kind of you to put me up in your own home and I felt I got to know a bit more about life in a German family. I *particularly* enjoyed the trip to the mountains; we were lucky to have *such* beautiful weather. Professionally, I was *delighted* that we had such fruitful discussions and feel that we can now proceed to the next stage of the project without delay.
Please *give my* regards to Bettina, and I look forward to seeing you in Milton Keynes in September. Until then, with kind *regards,*
Marion

3

The language analysis collects together a number of different points, some of which may be revision at this level. Give the pairs time and freedom to focus on the questions that interest them most, and listen to some of their discussion to gauge their understanding of the different points. At the end, conduct a feedback and add further examples on the board for clarification if necessary.

Answer key

1. This depends on the class.
2. We use *so* when followed by an adjective alone, and *such (a/an)* when followed by an adjective + noun. They are commonly used in contexts which include the need for emphasis and/or enthusiasm.
3. They emphasise or focus on certain points.
4. This depends on the class.

Option

With monolingual groups it would be interesting to take in similar letters written in the L1. Pairs or groups can use these for comparison with the letters in English. The L1 letters may also create the need for other English expressions, which you can provide.

4

Explain that each learner is writing their letter after the events shown in the pictures. They can do this individually or in pairs. When they have finished and shown it to a classmate, they may wish to change it.

If your group is particularly interested in letter writing, you could go on to Worksheet 3 on page 116, which recycles much of the language from this lesson and provides both models of and further practice in writing letters of sympathy and congratulations.

Personal Study Workbook

3: Studying is simply ..: focusing adverbs and *so* vs. *such*
5: I can't thank you enough: listening
7: Using *get* in a variety of ways: writing

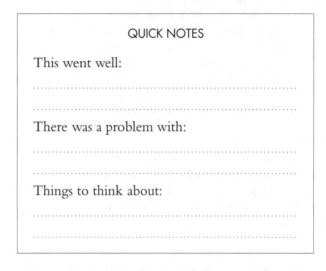

QUICK NOTES

This went well:

....
....

There was a problem with:

....
....

Things to think about:

....
....

I WAS REALLY EMBARRASSED ...

Introduction

This lesson introduces and practises the use of *wish* and *if only* + past perfect. The context is embarrassing situations, and there is both a listening text and personalised speaking activities around the topic.

Suggested steps

1

You could elicit more examples of embarrassing situations connected with the first photo before putting the learners into pairs for further discussion. You may also find that the photos suggest certain outcomes that learners have difficulty expressing, so you might be called upon to teach certain items, e.g. the person in the restaurant *spills* their meal in their *lap*; a swimmer's *swimsuit falls off*, etc.

Option

If one group appears to have finished while others are still talking, get the learners to write their ideas on the board. This not only keeps them occupied, but also gives the whole class something to consider at the end.

If there is a different, and potentially embarrassing context which would be particularly relevant to your teaching situation, you could adapt this exercise to fit it, e.g. for an in-company group.

2 ▢▢

Introduce the listening, then play the recording. Let learners compare answers (this gives you a chance to assess how much they have understood), then check with the whole group if you feel they have grasped most of the main points.

Answer key

1. In the house in the country belonging to his girlfriend's parents.
2. He felt nervous.
3. a) He was wearing the wrong clothes.
   b) He kissed his girlfriend's mother and she was shocked.
   c) He said the wrong thing about sentencing of criminals. (He said burglars should get long prison sentences, not realising that his girlfriend's father had been in prison for burglary.)

Tapescript

PAUL: I think, er, the most embarrassing thing that ever happened to me was when I met my in-laws for the, must have been the first time, (Mmm) and, er, Sally and I had been going out for about a year before we decided to get married, and, er, I didn't know anything about her family, hardly anything, so I was rather nervous, and, er, she suggested that we went down to their house, because they used to live in the country, (Yeah) and we went down there for the weekend. Er, so anyway, I agreed to go. And, er, the whole thing started really badly because I turned up wearing my suit, you know, wanted to look smart (Mm) and, erm, I looked really out of place because everyone else was wearing jeans or T-shirts and stuff. (Hm, hmm) And Sal's mother came, er, to meet us at the station – we went by train – and she kissed Sal, and she sort of came towards me in a very friendly way and so without really thinking about it, I, I kissed her on the cheek, and she just leapt back, you know, um, completely shocked and outraged, it seemed and I realised straightaway I'd got things wrong there. But, um, anyway, in the evening we had dinner, which was a total nightmare. Sal's dad wanted to know what I did for a living, right. Well, when he found out that I was a policeman, he started asking me what I thought about sentencing for, er, you know, criminals, burglars, whatever, and I kind of, I reckoned just by looking at him that he was the kind of, kind of guy who would, who would like to see thieves put away for life, you know, (Mm) so I suppose I took a rather strong line on it and I said I really hated burglars, I thought they were awful and I felt so bad about the victims, and, you know, all that kind of thing. And then I noticed there was this terrible silence. No one said a word and Sally suddenly got up and said that we had to go. I never even got the chance to thank them for the meal or anything; and, er, you know, I found myself more or less running out of the door. And it wasn't till we got home that Sally actually told me that her dad had spent three years in prison for housebreaking. (laughter, no!) I couldn't believe it. I just, I wished, you know, the whole thing had never happened. (Oh dear!)

We suggest giving learners a chance to listen a second time with the tapescript as learners can then focus on parts of the recording that interest them, e.g. new lexis, or passages of the text they didn't understand first time round.

3

Your learners should already be familiar with the use of *wish* + past simple. If not, you may want to follow this option before moving on.

Option

Write these sentences on the board and explain that you are unhappy about these situations and would like them to be different.
I don't have a brother or sister.
I can't play any musical instruments.
I'm quite shy.

You can then write *I wish* alongside each sentence and see if your learners can complete each one. If you don't get a correct answer quite quickly, feed in the first one, i.e. *I wish I had a brother or sister*, then see if the group can finish the others. Eventually you will get the right answers and you can then either elicit (if you have time) or explain why the past tense is used. You can also explain that *were* is considered the correct form of *be* after *wish*, but that *was* is acceptable in spoken English. Follow with some brief practice, e.g. asking them to write down wishes they have and discuss with a partner.

If your group are familiar with the use of *wish* + past simple, let them look through the sentences and correct them, first for grammar, then for meaning. Check answers carefully and use further examples if there are problems in understanding the grammar.

Answer key

1. I wish I hadn't worn formal clothes.
2. If only I hadn't kissed Sally's mother at the station.
3. correct
4. correct
5. If only I had kept quiet during the meal.
6. correct

We use *wish/if only* + past simple to talk about situations we would like to be different now or in future. We use *wish/if only* + past perfect to talk about situations we would like to have been different in the past.

4 ▭▭ ▰▰

Choose the appropriate version of the listening (or use both), and play the recording, but first emphasise that learners only have to note down the embarrassing things that happened, and not everything that happened. It may also be wise to forget about the sentences with *wish* until after you have checked their understanding. Play the recording twice if necessary. If you think the topic of version 2 is unsuitable for your class, don't use it.

Answer key

Version 1:

The man spilt some water over a customer when he was a waiter. He might have said: I wish I hadn't tried to carry all those glasses.

Version 2:

The girl tucked her skirt inside her tights, showing her underwear. She might have said: I wish I'd checked my skirt.

Tapescript

Version 1

NICK: This is something that happened when I was about 16, and I had a Saturday job, which was working in a, a small restaurant that was attached to a pub, er, in Yorkshire, and, erm, my duties were to, erm, really serve the wine, er, open the bottle, er, present the bottle first, then open it and serve the wine. I was a wine waiter, erm, but, erm, one, er, one day, they were understaffed and they asked if I'd do some serving as well, and they'd been promising to, to teach me how to do silver service, which is like, serving the food with a spoon and a fork, erm, and so I started to do that. And, er, obviously I wanted to be as good as the other waiters and waitresses, but I wasn't; and, um, this ... table of, er, it was a party of four, and it was a woman's birthday, 50th birthday or something, and she ordered, er, four glasses of iced water. And I thought I'd be able to carry that on a tray, but, er, it was beyond, beyond me, I'm afraid. And as I walked up to the table, I sort of tripped and it went all over her, all the water, and it was terribly, terribly embarrassing ... um, but she was really nice and, er, she gave me a huge tip at the end and I just felt terrible.

Version 2

CECILIA: Yeah, I remember when I was at college, a couple of years ago, that something that I'll never forget happened to me, and I always check because of this thing that happened. Um, on a Friday we all used to go out, it was like a ritual, we'd go to the disco, we'd go to the pub first, and then go to a club or a disco, and, um, this time we decided to like, go to the pub first. So we went to the pub, and there was like, some people from another college that we didn't really like or that didn't like us, we don't know, but there was a kind of 'vibe' there. And we were kind of, um, sussing each other out the whole night, and my friends decided that it was so awkward that they wanted to leave now, and just said, 'Come on, let's skip this bit and get on with the evening.' So I thought, OK, then, but I was really dying to go to the toilet, so I insisted that I went, and they were saying, 'No, you can go, you know, when we get there,' and I said, 'No, I have to go now,' and so I went, and I went very quickly, you know, and did everything quite quickly, I did wash my hands in fact, I did everything quickly. And, um, then when I came out, my friends were really pointing at me, and there was this, it was, like, a huge pool table in the middle of this room and the pub, the sort of bar was on one end and I had to walk from the toilets right to the other end where my friends were, and these other people from this other college, and erm, I noticed that they were staring and pointing, and some were laughing and some were kind of, telling me to hurry up. So I walked over as dignified as I could, and, um, they pointed to me, told me that I'd actually tucked my skirt into my tights at the back (Oh, no!) and everybody was staring at me, it wasn't in admiration; they were thinking I was looking really stupid, and I just quickly sort of pulled my skirt out and left quickly ...

5

Give the class time to think about this, then put them in small groups. Move round and monitor their stories and make notes. If you hear any particularly good stories, you could ask the learner to tell the whole group at the end. Don't force anyone to tell an embarrassing story if they don't want to; but in this situation, most people self-edit, and the situations described often make for very motivating listening.

Personal Study Workbook

1: Wish you were here: *wish* and *if only* + past perfect
4: Could you say that again?: pronunciation
8: Speaking partners

QUICK NOTES

This went well:

....

....

There was a problem with:

....

....

Things to think about:

....

....

REVIEW OF UNIT 1

1 ▭

Put the class in pairs and give them a few minutes to see if they can recognise the use of homonyms, i.e. words with the same form but different pronunciation. Elicit the answer, then make sure everyone understands and can pronounce each one. Finish with some quick practice of learners reading the sentences aloud, in pairs or small groups.

For part B, follow the instructions in the Class Book. The second part can again be done in pairs or groups.

Answer key and tapescript

1. flu   2. missed   3. rows   4. fare   5. flour   6. weak
7. allowed   8. peace

1. flew   2. mist   3. rose   4. fair   5. flower   6. week
7. aloud   8. piece

2

Look at the example together and then elicit the similarities and differences for one of the others, e.g. having a bath and having a shower (they are similar in that both serve the purpose of getting you clean; they are different in that you stand under running water for a shower, and sit immersed in still water for a bath). Then put the class in groups. Don't prolong the activity if they are struggling to think up pairs of words (three or even two pairs may be enough for the activity), but equally, encourage them to think up even more than five if they are fairly creative and seem to be enjoying themselves. For the second part, maintain the pace otherwise it will become very laboured.

REVIEW OF UNIT 2

1

Check the answers to the first part just to make sure everyone understands the vocabulary (there are several new items which did not appear in the unit).

Answer key

sunburn: exposed skin, mostly the face, shoulders, arms, back, legs and feet
asthma: lungs (breathing)
hangover: head, and possibly stomach
cough: throat and lungs
migraine: head
ulcers: different parts of the body, but often mouth or stomach
constipation: bottom (causing discomfort elsewhere as well)
eczema: skin
cold sores: lips or inside of the mouth
hiccups: diaphragm (but affecting the upper body)
cramp: usually the legs/feet
dandruff: hair/head
indigestion: stomach

hay fever: eyes and nose
jet lag: whole body
catarrh: nose and throat
blisters: mostly feet and hands

Remind learners not to mention the ailment when they write their advice. After pairs have guessed the ailments described, you may find that a general discussion develops on the subject of ailments and remedies. Be ready to feed in new language where appropriate.

2

Start with an example, and elicit one more from the group before learners complete the task, individually or in pairs. Let them compare in small groups to discuss the sentences and the use of tenses.

Answer key

Possible answers:
He has broken/hurt his arm.
He has shaved off his beard.
He has been painting the wall.
He has eaten some hamburgers.
He has been eating chocolates.
He has spilt the paint.
Someone has hit him in the eye.
He has read the newspaper.

QUICK NOTES

This went well:

....

....

There was a problem with:

....

....

Things to think about:

....

....

GETTING YOUR MESSAGE ACROSS

```
                        CONTENTS

Language focus:   modals of past deduction
                  (must've, could've, might've + past participle)
                  idioms: communication problems
                  character adjectives
                  phrasal verbs and idioms
                  functional language

       Skills:    Speaking:   talking about misunderstandings
                              pros and cons of answerphones
                              telephone roleplays
                  Listening:  people talking about communication breakdowns
                              telephone messages
                  Reading:    book extract: unrequited love
                  Writing:    correcting a text
                              telephone messages
```

WHAT ON EARTH DO YOU MEAN?

Introduction

The lesson provides a dual language focus: modal verbs
for making deductions about the past; and a wide range
of idioms and lexical phrases used to describe
communication problems. Several activities provide a
focus on meaning and controlled practice, and the lesson
concludes with a listening text about communication
breakdowns followed by a personalised speaking activity.

Suggested steps

1

Go over the examples given in the table first, then put
learners in pairs for the activity. Check answers at the
end and clarify any problems. One thing learners may
ask you is whether they can say *he didn't have the faintest
idea* as well as *he hadn't the faintest idea*. Both forms would
be acceptable, but we feel that in this particular
expression most native speakers are more likely to use
the latter form. Finish with some work on
pronunciation, paying attention to the main stress on
multi-syllable words, e.g. *incoherent* (prefixes do not affect
the stress unless particular emphasis is required), and the
overall rhythm of the expressions.

Option

You could begin by telling the class an anecdote of your
own about a breakdown in communication, especially
one which relates to English and your learners' mother
tongue. If you don't know one, you could tell the class
this old apocryphal story:

An Englishman was on the top bunk of a couchette on
an overnight train travelling through France. There was a
Frenchman on the lower bunk who spoke *quite* good
English, but not *very* good English. During the night,
the Englishman suddenly felt sick and realised he was
going to vomit. He shouted a warning to the Frenchman
below. 'Watch out!' he cried. The Frenchman responded
immediately and 'looked out' from his bunk to see what
the problem was!

Answer key

He didn't understand correctly:
He must have misunderstood.
He just couldn't grasp what she was saying.
He misinterpreted it.
He must've got the wrong end of the stick.
He didn't know:
He didn't know anything about it.
He hadn't got a clue.
He hadn't the faintest idea.
He didn't hear properly:
He couldn't catch what she said.
He had to tell her to speak up.
He must have misheard the name.
He wasn't able to communicate clearly:
He was incoherent.
He was unintelligible.
He was completely incomprehensible.
What he said was very misleading.

2

This activity provides a further check on meaning, some
controlled practice, and also an opportunity to extend the
expressions into the kind of utterance in which they are

likely to appear, i.e. the expression of a communication problem followed by the reason for it. Learners can work in pairs and it is probably sufficient if you just monitor their work to check they are producing some plausible sentences, then elicit some of their examples in feedback.

3

Before learners move on to further practice, there is a brief check on their understanding of *must have* + past participle, and *can't have* + past participle for making deductions. Put learners in pairs or small groups and monitor their discussion carefully. Conduct a feedback with the whole class and provide more examples if necessary.

Answer key

(The percentages in brackets give a general numerical indication of the degree of certainty in the speaker's mind.)
He must have misunderstood it. = I don't know for a fact that he misunderstood, but I assume he misunderstood because it is the most probable explanation. (90%)
He misunderstood it. = I know for a fact he misunderstood. (100%)
He can't have misunderstood it. = I don't know for a fact that he didn't, but it seems highly unlikely that he misunderstood it.(90%)
He could/might have misunderstood it. = It is possible that he misunderstood it. (50%)

We may use *must have* + past participle in the context of communication problems because it is in the nature of communication problems that we don't always know why they occur; therefore, we often make deductions to try to explain them.

4

If you wish, do the first picture together as a class, eliciting answers and writing them on the board. Then allow as much time for this activity as learners need, and bring it to an end when you sense they are running out of things to say. If you have heard a number of different answers during your monitoring, it would be worth listening to some of them round the class; otherwise move on quite quickly.

Answer key

Possible answers:
1. She must've overslept. She might've forgotten to set her alarm clock.
2. He must've had an accident. He might've fallen off his bike.
3. He must've received good news. He could've passed an exam.
4. They must've had an argument or disagreement. He might've been rude to her or forgotten to do something important.

5 ▭ ▬

If it hasn't come up already, you could teach the expression *communication breakdown* (or *breakdown in communication*). It is a useful lexical item, particularly for language learners, and is clearly relevant as an introduction to the listening. Give the group a minute to read through and digest the questions, then play version 1 and/or version 2 of the recording. Let learners compare, then check answers.

Answer key

Version 1:
First speaker
1. He was working in America and was invited to a reception.
2. The woman who took him to the reception.
3. The breakdown was connected with the difference between British English pronunciation and American English pronunciation: she mistook his *lock* for the American English *look*.
4. Amused or possibly confused.
Second speaker
1. She was at work making an excuse for a colleague who was absent.
2. Her colleague and her boss.
3. She misunderstood him: she thought he was leaving work completely, not just having a day off.
4. Angry.

Version 2:
First speaker
1. In a restaurant with friends.
2. The American with the strong accent.
3. When the American said *adorable*, the speaker understood *a doorbell* because of their different accents.
4. Amused.
Second speaker
1. First occasion in a tea house in China; later in the street in China.
2. The woman who served her at the counter; the people in the street.
3. The problem was obviously her Chinese pronunciation, which the people in China didn't understand.
4. A bit frustrated on the first occasion; amused and bewildered on the second.

Tapescript

Version 1
1. Gareth
I was working in the southern states of America, and, er, and I was asked to a reception, so I put on a suit and tie, and, you know, tried to look smart, and, er, a woman picked me up, er, and drove me to the reception, and we had a very nice chat on the way, and we got to the reception and I got out of the car, and of course American cars are a little bit different from, from ours in England, so I said, er, I said to her, 'How do I lock?' and she said, 'Why, you look fine.' (That's wonderful!)

2. Marcella
Well, one night this friend of mine rang me up and asked me to do him a favour, that when I went into work the next day, to tell our boss that he wasn't coming back to work. Well, you know, I really don't know why I actually agreed to do it, but I said yes. I didn't really

want to, but however, I said yes; went into work the next day, saw the boss, said to her that he wasn't coming back to work – she was raging, of course – erm, but I really couldn't give her any more explanation than that, and, er, so worked away, then the next day, there I am at my desk, and in he comes! (What?) As cool as a cucumber! And I said to him, 'I thought you weren't coming back! You told me to tell the boss that you weren't coming back!' and he said that I was wrong, that what he meant was that he wasn't coming back the next day. (Oh) So he gave me the impression that I had completely got the wrong end of the stick, but actually I didn't; I'm convinced that he totally misled me, so, I mean, it was a really embarrassing situation, and, er, I've never spoken to him since. (I'm not surprised!)

Version 2
1. Marcella
There was a few of us out one night in a restaurant, about six of us altogether, and, er, there were some visitors in from the southern states [of America], and one of them had a very strong accent, and she was talking about a friend of hers who was really quite zany, and she went on to describe all the things she said and did, and she said she was 'a doorbell'. And I said, 'God!' You know, a doorbell? And she said, 'Yes, she was, she was a doorbell,' and I said, 'I've never heard that expression before, it's wild, you know, a doorbell – what does "a doorbell" mean?' She looked at me blankly and went 'a doorbell'. (laughter) So this exchange took place where she was saying 'a doorbell' and I was saying 'a doorbell', and everybody looking completely blank round the table … (Adorable!) it was 'adorable'! So since then, all my friends whenever we're describing somebody say, 'Oh, she's a doorbell!'

2. Lynne
Well, I experienced a couple of misunderstandings when I was in China; (Hmm) the first time that comes to mind was when I was in a tea house, and I went into the tea house and I had a bit of Chinese, I'd learnt a few words. I went up to the counter and I said, erm, 'I'd like a tea, please,' politely, and they have a phrase in China which means 'we don't have it,' and you hear it quite a lot, and so the woman at the counter said, 'we don't have it,' and I was looking around, and everyone was drinking tea, it was a tea house, so I said, 'No, no, no, I'd like a cup of tea, please,' and she just kept saying, 'We don't have it,' like she couldn't seem to grasp what I was getting at or maybe she didn't want to grasp what I was getting at, so I stood there and I didn't have any means of telling her what I wanted, of communicating with her, and so I just had to leave. I just felt really pathetic. And then on another occasion I remember I was asking for the People's Hotel, but because of the tonal thing in the Chinese language, it turned out that I was asking for the People's Prawn and I think they were pointing to the river in Guang Jo and saying, 'it's in there,' and laughing a lot. (Right)

Refer learners to the tapescript on page 161 of the Class Book, then play the recording a second time for them to follow.

6
Providing a sample story yourself is often the best way into this kind of personalised activity, although the recordings will have given them several anecdotes which may help to trigger their memories for similar embarrassments. Learners can and obviously will self-censor here, but you could still reassure learners that you do not want them to reveal anything about themselves or others which will make them feel uncomfortable.

Personal Study Workbook

1: What are they talking about?: phrasal verbs and idioms
4: She must have got held up: past deduction

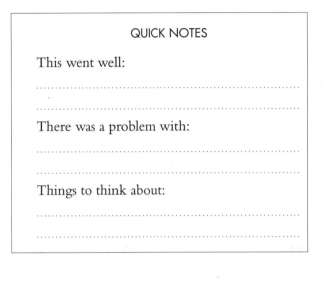

QUICK NOTES

This went well:
....
....

There was a problem with:
....
....

Things to think about:
....
....

UNREQUITED LOVE

Introduction

The lesson revolves round an extract from a book in which a foreign language learner becomes infatuated with his female teacher and sends her unintentionally humorous love letters. This is the context for the presentation and practice of a group of adjectives describing character, and learners also have the opportunity for some language reformulation (correcting and improving the love letter), plus reading comprehension and summarising.

Suggested steps

1

Using the example of *Fatal Attraction* in the Class Book, or choosing your own, explain what happened in the story, then tell the group it was an example of *unrequited love*. Can they think of more examples?

Option

If you know the group quite well and feel they are comfortable with each other, you could ask them if they have any experience themselves of writing or receiving love letters. It must be stressed that learners should never feel pressurised into talking about a subject if they feel uncomfortable about it. This is only a decision you can take, knowing your own group as you do.

2

Go over the background to the book, let the learners read the letter (give them time to digest it and look up new words if necessary), then put them in pairs to answer the questions. Get some feedback from them. If they are perplexed by the letter or find it very difficult, move on to Exercise 3; if they are amused or intrigued by it, you could ask them to have a go at improving the grammar and the way it is expressed. In this case give them as much freedom as they wish to make changes. This could actually be quite time consuming, but learners may find it both challenging and fun, and they should have an opportunity to read different letters to see if they can improve their own.

Answer key

1. He's trying to tell her he loves her very much.
2. His language is very emotional and extravagant.

There is clearly no single way to correct the letter, but learners may be interested to compare their letter with one possible answer.

Answer key

Possible answer:
Darling (name),
Do you know why my eyes never meet yours in class? It is because if they do, I will be too overcome with emotion.
Do you know I walk through London and think only of you? I don't notice traffic or noise or other people – on one occasion a car almost ran me over because I was thinking of you.
(Name), please give me your telephone number so that we can arrange to meet alone one evening. You are like the most beautiful sun that has ever shone on London. I promise you, I just want to hold you in my arms and protect you.
Love,
F

3

You will need to give the class five to ten minutes to read the full text carefully and digest the information. Then tell them to shut their books and recap. Let one partner start, then tell the other to take over after one minute. Have they included all the key information? You could let them return to the text to check for one more minute.

Option

You could do the reformulation round the class. Ask the group to read the text, then ask one learner to start recapping. After a few seconds, ask another learner to take over, and so on. When you have got to the end of the story, ask another learner if they have anything to add. Then ask another learner if they have anything to add, and so on. Within two or three minutes you should have had a paraphrase of most of the text and story.

4

Encourage learners to do as much as they can without dictionaries, and then use them to check their answers and look up words they don't know. If they are using English–English dictionaries, they could compare the dictionary definition with the one we have provided. Check that they can pronounce the words accurately, and drill where necessary.

Answer key

a. 3   b. 6   c. 8   d. 2   e. 7   f. 5   g. 4   h. 1
Definitions:
A *generous* person is happy to give time or money to help others.
An *unreliable* person or machine is one you cannot trust or depend on.
A *violent* action is intended to hurt someone; a *violent* person is likely to attack and hurt others.
A *passionate* kiss or embrace is one with strong sexual feeling.
A *sensible* action is logical, practical and most of all, reasonable and intelligent.
If someone is *kind*, they are warm and friendly and willing to help others.

Option

With a monolingual group you could make this an interesting dictionary exercise if you have access to English–English dictionaries and bilingual dictionaries.

Split the group in half and give one half a selection of English–English dictionaries, and the other half bilingual dictionaries. The first group should do the activity with the help of their dictionaries and then write down the best translation for each word in the list. The other half should do the exercise making use of translation from their bilingual dictionaries, but without the aid of the definitions we have provided. At the end, let them compare answers and also compare L1 translations. If their answers are different, which group has the best translation, and what conclusion does the group draw about their bilingual dictionaries?

Writing definitions is a challenging task, and you could do this as a whole class activity to speed things up if you wish.

5

Put the learners in groups for this activity and encourage them to justify their answers with reference to the text. Be prepared to help them with new vocabulary which may not have appeared in the lesson.

Personal Study Workbook

2: Shall we give her the job?: character adjectives
3: Say it another way: reformulation
5: Conversation: reading and listening
8: Speaking partners

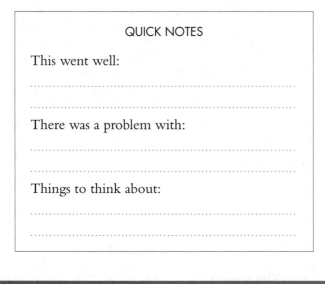

QUICK NOTES

This went well:

....

....

There was a problem with:

....

....

Things to think about:

....

....

PLEASE LEAVE A MESSAGE

Introduction

Learners of all levels usually want to practise common everyday language used in telephone conversations, and to this we have added a range of phrasal verbs as well. There is a selection of telephone messages for the learners to listen to and an opportunity for some extended speaking with a series of roleplay activities at the end of the lesson.

Suggested steps

1

Setting a time limit for this warm-up activity is a good way to focus the learners' minds, and ensures the activity does not take up too much of the lesson.

Answer key

Possible answers:
1. Advantages of answerphones:
   People can leave messages for you when you are out, so you know who has called you.
   You can leave messages for yourself to remind you to do something.
   You can be at home, listen to the message on the answerphone and decide if you want to pick up the phone and speak to the caller.
   Disadvantages of answerphones:
   It is more difficult to avoid people you do not want to talk to.
   People often call but don't leave a message; it can be frustrating.
2. Advantages of leaving a message:
   If you don't speak the language very well, you have time to compose your message. Also, the other person cannot reply, disagree, contradict you, etc.
   Disadvantages of leaving a message:
   You cannot erase your message and later you may regret you left it.

2 📼

Give learners time to read through the sentence beginnings for each conversation. You could also ask them to guess the content of each message by looking at the surrounding artwork. Then play the recording once and let learners compare answers. You could play the recording a second time before you check answers, but bear in mind that the next exercise has a task which requires learners to listen to the recording again.

Answer key

1. She apologised for not turning up on a previous evening, and would like to invite Sally to a restaurant for Sunday lunch.
   Please ring before the weekend.
   Phone number: 0171 886 9430
2. Derek rang to check everything was OK for the babysitting.
   At the moment he is at work.
   He wants Sally to ring him at work or pop round later.
   Phone number: 0987 498087
3. Patience rang to say that she has split up with Jonathan and the wedding is off.
   She wants Sally to ring her this evening at her sister's.
   Phone number: 456 9920
4. Martin Bellingham rang. He is going to help Paula to move her belongings into Dave's.
   He can't do it this evening as arranged but he'll come tomorrow morning.
   He needs more information about how to get there.
   Phone number: 08954 88023

Tapescript

Hiya, this is Sally. Sorry I can't take your call right now, but if you'd like to leave a message and your name and number, I'll get back to you as soon as I can. Please speak after the tone. Thanks for calling. Bye!

Sally – this is Alice. Listen, I'm so sorry for not turning up the other night. I'm sorry I let you down. Um, listen, I'd like to invite you to Sunday lunch, right? We're going to the Waterfront Restaurant. I want to make up for it. Um, I hope you can call me back before the weekend – 886 9430, that's 0171 886 9430. I'd really like to see you there – hope you can make it. OK, speak to you soon …

Oh, hello, Sally, erm, is it working? Yeah, it's Derek here, Sally, next door. Look, I'm phoning up, it's about the babysitting tomorrow you said you'd do for us. I want to double-check everything is OK. Erm, oh what … yeah, I'm working late at the office tonight, what's new, so, er, you can ring me here, er, 0987 498087 or, er, maybe, well, could you pop round later? Just put a note through the door or something. Er, thanks very much. Did I – it's Derek – did I say that? Yeah. Bye!

Oh, Sally, you're not there. Hi, it's, it's Patience. Erm, I really need to talk to you. Erm, listen, Jonathan and I have split up. We've split up and the wedding's off. Oh God, I'm in such a mess, it's a disaster! Erm, I've got to cancel all these arrangements. Look, I'm really desperate to talk to you. Can you, can you ring me at my sister's this evening? What's the num ... oh yeah, the number's, er, 456 9920 just, any time, doesn't matter how late, as soon as you get in. All right, speak to you soon. Bye!

Hi, Sally – my name's Martin Bellingham. I'm the poor bloke that, er, Paula's asked to help move her stuff from your place into, er, Dave's. Um, if you can give me a call back, er, later on this evening, because unfortunately, I won't be able to make it tonight as arranged, erm, I need to know if you'll be in tomorrow at about 10 a.m. Erm, I also need to know how to get to your place, I know it's near the church, but there's a one-way system which I'm not sure about, and I don't want to get stuck in the traffic. So if you could give me a call on my mobile number which is 08954 88023, before 11.00 tonight, that would be great. Thanks.

3 ▭

Put the group into pairs and see how much they can answer before you play the recording again. (They could write *yes*, *no* or *not sure* next to each sentence.) At this stage you could explain the meaning of any new vocabulary. Play the recording again so they can complete the task, then let them check their answers using the tapescript at the back of the Class Book. In context, the meaning of most of the new vocabulary should be fairly transparent, so see if your learners can explain the new vocabulary to you, e.g. *to call something off*, *to get stuck*, etc.

Option

Put learners into pairs. Partner A has to memorise (and pronounce correctly) the first eight phrases; Partner B the second eight phrases. Set a 2–3-minute time limit, then they can test each other.

4

It is important that learners are familiar with the situations and understand exactly what they have to do, so don't rush the preparation in your desire to get them speaking. You could put learners with the same role cards together so that they can prepare what they are going to say and rehearse one or two key sentences. If necessary, ask one or two confident learners to act out the first conversation in front of the group to check that everyone knows what to do. Put them in pairs to roleplay each situation. Listen and make notes on their performance, then give them some feedback – this may involve some error correction but remember also to use this opportunity to feed in new language that would have helped them, and give praise for the appropriate use of new language from the lesson.

Option

If your group is not too big, and time, space and the technical facilities permit, you could try this alternative. Record each pair roleplaying one of the situations, then let them listen to their conversation in a language lab (they could do this in different rooms if you have lots of space). As they listen, they must write the transcript of their conversation. When they have finished, put them

back into their pairs to a) compare their transcripts, and b) make improvements to it using a different coloured pen. When they are happy with their amendments, collect them in and check them. In the next lesson give the transcripts back with your amendments, allow time for them to read through them carefully, then take them away and get them to roleplay the situation again.

If you would like to spend more time thinking about everyday phrases, you could try Worksheet 4 on page 117.

Personal Study Workbook

6: Don't be so rude!: listening
7: I'd better tone it down: writing

```
┌─────────────────────────────────────────┐
│              QUICK NOTES                  │
│                                           │
│   This went well:                         │
│   ......................................  │
│                                           │
│   ......................................  │
│                                           │
│   There was a problem with:               │
│                                           │
│   ......................................  │
│                                           │
│   ......................................  │
│                                           │
│   Things to think about:                  │
│                                           │
│   ......................................  │
│                                           │
│   ......................................  │
└─────────────────────────────────────────┘
```

REVIEW AND DEVELOPMENT

REVIEW OF UNIT 2

1

Follow the instructions in the Class Book.

Answer key

The words which do not collocate are:
have: tiredness
set: the TV
suffer from: a cough
feel: asleep
lie: out

You could then extend the collocations. Take the wrong answers and ask learners for verbs which do collocate with them. Answers could include: suffer from tiredness; turn on/off the TV; have (got) a cough; fall asleep; get/take/put out, etc.

2

Encourage your learners to let their imaginations run free in this activity, and do allow plenty of time for preparation. One idea that helps some learners is for them to go through the whole talk in their head, i.e. rehearse it as they would a part in a play. You can also run the activity twice: after the first time, give some language feedback, then form new groups and do it again. This gives learners an opportunity to benefit immediately from your feedback, and many enjoy doing an activity twice in order to feel a sense of progress. Obviously this requires careful monitoring – it can be very demotivating if activities are repeated too often.

REVIEW OF UNIT 3

1

Explain the rubric clearly – each pair chooses one situation only, then prepares the roleplay, e.g. B phones A (aunt or uncle) to thank them for the leather diary he/she received from them. If it is not possible for pairs to record their conversations, they can obviously repeat the activity by selecting another gift from the left and relationship from the right.

2

You could see if your learners can identify the people in the picture and suggest a sentence expressing a personal regret using *wish* + past perfect. If they are unable to do this, go through the examples, then follow the instructions. If anyone cannot think of a personal regret of a famous person, ask them to think of an example of someone who may be known to the rest of the group, e.g. the man or woman who runs the coffee bar in the school.

QUICK NOTES

This went well:

....

....

There was a problem with:

....

....

Things to think about:

....

....

BUILDINGS

CONTENTS

Language focus: plural nouns, compounds, collective nouns, uncountable nouns, adjectives as nouns
past perfect simple/continuous
present perfect review
building vocabulary
compound adjectives

Skills: Speaking: discussing facilities and services in your home town
creating a story around a house you have bought
and converted
designing a school
Listening: a description of two buildings
Reading: an article about the conversion of a public lavatory
into a house

NOUNS ARE BUILDING BLOCKS

Introduction

This lesson looks at many types of noun and the problems associated with them, but the presentation is in the form of a quiz, which we hope learners will find motivating and challenging. Naturally, there is also quite a lot of lexical input, e.g. common compounds, plural nouns, collective nouns, etc. The second part of the lesson offers a range of activities which allow learners to practise the new language.

Suggested steps

1 ▭

This first exercise is an opportunity to focus on one type of noun and discuss the problems as a class, before setting learners to work on the entire quiz on their own.

Some of the lexical items will be new, so ensure the group have access to dictionaries. If that isn't possible, you will need to provide a brief explanation yourself. Either way, see if they can work out the reason why these nouns all end in s. If they cannot answer that, go on to the listening. Check the answers after the dictation (or refer the learners to the tapescript on page 162), then ask learners again if they can explain the s.

Answer key

These are all plural nouns, which means they only have a plural form and end in s, and they almost always take a plural verb. See the language point below.

Tapescript

1. The factory was too small, so the company has decided to move to new premises on the outskirts of town where the surroundings are also more pleasant.
2. The facilities in the sports centre include not only an outdoor swimming pool and gym, but also an attractive seating area near the squash courts where you can get refreshments.
3. Our company has branches all over the country, but the most important decisions are taken at our headquarters in New York.

Language Point: plural nouns

The plural nouns in the box may be new, but your learners will already be familiar with many others (they may not realise they are plural nouns), e.g. *stairs, headphones, jeans, trousers,* etc.

Two of the plural nouns in the box can be made singular (*premise* and *facility*), but the meaning is different:
facility 1. a special part of a piece of equipment or service, e.g. a *locking facility, an overdraft facility*
2. a natural ability, e.g. *a facility for lateral thinking*
premise (also spelt *premiss*): an idea which you accept as true and use as the basis for developing another idea, e.g. *The system works on the premise that men and women are equal.*

Learners don't need to know these meanings, but if they are using dictionaries they may want some clarification.

2

Put the learners in small groups and try to give them access to good dictionaries, both English–English and bilingual. Tell them they can do the questions in any order, and set a time limit if you wish to make the activity more competitive (some groups respond well to this, others don't). Move round and monitor while they are working, provide help where necessary, and deal with pronunciation problems as they arise; but don't become too intrusive. When you feel the groups have done as much as they can, conduct feedback and clarify problems where necessary. Worksheet 5 on page 118 gives more practice with compound nouns. The answers are on page 29.

Answer key

Countable and uncountable nouns
1. forms of transport   2. the traffic is ...   3. a lot of trouble   4. correct   5. the accommodation we were given was ...

Compound nouns
1. hostel   2. precinct   3. lavatory/convenience/toilet
4. lost-property   5. agent   6. rank   7. court(s)
8. centre/mall

Collective nouns
1. staff/workforce   2. jury   3. audience   4. committee
5. council   6. the public

Places and articles
1. to prison = to serve a sentence for committing a crime; to the prison = to go there physically, e.g. to visit
2. to church = to pray/worship; to the church = to go there physically
3. into hospital = as a patient; to the hospital = to go there physically, e.g. to visit someone or work
4. to university = to study; to the university = to go there physically
5. at school = when we were students; at the school = the school was the location, e.g. for our meeting

Adjectives as nouns
1. the disabled   2. the unemployed   3. the injured
4. the rich   5. the retired/the elderly   6. the blind

Option

If time is limited, or if you wish to make the quiz more interactive, you could divide the class into five groups and give each group responsibility for one section only. Make sure they do it thoroughly and monitor to check their answers are correct. When they have finished, recreate five new groups with one person from each of the previous groups. They must now take it in turns to teach the others in the group about their particular type of noun, and the meaning of the new lexis. Monitor carefully.

3

Mix up the groups a little for extra variety, then let them discuss the questions in whatever order they wish. You should not expect learners to incorporate a great many new items from the lesson in this activity, but simply talking about the places and people introduced in the lesson will provide useful reinforcement, and it may be interesting to notice which new items are being used quite freely.

Personal Study Workbook

2: Shall I put an *s* here?: plural nouns and uncountable nouns
3: What's missing?: compounds

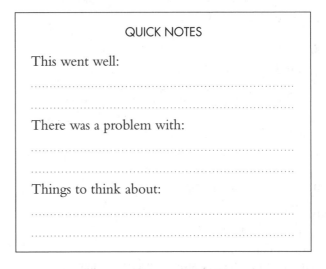

```
QUICK NOTES

This went well:
.....................................................
.....................................................

There was a problem with:
.....................................................
.....................................................

Things to think about:
.....................................................
.....................................................
```

NO PLACE LIKE HOME

Introduction

Learners read and discuss a text about a man who bought an old public lavatory and converted it into a house. A comprehension task on the text also highlights the main language point (the past perfect simple and continuous alongside revision of the present perfect), and this is followed by an extended guided speaking activity in which learners can use the different tenses quite naturally.

Suggested steps

1

Write the six items on the board, explaining any that are new, and check that learners understand the meaning of *convert* and *renovate* which are crucial to the lesson. Then let them discuss whether they would like to live in any of these converted buildings. If you have any examples in your vicinity, these would make an interesting starting point.

2

Use the photo in the Class Book to teach or elicit the lexical items, then let learners read the text with a dictionary if necessary. Follow with a brief reaction.

3

This activity tests understanding of the text but also highlights the chronology of events which gives rise to the use of the past perfect in the text. First see if your learners can find the mistakes without referring back to the text.

Answer key

1. The graffiti has not remained on the walls until the present day (the owner cleaned it off when he bought the property).
2. The safe was only discovered after the renovation began (not before).

4

You could set this task without any reference to the past perfect, or you could tell the group that they will need to use the past perfect in many of their answers. It is your decision, based on your knowledge of the group and how well you think they will cope.

Let learners compare answers, then check them and refer the group to the Language Reference on page 144. Give them time to read through and ask questions.

Answer key

1. had been looking
2. hadn't been used
3. have asked for permission to use the toilet
4. had travelled down
5. had been scrawled (written) on the cubicle partitions
6. attendant had put some jewellery in it, with a note as well.

5

The guidelines to the task make it clear that we are creating opportunities for the use of the present perfect, and past perfect simple and continuous, but you must decide whether you want to remind learners of this or just see if they can use the forms naturally. You will also need to decide how much preparation time is required. This will depend on the level and confidence of the group, but we feel it is important not to rush this planning and rehearsal time. Move round and help where necessary, and suggest to pairs that they can also prepare the question forms they will need as well as the information they are going to impart.

Personal Study Workbook

4: Let's do it up: vocabulary
5: A watery home: reading; narrative tenses
6: I'd love to live there: listening
7: I saw this amazing house today ...: writing

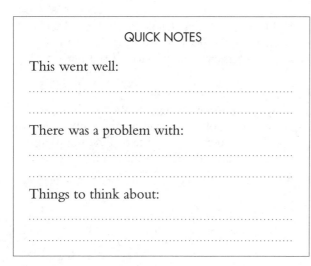

QUICK NOTES

This went well:

....

....

There was a problem with:

....

....

Things to think about:

....

....

DESIGN YOUR OWN SCHOOL

Introduction

The main focus of the lesson is an extended speaking activity in which small groups are given the outline plan for a language school and then have to redesign it, including a limited range of equipment and resources, but within certain constraints. Before the activity there is quite a lot of preparation in terms of lexical pre-teaching, a listening passage, and key information for the task.

Suggested steps

1

You could start by asking for a general description of the two buildings in the pictures – both the general location and the buildings themselves. This might throw up the need for certain lexical items which will occur during the lesson or might be useful later on in the lesson. Then organise pairs for the brief discussion and conduct feedback.

Option

You could divide the class into pairs. One learner has to speak in favour of Amora House, with reasons; the other learner has to argue for Dado Court.

2

This short vocabulary activity focuses on compound adjectives which will all come up again later in the listening passage. In other words, they are important for the lesson, and learners will have an opportunity to hear them and use them. Point out that they are required to form compound adjectives (not compound nouns), and that they should all be connected with the topic of buildings (in other words, you are not looking for *self-conscious* or *well-off*, etc.).

Answer key

air-conditioned	old-fashioned
self-contained	brand-new
semi-detached	run-down
built-up	well-known/well-built/
	well-designed/well-maintained

3 ⊡ ▣

Choose the appropriate version and play the recording. (As both versions contain the same information, there is no purpose served in this case in playing both versions.) Check answers, and then return to the earlier topic of conversation. Would anyone change their minds about the best building for a language school after listening to the additional information?

Version 1:

Amora House

✓: in a built-up area; shares the building with other companies; is centrally-heated; is in good condition; is near a bus stop; has a lift

✗: is air-conditioned

?: is in a residential area; has snack bars nearby

Dado Court

✓: is in a residential area; is centrally-heated; has snack bars nearby

✗: is in a built-up area; shares the building with other companies; is air-conditioned; is in good condition; is near a bus stop

?: has a lift

Version 2:

Amora House

✓: in a built-up area; shares the building with other companies; is centrally-heated; is in good condition; is near a bus stop; has a lift

✗: is air-conditioned

?: is in a residential area; has snack bars nearby
They don't mention the fact that it is or isn't in a residential area (we can probably assume it isn't); and they do not discuss snack bars (we can probably assume there are many in the area).

Dado Court

✓: is in a residential area; is centrally-heated; has snack bars nearby

✗: is in a built-up area; shares the building with other companies; is air-conditioned; is in good condition; is near a bus stop

?: has a lift

Tapescript

Version 1

CUSTOMER: What can you tell me about this first one, erm, Amora House?

ESTATE AGENT: Ah, Amora House, well, I think you'll like this. It's very conveniently situated. There are quite a few buses that stop outside and the underground is only a minute's walk.

CUSTOMER: Oh!

ESTATE AGENT: Erm, it is in a built-up area, as you can see from the picture. It's this modern office block, it's the whole of the third floor, so it's quite spacious, (yes) and you needn't worry about running up and down the stairs – there is a small lift, it's not big but, erm, you know, there is a lift. Erm, it's also, it's also centrally-heated, er, and it's in very good condition, really. Erm, the plumbing and the electrics are recently renewed, so that's good. Erm, oh, there's no air conditioning ...

CUSTOMER: Ah, right.

ESTATE AGENT: ... forgot to tell you that. And, er, just really needs a little bit of renovation, a bit of paint, that's all really.

CUSTOMER: OK, it's in a built-up area. Is there a problem with noise, traffic?

ESTATE AGENT: Oh, no, no, no, no, none at all, it's very well insulated and it's double glazed, so there's no problem at all.

CUSTOMER: Double glazed? That's excellent. And this second one, Dado Court, what can you tell me about that?

ESTATE AGENT: Ah, Dado Court, yes, it's in a very quiet area, erm, it's a residential area, almost in the country, really. It's been very, very well built and as you can see from the picture, it has lovely grounds. It's, er, it's even got a tennis court, which should please the students!

CUSTOMER: Excellent.

ESTATE AGENT: It's completely self-contained. Erm, it is on a bus route, there's only one bus, I'm afraid, and also it's about a 15-minute walk to the bus stop, but, er, it is accessible. Erm, the building itself is a little run-down. It does need some renovation, a little more than just a bit of paint, er, but the central heating system is absolutely brand new, so I can guarantee that that works.

CUSTOMER: Right. And air conditioning?

ESTATE AGENT: No. No, no air conditioning. Erm, so I think that might, oh, and also, there are, just up the road, erm, a few, I think there are two or three coffee bars, and there's a pub, so plenty of places for the students to eat in.

CUSTOMER: Good.

Version 2

ESTATE AGENT: Well, we've got two properties which would be suitable for the language school; the first one here, you see the picture, it's Amora House. It's very conveniently situated to bus and underground routes, in a built-up area ...

CUSTOMER: Right.

ESTATE AGENT: Erm, as you can see, it's, it's quite a tall building, and the vacant space is on the third floor.

CUSTOMER: Ah, so is there, is there a lift, or ...

ESTATE AGENT: Oh, yes, there's a lift.

CUSTOMER: Oh, good, what's that like?

ESTATE AGENT: It's a good lift, I mean, it's a pretty new building. Erm, it takes three people at a time, so I don't know what the class sizes are, obviously there's stairs, so ...

CUSTOMER: You mentioned that it's, it's a built-up area. Now is it a very noisy area?

ESTATE AGENT: No, no, not too noisy, I mean obviously, it's quite a new building, so there's double glazing and everything ...

CUSTOMER: No, but we will need to ... I mean, for instance, in the summer, we will need to open the windows, if the weather's hot, and get some air in the classrooms.

ESTATE AGENT: Oh, right.

CUSTOMER:	I'm thinking of the noise element for concentration.
ESTATE AGENT:	Right, well it's not air-conditioned, um, but other floors do have air conditioning, so it's not impossible to install it if you wanted to.
CUSTOMER:	Right.
ESTATE AGENT:	Um, the building itself is in good condition; the plumbing and the electrics are OK. Um, obviously in the winter it's OK because it's centrally-heated. One of the problems is the entrance is shared with the other companies, so I don't know if there's a problem with, you know, some of the students ...
CUSTOMER:	I shouldn't think that should be too much of a problem.
ESTATE AGENT:	Right. Well, I think it's a, I think it's a good property. The other one here is Dado Court which is an older building; it's in a quiet, residential area, beautiful building, as you can see ...
CUSTOMER:	Lovely, yes, yeah.
ESTATE AGENT:	... very well built, lovely grounds; there's a tennis court in the back ...
CUSTOMER:	Hmmm!
ESTATE AGENT:	... parking facilities, no problem there; you've got the whole building to yourselves, it's completely self-contained.
CUSTOMER:	Right. Whereabouts is it situated? It's not in the city centre, is it?
ESTATE AGENT:	No, it's not, I mean, it's a bus, bus ride away, (ah, ah) it's on a bus route. It is a bit of a walk to the bus stop, but, you know, if people can drive or ...
CUSTOMER:	Yeah, just thinking about the students needing, you know, facilities such as, you know, café, bars, restaurants. I mean, what's in the surrounding area?
ESTATE AGENT:	It's not a problem because there are two or three snack bars in the area, so that's, that's OK.
CUSTOMER:	Right.
ESTATE AGENT:	The building itself is a little bit run down. It needs a bit of renovation.
CUSTOMER:	I see. Well, that would explain the price, which is quite reasonable.
ESTATE AGENT:	Yeah, but I mean certain aspects are, you know, brand new, the central heating is brand new.
CUSTOMER:	Oh, well, that's something.
ESTATE AGENT:	There's no air conditioning, unfortunately, but, you know, with big windows like that, it would be fine in the summer.
CUSTOMER:	Yes. Lovely and quiet. Well, gosh, it's a difficult decision ...

4

This is the main activity in the lesson and learners should be very clear about their objective, so make sure they know what they have to do and what constraints they are under. For example, they must understand that they cannot include all the facilities listed as they don't have enough rooms, so they may have to think about priorities before even coming to the practical consideration of where to place the facilities. You could form groups immediately, but it may be wise to allow the class some time to think about the issues individually before establishing the groups. Either way, don't be too alarmed if the discussion gets off to a fairly slow start – it often takes a while for learners to be sufficiently familiar with the facts to marshal their arguments very quickly. Intervene and give encouragement if you think it is absolutely necessary; otherwise take a back seat and just observe for a while.

5

Make sure that each group finishes with a large clear copy of their design, which they can pin up on the wall or explain to other groups. Which option you choose may depend on time and the degree of enthusiasm generated by the activity. Ideally, it would be nice if the class could try to agree on the best design. Afterwards, give the group some feedback on their use of language. If resources permit, you could also record part of one of the conversations, and then get members of that group to transcribe the conversation, try to correct it, and then submit it to the teacher and the rest of the class for analysis.

Option

If this activity is very successful, you could consider trying to create a similar activity – using a similar plan – in which learners design, for example, a leisure centre. You could give them a list of facilities such as basketball court, swimming pool, gymnasium, squash court, café, etc., and provide a floor plan which will only allow a limited number of these facilities.

Personal Study Workbook

1: Spiral word: building vocabulary
8: Speaking partners

QUICK NOTES
This went well:
....
....
There was a problem with:
....
....
Things to think about:
....
....

Unit 5 BUILDINGS

REVIEW OF UNIT 3

1

You could ask the group to scan the text quickly and then discuss any new vocabulary. After that, introduce the task, and, if you think it is necessary, discuss one example with the class, e.g. if a box of mints would be a normal house present to take in your country. Learners can then continue through the text and discuss it in groups afterwards. If the text generates a good deal of discussion, you could mix the groups so they can give each other feedback on the outcome of their discussion.

2 ▭

You could ask learners to complete the first column in pairs so they discuss the subjects and give each other ideas. Then play the recording, pausing where necessary to give learners time to write down the speaker's exact words. At the end, highlight and clarify the use of *wish + would*, although we would not recommend becoming too involved with the structure at this stage as there are instances where the distinction between *wish* + past tense and *wish* + *would* can be very tricky.

Answer key and tapescript

1. I wish I could speak French really well because I love France.
2. I wish I had loads of money – that would be nice.
3. I wish I was more patient. I have no patience whatsoever.
4. I wish my brother wouldn't come in late at night and start banging around – [it] really annoys me.
5. I wish I hadn't cheated in my driving test – I might have passed.
6. I wish I had gone to university because I think education's really important.

If necessary do one example with the class to show them how they should transform their ideas. For example, a learner who wrote *I don't know how to cook*, would tell their partner: *I wish I knew how to cook.*

REVIEW OF UNIT 4

▭

Follow the instructions in the Class Book. As the class tells you their sentences for part A, write them on the board or OHT and ask learners to rank them according to how polite they are. In part B, force them to listen very carefully and write down sentences which are in any way different to their own. Finally, move round the class during the pairwork activity in part C to check on your learners' pronunciation.

Tapescript

I beg your pardon?
Pardon?
What did you say?
Hmmm?
What?
Could you repeat that?
Could you speak up a bit, please?
Sorry, can you slow down a bit?
I didn't get that.
I didn't follow that.
I didn't quite catch that.
I can't make out what you're saying.
Sorry – I must have misheard you.

Answer key

The imaptient/angry sounding sentences are:
I beg your pardon?
Could you speak up a bit, please?
I can't make out what you're saying.

```
QUICK NOTES

This went well:
......................................................................
......................................................................

There was a problem with:
......................................................................
......................................................................

Things to think about:
......................................................................
......................................................................
```

Worksheet 5 Answer key

2. 1. cutbacks   2. write-off   3. check-in   4. outcome
   5. sell-out   6. breakthrough   7. takeover
   8. cover-up

PROJECT: WRITING BIOGRAPHIES

Introduction

The topic is summed up very concisely in Exercise 1, and if you do the project with your group, it will probably take 2–3 hours, although that could be cut to about one and a half hours of class time if you give Exercise 6 as homework. As with many projects, learners may take a little while to get involved, but it does soon become an absorbing activity for most learners. When you have done this project once, keep a copy of the biographies to show a future class – it is an excellent way of motivating them.

Suggested steps

1

Try to ensure compatible pairs. If you have an odd number, you can have one group of three, but they will probably require more assistance from you in structuring the different activities. If you decide to divide the project over two different class sessions (or have to do it that way), another potential difficulty is with learners who miss the first session or alternatively miss the second session. When that has happened with us, we have asked the learners on their own to write their own autobiography.

2

This activity serves to introduce some ideas for content for the biography and also introduces some lexical items which will be very useful in the biography. You may be surprised to discover how many of these will be new for your learners. Note too that these adjectives often form quite strong collocations with the nouns that follow, e.g. *key influence* and *major achievement*.

Answer key

crucial, key, major, main

3

Learners must now choose from the list of contents. This gives them a chance to structure their biography, and at the same time remove any topics they do not wish to talk about. It is very important that nobody in the group feels threatened by the topics which will form the basis of the profile. The example in the Class Book will give you some idea of typical content you could include.

4

This also serves a dual purpose: it will provide learners with some useful and interesting expressions to begin their profile, and we hope will also prompt discussion which will lead them to realise that the regurgitation of dull factual material (e.g. *Carlos was born in 1972. He went to school at the age of six …*) will not be very effective in capturing the interest of the reader.

5

Some teachers find that this correction activity interrupts the development of the personal narrative, and so they omit it at this stage and return to it after learners have completed their first draft in Exercise 6. You could do that if you wish. The advantage of doing it now, of course, is that it may help learners to avoid typical errors when they write (e.g. *succeeded to pass*), and it also introduces some useful language they may be able to use (e.g. *quite a* + adjective + noun).

Answer key

… exam again, which was quite *a* frustrating experience for her. However, she carried on studying *on her own/by herself*, and finally she succeeded *in passing* her accountancy exams. She got a *very well-paid job* in a large firm where she *still works*. She *thinks she has been* very lucky because she was *a junior member of staff when she started*, but several people *left the company* and she got promotion very quickly.

6

Learners should now have the information, the structure and some useful language to have a go at the biography. Encourage them to write and then go back and edit/correct afterwards. After this first draft, they can show it to their partner for comments, both on the information and the way it is expressed. This may lead to a second stage of redrafting or refining, and it can be submitted to you.

We do not feel that the teacher should remove every single mistake if that means making significant changes to the profile. The main purpose of looking at the biography is to see if there are simple ways a learner can make an improvement to the piece of work, and also to recognise that learners would probably not wish to see their biographies displayed if they contained 'silly' mistakes that might be humiliating for the writer. Otherwise, try to leave them as they are.

If your learners do complete a booklet of their biographies, ask them to read them all for homework and write one or two questions for each profile. In the next lesson, give them time to mingle and ask/answer their questions.

6

TRAVELLING CAN BE HARD WORK

CONTENTS

Language focus:	emphasising structures (e.g. *the thing that annoys me is ...*)	
	making/changing arrangements	
	present continuous and future continuous	
	different uses of *would*	
	phrasal verbs and idioms	
Skills:	Speaking:	the way people behave on trains and buses
		pros and cons of being a tour rep
	Listening:	people describe annoying behaviour on trains
		phone calls about travel plans
	Reading:	a fax and a formal letter
		a magazine article about tour reps
	Writing:	a letter confirming travel plans

SEAT HOG!

Introduction

Learners talk about annoying behaviour on buses and trains and then listen to native speakers talking about the same subject. This leads into the use of emphasising structures (e.g. *the thing that annoys me is ...*), and then personalisation for further practice. The lesson ends with a cross-cultural discussion about other aspects of behaviour on public transport in different countries.

Suggested steps

1

You don't need to mention the listening at first. Just ask the group for the type of behaviour they find annoying on long train and bus journeys. Give one or two examples yourself to set the conversation going, e.g. people digging their elbows in your ribs or eating smelly food, then let them continue in small groups for several minutes. At the end, put their ideas on the board, then introduce the listening.

2 ⬚⬚ ⬛⬛

Choose the appropriate version of the listening (or use both if you have the time and want learners to have as much listening practice as possible), then play the recording once. They will need to listen to the recording again for the next exercise, so refrain from playing the recording a second time at this stage unless it is absolutely necessary. Let them compare with a partner, then check with the group.

Answer key

Version 1:
Speaker 1: People using headphones, because the noise is irritating and you can't concentrate if, for example, you are reading.
Speaker 2: People eating, because it smells and causes litter.
Speaker 3: People who sit beside you and want to talk, because you cannot sit quietly or sleep.
Speaker 4: People who pick their nose and scratch, because it's horrible.

Version 2:
Speaker 1: People who spread their belongings over two seats and obviously don't want others to sit next to them. The speaker dislikes this because it is selfish.
Speaker 2: People who use mobile phones, because he doesn't want to have to listen to other people's conversations.
Speaker 3: Children who run around and make a noise, because it prevents you from sleeping or relaxing.
Speaker 4: The noise from headphones, because it's so irritating.

Tapescript

Version 1
1.
SHEILA: The thing that annoys me is people using headphones. I'm sitting there, trying to read my book, and this insistent 'ttittittittitti' goes on and you just can't concentrate.

2.
IAN: The thing I find most irritating is people eating on train and bus journeys. Why is it that they have to chomp their way through two hamburgers and two cups of coffee and then throw their discarded wrappings all over the floor? It's not necessary and it smells and it's disgusting.

3.

NIGEL: The thing that really annoys me is when you're going on a long coach or train journey, and somebody comes along, and perches themselves down beside you and tries to strike up a conversation; and it usually goes something like, 'Hello, let me tell you about me,' and you spend the next three hours being talked at by this person. It annoys me so much because I don't like travelling anyway, and I'd rather just sort of sit quietly on my own and, you know, try and go to sleep or something.

4.

CECILIA: The thing that really gets to me is when I'm travelling, and there is somebody who is near me, or opposite me or anywhere around me that's picking their nose, as if I can't see them, or scratching. It just makes me feel really ... I want to say to them, 'Can you stop doing that, please, or wait till you get off?'

DENICA: Yeah, I know what you mean.

CECILIA: It's horrible, disgusting!

DENICA: I know – disgusting! Yeah! (laughter)

Version 2

1.

KAREN: The thing that gets me is when you get on a long distance train that's absolutely packed and you haven't reserved a seat and there's one seat left and someone's spread all of their belongings and possessions right across it, and you stand there and say, 'Is that seat taken?' and then very disgruntled, they will just about move you a tiny space. And you've paid for your ticket just as much as they have, and you have to squeeze yourself in. It's, it's just dreadful, really selfish.

2.

NICK: I think the thing that really annoys me on a train is people who use mobile phones.

DENICA: Oh, yeah ...

NICK: But I mean, 'cos, I have a mobile phone, and if I use it I'm quite discreet, but they seem to ... some people seem to feel they've got to talk at four times the normal volume, and so they're shouting away. Usually they're just saying, 'I'm on the 8.47' you know, and it's like they're just wanting to share their life with you, and I don't want it, and it just annoys me because I don't want to be hearing what other people are thinking.

DENICA: No, I know.

3.

DENICA: I mean, the thing that I find irritating as well is when people's kids just won't shut up, when you're trying to, you know, sleep or relax on the train, and these kids are running up and down the corridors, and you know, you don't want to have to be involved in other people's lives to that extent.

4.

WILLIE: Yeah, well, what really annoys me, though, is, um, when you're on the train and someone gets on, and they're wearing those, like, headphones, 'cos they've got ...

DENICA: Oh, yeah ...

WILLIE: ... a Walkman or a portable cassette, and you can hear the music's up really loud, but you can't hear the music, all you hear is the kind of squeaking noise from their headphones ...

CECILIA: Tststststst ...

WILLIE: ... that's right, and they're making noises too. And it just goes on and on and on ...

CECILIA: I hate that!

WILLIE: You either want to switch it off, or you want to listen to it yourself, preferably switch it off!

DENICA: Yeah, so irritating.

3

When you go through the rubric, make it clear that the words in brackets in the sentence beginnings can be added or omitted – the learners' task in the listening is to note down exactly the sentence beginnings that are used. To check answers, refer them to the tapescript on page 163.

For the controlled practice, you could ask learners to write down three or four examples and then exchange sentences with a partner. If you want to focus on stress and intonation, you could drill some of the sentences using the tape as a model, or saying them yourself.

4

Exercise 3 presents a number of ways of saying the same thing. If you sense learners might get confused with these different forms, suggest that they just concentrate on two examples for the further practice activity. Give each group a few minutes to gather their thoughts, and also allow them to choose the topics they wish to talk about. Monitor and conduct a brief feedback at the end.

Option

Be prepared to change the topics of conversation if you think it would be appropriate for the group, e.g. for a monolingual group of Italians studying in Venice, you could ask them to note down what annoys them most about living in a city that is so popular with tourists.

5

This may be more generative with a multinational group where differences in behaviour from one culture to another may be more marked. With a monolingual group though, there will still be differences of opinion on whether these things are common or acceptable, and you could also ask the learners if they personally do any of the things in the list when they travel.

Personal Study Workbook

1: What shocks me is this...: emphasising structures
5: Road rage: reading

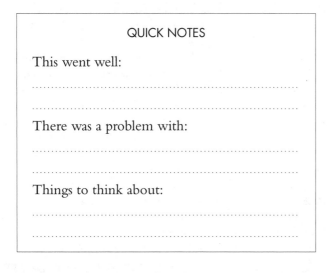

I'LL BE ARRIVING AT ELEVEN

Introduction

The focus here is on writing and differences in style between formal and informal letters. The context is writing about travel arrangements, out of which the use of the present continuous and future continuous arise very naturally. A listening passage provides further skills work and also additional variety.

Suggested steps

1

Ask the group if they would expect a formal letter in English to be different from an informal letter. If so, how would it be different? Elicit one or two ideas to get them warmed up, then give them the task to complete, individually or in pairs.

Answer key

Some of the differences between formal and informal letters in British English are as follows:
- Informal letters may be handwritten; this is most unusual for a formal letter.
- A full address is essential in a formal letter, including the address of the person you are writing to. (Company letters, of course, will have their own headed notepaper.) In an informal letter, the sender may or may not put their own address, but they would not include the address of the person they are writing to.
- A formal letter will always begin *Dear Mr/Mrs/Ms/Dr*, etc. An informal letter may or may not include this. First names are also much more likely in an informal letter.
- A formal letter will end *Yours faithfully,* or *Yours sincerely* (if we know the name of the person we are writing to); informal letters may end *Best wishes, Love,* etc.
- Certain pronouns and verbs are often omitted in informal letters, e.g. *Sorry it's so late* (Not *I am sorry it is so …*).
- Note the use of contractions in the informal letters,

e.g. *I'll, I've,* etc. This is not common in a formal letter.
- There is more formal language in a formal letter, e.g. *Should you require any further information.* In an informal letter, we would probably say *If there's anything else you need to know.*

Option

With a group from the same country, you could make this more of a cross-cultural comparison. Ask them how a formal and informal letter would be different in their own language (in as much detail as possible), then see if the group can find similar differences in the two examples in English in the Class Book.

2

It may be more effective for you to explain this from the board, with examples from the fax and letter, rather than have the whole group with their heads buried in the book. Emphasise that we are talking about language preference here and not rules, and elicit one or two answers from the group if you think further exemplification is necessary.

Answer key

Possible answers:
you should recognise me
I can give him your message
we can meet very easily
hurry up
you don't need to bring any money with you

3 🔲

As the phone calls concern changes to the arrangements, the learners should have the fax and letter in front of them while they listen. They can then amend them while they listen. Play the recording a second time if necessary, then check answers with the group.

Answer key

1. Derek isn't now seeing Bob and Jean because they have a meeting, so he's getting an earlier flight, arriving at 7 p.m. Margot is busy then (she has to pick up Shelley from her class), but she arranges to come to the airport and meet Derek at 8 p.m. at the information desk.
2. Dr Robinson's visit to KJP Trading has been cancelled, so she will now spend the whole time at Pansing, and will need to have her hotel reservation extended for two more nights. She would also like some extra appointments arranged. Mr Lea will also have to arrange a car to take Dr Robinson to the airport for her return flight on 14 July at 15.00.

Tapescript

1.
MARGOT: Hi.
DEREK: Hello, Margot, it's Derek here.
MARGOT: Oh, Derek, hi! Hi, sweetie, how are you?
DEREK: I … I'm fine. Er, a slight change of plan …

MARGOT: Mm hm ...

DEREK: I was meant to be meeting Bob and Jean, and, um, getting a plane in the evening ...

MARGOT: Yeah, sure.

DEREK: ... and they're actually, they've got a meeting or something, so I can come earlier. I've actually managed to get ...

MARGOT: Oh, great!

DEREK: ... an earlier flight so ...

MARGOT: Oh, what time?

DEREK: Well, I'll be getting into JFK at 7.00 p.m. now.

MARGOT: OK, OK, now let's think. Now, I can't meet you at seven, because I, I've got to pick up Shelley from her class. I can get to JFK by eight o'clock ...

DEREK: Um, well, er, that's OK, I tell you what I'll do, I'll get the airport bus.

MARGOT: Oh, no, no, no, no, you're going to have all this, all this luggage, you've got all your stuff with you, no, no, no, I'll pick you up, don't worry about it, don't get a taxi or anything, just meet me at the information desk, OK ...

DEREK: Yeah ...

MARGOT: ... there's a coffee shop right there, and I'll be there at eight o'clock.

DEREK: OK, yeah, OK, that's what I'll do, I'll get a coffee and I'll just wait for you.

MARGOT: Have a great flight.

DEREK: Thank you. All right – see you!

MARGOT: Bye!

2.

JACKSON LOMAX: Hello, could I speak to Mr Lea, please?

MR LEA: Mr Lea speaking.

JACKSON LOMAX: Mr Lea, it's Jackson Lomax here of Merson Electronics.

MR LEA: Ah, Mr Lomax – nice to talk to you. How are you?

JACKSON LOMAX: I'm very well – how are you?

MR LEA: Very well indeed. What can I do for you?

JACKSON LOMAX: Did you get my letter of the 10th of June?

MR LEA: Yes, I did.

JACKSON LOMAX: About Dr Robinson's visit?

MR LEA: That's correct, yes.

JACKSON LOMAX: Right, well, now, there have been a couple of changes, I'm afraid, so I'm just calling you to tell you about those ...

MR LEA: Uh, hm.

JACKSON LOMAX: Er, Dr Robinson's visit to KJP Trading ...

MR LEA: Hmm?

JACKSON LOMAX: ... unfortunately has had to be cancelled.

MR LEA: I see.

JACKSON LOMAX: So Dr Robinson would like to spend the whole time at Pansing International with you. Would that be all right?

MR LEA: That's an extra two days, yes, yes, that would be possible, yes.

JACKSON LOMAX: That's great. So could you possibly extend the booking at the Raffles Hotel for an extra two nights?

MR LEA: Another two nights for Dr Robinson. Yes, I'll get my secretary on to that at once, yes.

JACKSON LOMAX: And if you could make some appointments for her to see a few more people while she's there ... as this part of the visit has now been cancelled, that would be good as well.

MR LEA: Yes, I think that will be possible.

JACKSON LOMAX: Well, do what you can, anyway.

MR LEA: I certainly will.

JACKSON LOMAX: Now there's just one other thing. Could you, um, be responsible for making sure Dr Robinson can get her return flight?

MR LEA: Yes, yes.

JACKSON LOMAX: It just simply means getting, getting her a car to the airport, er, on July the 14th.

MR LEA: Yes, that'll be the 14th, and what time is her flight?

JACKSON LOMAX: The flight is 15.00.

MR LEA: 15.00, so if I arrange for a car to deliver her at the airport for check-in at about 14.00, that would be ...

JACKSON LOMAX: At the latest, I would have thought ...

MR LEA: Yes, yes.

JACKSON LOMAX: So that's July 14th at 15.00.

MR LEA: July 14th, 15.00 is the flight. Yes, I think so, Mr Lomax, that shouldn't be a problem. Anything else?

JACKSON LOMAX: No, I think that's it. You are aware that Dr Robinson is a strict vegetarian; I put that in the letter, did I?

MR LEA: Yes, yes, you mentioned that in your letter, yes.

JACKSON LOMAX: Good, well, thank you very much, Mr Lea.

MR LEA: Thank you, Mr Lomax.

JACKSON LOMAX: I'll be in touch again soon.

MR LEA: Pleasure speaking to you.

JACKSON LOMAX: Bye bye.

MR LEA: Bye bye.

4

Follow the instructions in the Class Book. Move round and monitor the pairs while they work and provide help if necessary.

When learners show each other their work, make it very clear that the purpose is not to find fault, but to make positive suggestions that will improve another piece of work, and to look for ideas in other people's letters which will improve their own work. You could collect the letters at the end to correct and give feedback.

Personal Study Workbook

2: We'll be seeing you: expressing the future
6: Making arrangements: listening

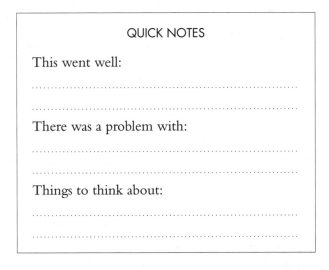

TOURISTS AND TOUR REPS

Introduction

A reading text about the difficulties faced by tour reps is the basis for the lesson, as it provides the springboard for speaking activities, and contains the main language input: a group of idioms and phrasal verbs, and different uses of *would*. Learners have an opportunity to practise these uses of *would* at the end of the lesson.

Suggested steps

1

You could elicit answers to the question from the whole class and put them on the board. You may find learners will give you a couple of the phrasal verbs which come up in the next exercise; or they will try to express the concepts without knowing the best verb to do it, e.g. they may say that tour reps go to the airport to meet groups of tourists. If this happens, feed in the vocabulary that would be useful to them (in this case *to pick people up*).

2

Learners will need dictionaries to help them, as it is their task to contextualise these phrasal verbs and expressions and elucidate the meaning of each one. Go through the examples first to show them what is meant by contextualising them, and then let them work on the lexis individually or in pairs. Conduct a short feedback by eliciting their answers and clarify any problems.

3

Now let them read the text to find out how the target items from Exercise 2 are used in the text. See if their ideas in Exercises 1 and 2 were the same as the text.

4

This speaking activity involves learners responding to the text by putting themselves in the same position (that of tour rep), and talking about the parts of the job they would love or hate if they were doing it. Elicit one or two examples to check they recognise the need for *would*

in this hypothetical situation, and correct if necessary. Then let them carry on with a partner or in small groups and monitor their ideas and language while they talk. Make sure to praise the effective use of the target lexis from the earlier exercise as well.

Option

You could omit Exercise 4 at this stage and move on to the analysis in Exercise 5. This has the advantage of allowing you a more thorough opportunity to check that your learners can manipulate *would* in imaginary situations, before moving on to the practice; but the disadvantage is that it concentrates all the language analysis into one lengthy session in the middle of the lesson, and relegates much of the freer speaking to the end of the lesson where it might get squeezed out if you are short of time.

5

Learners now have the opportunity to look at other uses of *would* in the text. Go through the examples, starting with the example they have already encountered and used, and remember to make it clear to the group when *would* and *used to* are not interchangeable. Then let them work on the text individually or with a partner. Check answers.

Answer key

wouldn't take him (3)
wouldn't press charges (3)
wouldn't be easy (4)
would get (2)
would usually go (2)
would arrive (2)
I'd have to (2)
I'd visit (2)
would try (2)
wouldn't give (3)
they'd come (4)
would certainly do it (1)
would recommend (1)

6

Finally, put learners in pairs or small groups to discuss either (or both) of the situations. Give them a few minutes to collect their ideas, then let them talk freely. Conduct a feedback at the end if there is time

If the group enjoyed the lessons *Seat hog!* and *Tourists and tour reps*, Worksheet 6 on page 119 draws together the two themes and provides both recycling of language from the two lessons and additional new lexis to describe annoyance and surprise.

Personal Study Workbook

3: Don't worry, I'll sort them out: phrasal verbs
4: A few days off: pronunciation: linking
7: The holiday from hell: writing
8: Speaking partners

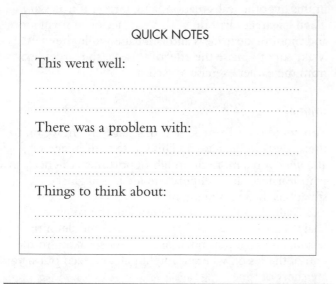

Answer key

Possible answers:

1. Someone might've tried to get across a small river by climbing along the overhanging branch of a tree, which then broke under his weight.
2. Someone must've passed his exam despite the fact that he didn't study very hard.
3. This suggests there was some kind of accident – there might've been an explosion.
4. Obviously someone must have left the bicycle out in the rain or left it unprotected for a long time.
5. The people who moved might have been in trouble with the police, or possibly they wanted to keep the move a secret.

REVIEW AND DEVELOPMENT

REVIEW OF UNIT 4

1

Follow the instructions in the Class Book for the first part. When you have checked the answers, the pairs can memorise their exchanges. In our experience, learners not only enjoy the challenge of memorisation, but in this case (and in many other parts of the book), the sentences provide variations on chunks of language that frequently co-occur – to such an extent that native speakers would store them together as items of vocabulary, e.g. *I/We won't be able to make it, (I'm afraid)*; *Could you double-check ..?; I'll pop round and see you ...*; etc.

The final part allows learners to explore these exchanges and develop their own situations and dialogues.

Answer key

I'll pop round and see you after ten o'clock. Can't you make it a bit earlier?
Could you double-check the holiday dates? I already have.
We got stuck in a traffic jam by the station. Yes, I'm always getting held up there too.
I won't let you down again. Is that a promise?
We won't be able to make it, I'm afraid. That's a pity – oh, well, never mind.
Derek and Jill have split up. They'll probably get back together again.
Didn't he turn up last week? No, that's the second time he's let me down.
The match is off this evening. Yes, they're playing next week instead.

2

It is important that learners have the freedom to respond to these situations as they wish, but you can encourage them (without labouring the point too much) to use modals of deduction in speculating about the possible explanation for each of the statements. Monitor the pairs or groups and listen to some of the more interesting or imaginative explanations at the end.

REVIEW OF UNIT 5

1

If you want to allow each learner an opportunity to rehearse and improve their talk before they give it to their group, you could put learners who are talking about the same picture together. They can then tell each other what they are going to say and help to improve each other's talks. Then, mix the groups so that each group consists of someone who is going to describe a different painting. Collect examples of well-expressed ideas, or language errors, and give feedback at the end.

2

You could play a few rounds of the game to see what questions the learners produce, and intervene only if you sense certain likely questions are not being asked. In that case, draw the learners' attention to these questions and carry on.

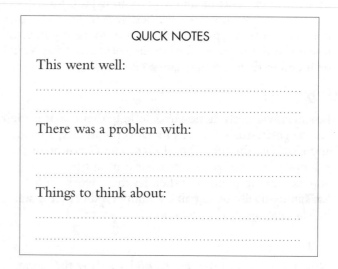

7

HOW DOES IT LOOK?

```
                              CONTENTS
  Language focus:   prepositions of place
                    look + adjective, look like + noun, look as if/though
                    modal verbs:  hypothesising
                    adjective word order
                    describing clothes
                    vocabulary: colour and materials

         Skills:    Speaking:  describing a painting
                               how colour affects our work
                               attitudes to clothes and fashion
                    Listening: facts about colour blindness
                               clothes people wear at weddings
                    Reading:   information about a painting
                               a questionnaire
```

MANET'S MASTERPIECE

Introduction

First, learners are asked for their impression of Manet's famous painting 'A Bar at the Folies-Bergère'. This is followed by exercises on prepositions and *look* + adjective, *look like* + noun, and *looks as if/though* + clause, which practise and revise language that learners often need to talk about a painting. A reading text gives more background information to the painting and is used for the development of the reading skill, and then learners have an opportunity to talk about some different paintings, using language from the lesson if they wish.

The lesson will obviously be of most interest to learners who enjoy art, but the target language will also be very relevant for learners studying for Cambridge exams.

Suggested steps

1

If you have a class that may have an interest in art or at least be able to identify the style of the painting, you could start with the option below. If not, it is a good idea to do the vocabulary activity and check it before you ask for any opinions of the painting (otherwise the two activities become confused). Let learners use dictionaries to help them, and after you have checked the answers you could also check or teach other items which come up later in the lesson, e.g. *balcony, counter, label, buttons, barmaid,* etc.

Answer key

greyish-blue: the marble counter or the barmaid's skirt
pale pink: one of the roses on the counter or parts of the balcony
beige: the woman's gloves in the front row of the balcony
dark green: one of the bottles on the marble counter
marble: the counter
velvet: the top half of the barmaid's dress
lace: the decorative collar of the barmaid's dress
glass: the bottles or the vase on the counter; the chandelier

Option

Try to get hold of a number of pictures of paintings from different periods, but including two or three from the Impressionist period. Pin them up on the walls and divide the class into small groups. Ask the group if they can a) identify the painting or painter in their Class Book, b) select paintings on the wall from the same period, and c) identify the period (or century) in which the other paintings were painted. You should obviously make this easier or more difficult based on your knowledge of the group and their likely knowledge of art. If you are teaching a multilingual group, make sure you have a range of paintings from the countries represented in the class.

After the vocabulary activity, put learners in pairs or small groups to give their impression of the painting. Conduct a short feedback and feed in new language where appropriate.

2

Parts of this gap-fill exercise are deceptively difficult, so be prepared for it to take longer than you think. Not only are there some prepositional phrases which may be new, e.g. *in the foreground/background*; some of the concepts here may also be new to learners, e.g. that you can wear something *round your neck*, and have buttons *down the front of a dress*.

Answer key

1. in   2. on; in   3. in   4. round; on (*round* is also possible)   5. on; in   6. on   7. down   8. down/across   9. in; on

At this point you may wish to highlight the use of certain phrases from the exercise on the board. For example:
in the foreground/background
in the top left-hand corner / bottom right-hand corner, etc.

The second part of this exercise shouldn't take long, but it is a further opportunity for learners to practise describing the painting and also tests them on some of the vocabulary you may have taught earlier.

Answer key

1. The legs and feet of an acrobat.
2. It has Manet's signature and the year of the painting.
3. The audience, a chandelier and two pillars.
4. A necklace and a bracelet.
5. Wine bottles, beer bottles, a vase of flowers, a bowl of tangerines (or similar fruit), a green bottle.
6. The woman wearing the beige gloves.
7. The barmaid.
8. (down) The buttons on the barmaid's dress; (across) The balcony.
9. Looking at someone or something through binoculars.

3

Highlight the target language on the board and elicit further examples if you think it is necessary. Then let learners work on their own examples based on the picture, and conduct a brief feedback at the end.

4

Before learners read, point out that you are going to test them on their memory of the passage afterwards – this may prompt a careful reading of the text. They will need to look back at the painting while reading. Put them in pairs or small groups to look at the picture and provide a summary of what they have read, and then refer them back to the text to find anything they have forgotten.

5

Follow the instructions in the Class Book.

Answer key

1. Paris, much loved by artists. They ...
2. a few minutes earlier and which she is now thinking about. Perhaps ...

3. in his pictures, preferring instead to show modern life in a factual way, the bottles ...
4. in two. Other strong horizontals are created by the bar counter and its reflection in the mirror. There is a strong ...

Option

If the group has enjoyed the topic of the lesson, you could ask them to bring in some pictures of famous paintings (from books, magazines or greeting cards) and then discuss them in pairs or groups. Exercise 7 in the Personal Study Workbook has a description and evaluation of a painting done by an Italian learner – you may wish to show this to your learners as an example of something they could do with a painting of their own choice.

Personal Study Workbook

3: Free at last: prepositions and prepositional phrases
7: That's a good description ...: writing

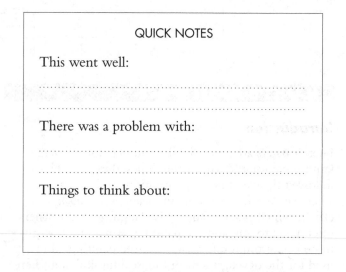

QUICK NOTES

This went well:
....
....

There was a problem with:
....
....

Things to think about:
....
....

COLOUR BLIND

Introduction

The topic of the lesson is colour blindness. Learners first discuss the effect that colour blindness *would* or *might have* on one's ability to do certain jobs (focus on different modal verbs), and then they find out what they know about the subject. A listening passage provides the facts about colour blindness, and the lesson then ends with a colour quiz for learners to do in groups.

Suggested steps

1

This is best done from the board rather than the book, but it would be too time-consuming to write all these questions on the board. The best option, if available, is probably an OHP. If you can prepare an OHT of the questions beforehand, you could discuss the questions in groups or as a whole class, and afterwards you could elicit the meaning of *tell* in these sentences. With a monolingual group, find out if one verb would translate *tell* in all of the sentences.

2

You could introduce this activity using the pictures in the Class Book. Ask the learners what problems they would have if they couldn't distinguish different colours at traffic lights or on a snooker (or pool) table. If they use *couldn't* all the time, ask them if they really mean *couldn't*, or *might not be able to*, i.e. are they sure about this or is it just a possibility? Similarly, make them aware of the alternative to *couldn't*, i.e. *wouldn't be able to*.

Move on to the list of jobs. Look at the examples and elicit one or two more if possible. Put learners in groups or pairs for the rest of the activity, monitor, and conduct a brief feedback of their answers with some language feedback as well.

Answer key

Possible answers:
A football referee couldn't/might not be able to tell one team from the other.
A gardener wouldn't be able to enjoy his garden as much and couldn't make effective planting plans.
A fashion designer wouldn't be able to match different garments and colours effectively.
A police officer wouldn't be able to describe or identify people with any accuracy.
A train driver might not be able to understand signals.

3

You could ask if anyone in the group is colour blind or knows someone who is colour blind. If so, ask them not to tell the group about the condition at this stage, but simply listen to what the others know or think. After a few minutes, conduct a feedback to put some of their ideas on the board, then move on to the listening.

4 ▭

Play the recording and let learners compare answers in pairs. Play it again if you think they could retrieve more information from a second listening; otherwise check answers. If you have anyone with a special knowledge of the subject, you could then invite them to talk about their own experience, **but only if they appear quite prepared to do so.**

Answer key

1. No.
2. Distinguishing red from green.
3. Men; and it is more common among white men than black or Asian men.
4. They are usually born with the condition.
5. No.

Tapescript

INTERVIEWER: Dr Smith, what exactly is 'colour blindness' and how many people does it affect?

DR SMITH: Well, essentially it's the inability to distinguish one colour from another, although the most common form of the condition usually involves difficulty with the colours red and green. And it's an interesting fact that the condition affects men far more than women.

INTERVIEWER: Really?

DR SMITH: Hmm, about one in 12 boys is affected, but only one in 100 girls. And also it's much more common amongst white people than black or Asian people.

INTERVIEWER: Right. But what exactly is colour blindness?

DR SMITH: Colour blindness means that the light-sensitive structures at the back of the eye don't work well. As I said, most people have difficulty with red and green. For some of them, reds look dull, almost grey. Others have problems with green, which looks grey, and they also find it hard to distinguish oranges and browns.

INTERVIEWER: So it's just those colours.

DR SMITH: Well, there is a more unusual condition which may develop as a result of poisoning from chemicals or drugs, and that affects blue. Complete colour blindness where the victim sees the world in black and white is fortunately extremely rare.

INTERVIEWER: OK. Is colour blindness something you can inherit from your parents, and is there a cure?

DR SMITH: It is hereditary, yes, apart from the cases of poisoning I mentioned. A lot of people with colour blindness in fact don't even realise there's anything wrong with them, though nowadays children are tested for the condition using coloured dots and plates.

INTERVIEWER: Right. And the cure?

DR SMITH: I'm afraid there is no cure. The only thing people can do is recognise they have the defect, and then use this knowledge in their choice of career – for example, you can't become a sailor, or a pilot or an engine driver if you suffer from colour blindness.

INTERVIEWER: Really?

DR SMITH: Yes, and, and when you're doing certain tasks, however simple they may seem, you do need that ability to distinguish colour; for example, changing an electric plug.

INTERVIEWER: OK, well, thank you very much, Dr Smith.

Option

If Exercise 3 prompted quite a lot of discussion, and/or you think your group would benefit from more discussion using different modal verbs, you could omit Exercise 5 and instead use Worksheet 7A on page 120.

5

There may be some new vocabulary in the questions in the quiz, or new items required to answer them, but it is probably more fun and more memorable if learners can find these things out for themselves. Just make sure they have dictionaries to help them. A time limit is also a good idea to add a bit of spice to the quiz.

Go over the answers and highlight some of the more difficult lexical items and sentence patterns on the board. For example:

What colour *do you associate with ...*
What colour *does/do X go ...*
What colour *represents ...*
What colour *is formed by mixing ...*

Encourage learners to use these patterns in their questions, but allow others as well. When they have had time to add four or five of their own, put them in groups to ask each other their questions. You could also try Worksheet 7B on page 120, which practises some figurative meanings of different colour words, and some idioms.

Personal Study Workbook

5: Cars and colour: reading
6: I wouldn't have to buy a ticket: listening

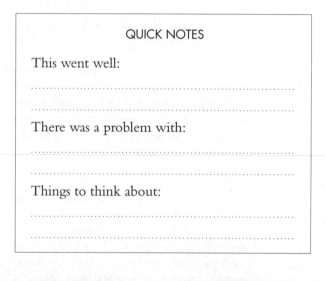

QUICK NOTES

This went well:

....

....

There was a problem with:

....

....

Things to think about:

....

....

THAT REALLY SUITS YOU

Introduction

There is a lot of vocabulary connected with clothes in this lesson (garments, colours, material, patterns, etc.), but we would expect your learners to know quite a lot already, so this is an opportunity to fill some gaps in a lexical area which is perceived to be both useful and important by many learners. The vocabulary is then practised in several personalised speaking activities which also introduce other common lexical patterns such as *X goes well with Y, X and Y look good together*, etc. The lesson finishes with a listening passage for further skills development and language reinforcement.

Suggested steps

1

This is a large list, but many items will not be new so there shouldn't be an overload of new vocabulary. If your learners are not familiar with phonemic transcriptions in dictionaries, they will have to rely on other learners, or you, to check pronunciation. Likely problems here are: *fur, purple, fashionable, suede* and *mauve.*

Putting the items into the correct box provides an initial guide to meaning, but you will need to provide some reinforcement. The pictures in Exercise 2 will help here, but if you make too much use of them, the later exercise will lose some of its impact. If possible, therefore, take in some examples of your own, e.g. a silk blouse, a picture of a tartan skirt, etc. This may not be easy, but for this lexical set no amount of explanation will compensate for the real thing. Translation will also be very useful here with a monolingual group.

When you have checked learners' answers, and their pronunciation, see if they can add more examples to each category. At this level they should know, for example: *elegant, smart, casual, untidy, red, green, blue, grey, leather, nylon, velvet* and *lace* (from the first lesson in the unit), and possibly *striped.*

Answer key

opinion	colour	pattern	material
scruffy	purple	tartan	suede
stylish	pale lemon	plain★	cord(uroy)
fashionable	mauve	spotted	denim
lovely	brownish	check(ed)	silk
revolting	bright red	patterned	fur
			wool/woollen
			cotton

★*Plain* would, in fact, normally precede a colour, e.g. *a plain grey dress.*

2

Ask learners if they can see any significance to the order of the categories in Exercise 1 (somebody should give you the right answer that they are the most common order of adjectives in English). Unfortunately, this is a case where the rules are made to be broken, so it is important to point out that this order will help learners if they are uncertain, but they should be prepared to hear other possibilities which are not wrong.

Language Point

Adjective word order can become very complicated. If you want to talk about the size of something, it commonly precedes the age of something, then the shape and then the colour. For example:
an enormous old TV   an old square table
a new black overcoat   an oval-shaped silver mirror
It is important to stress, once again, that these are useful guidelines but not strict rules. It is also generally true (but not a rule) that we don't commonly put more than two adjectives before a noun.

The activity should not take long, but elicit examples quickly from the pairs to make sure they can use the adjectives accurately with an appropriate order.

Answer key

(Possible answers in some cases)
blue cord(uroy) jeans
a purple silk shirt
a checked cotton jacket
a red silk blouse
red suede shoes
a revolting patterned waistcoat
colourful cotton trousers
a blue spotted top
a spotted woollen jumper
a lovely tartan scarf

3

The meaning of the lexis in bold should be fairly transparent. If you are feeling brave, you could check the concepts by asking your learners to comment on your own clothes. If not, just use the pictures in the Class Book.

4

This questionnaire provides an extended personalised speaking activity and teaches a useful lexical set. Make sure learners understand the questions (you may need to check items such as *match, suit someone, fit, vice versa* or *on impulse*).

5 ▢▢   �▢▢

Play the appropriate recording, or play both, and elicit answers. If you decide to play both versions, check answers to the first version before proceeding with the second.

Answer key

Version 1:
Conventional clothes: smart hat, gloves, suit and tie, top hat
Unusual clothes: flowing dresses, trouser suits, shorts
Version 2:
Conventional clothes: suit and tie, hat, gloves, morning suit (long jacket and waistcoat)
Unusual clothes: denim dresses, garlands of flowers, a kilt

Tapescript

Version 1

JACQUI: You know, I really, really like going to weddings; not, not just because they're happy occasions, or normally happy occasions, but because you can watch everybody and watch what they're wearing (Hmm) and nowadays, I think it's quite different from in our parents' day, when you always, well, women always wore very smart hat, gloves, suit – nowadays you see all sorts of fashions on women, you see very flowing dresses, trouser suits. I even saw someone wear shorts! (Hmm) I mean, they were quite smart shorts, and not, really, not everyone wears hats any more, and hardly anyone wears gloves.

LINFORD: Yeah. Well, I like going to weddings, 'cos it's one of the very few times you actually get a chance to dress up (Hmm) because most of the time I find myself wearing jeans or sweatshirts, or casual things, so it's really nice to actually be able to put on a suit and a tie for me, personally, so I really enjoy the occasion and the event because you get to dress up and play the role of, you know, being at a wedding.

JACQUI: Have you ever worn a top hat? Because men wear top hats sometimes.

LINFORD: Not really, but, erm, I'm sure I'll get to wear one if I ever get to be someone's best man or maybe even my own wedding! (Hmm)

Version 2

KATHERINE: I think it's much easier for men going to weddings, because you just have to put on your suit and your tie, and you look smart. (Hmm) Women have a whole rigmarole of deciding what to wear – should I wear a hat? And should I wear gloves? And … it's very difficult for a woman to look, look the part, I think.

PAUL: Well, I'm not sure I agree with you there, I mean, speaking from my personal experience, I was an usher at my sister's wedding, a few years ago, and she wanted us all in morning suit (Yes) so it was the full thing, you know, the trousers, the long jacket, the long waistcoat …

KATHERINE: Very smart …

PAUL: … very, very smart, and it was in August, (Oh!) and it was boiling hot, and I found it very, very restricting and didn't really enjoy wearing it at all. (Hmm) I was really, really happy to be at the reception in slightly more casual clothes.

KATHERINE: Yes, well, I once went to a very informal wedding, where the bride and the bridesmaids were wearing denim dresses and bare feet, and everybody was wearing garlands of flowers, and it was all set in a garden (Oh, brilliant!) so it was rather lovely.

PAUL: Hmm. What did you wear?

KATHERINE: Erm, well, I wore, um, I was probably one of the smartest people there, because I didn't realise that it was so informal, so I quickly took my jacket off and, um, took my shoes off eventually as well, so that I fitted in more.

PAUL: Brilliant. I've worn a kilt!

KATHERINE: Have you?

PAUL: Yes. Unfortunately, at this particular wedding, it was freezing and I froze. (laughter) I did have something on underneath.

KATHERINE: I wasn't going to ask. Are you Scottish?

PAUL: No, no, but the friend who was marrying was.

KATHERINE: Right.

Now form groups for the discussion. Monitor learners' language, and select one person from each group to summarise the comments from the group on one or two of the questions. At the end, give your own language feedback on the discussion.

Personal Study Workbook

1: Woollen, fashionable, pullover: adjective word order
2. Does it suit me?: clothes vocabulary
4: Longish hair and a roundish face: vocabulary and *-ish* suffix
8: Speaking partners

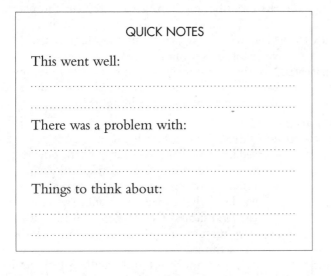

QUICK NOTES

This went well:

....

....

There was a problem with:

....

....

Things to think about:

....

....

REVIEW AND DEVELOPMENT

REVIEW OF UNIT 5

1

You will need to allow some time for learners to read and complete each story. An alternative would be to give the reading and completion activity for homework (and ask learners to be able to retell at least one of the stories from memory), then use class time for the retelling, with their own endings.

For the second part, follow the instructions in the Class Book.

Answer key

1. No, because clearly he had not finished cooking the chips when he fell asleep.
2. No, it would be wrong.
3. Yes, and there is little difference in meaning.
4. No, *see* is rarely used in the continuous form with this meaning.

2 ▢

Follow the instructions in the Class Book for the first two parts, and refer the group to the tapescript on page 165 if necessary. In the third part, try to encourage your learners not to think about individual words or sounds, but instead to think about producing the whole phrase or sentence as it appears on the recording. This way they focus on more global aspects of pronunciation such as the overall rhythm of the language. Sometimes learners find that if they can recreate the rhythm of a phrase, the sounds and stress fall into place more easily.

Tapescript

I'd been staying with some friends in Madrid and it was the last night of the holiday. We decided to go and see a thriller which had been filmed in a ruined castle in Scotland. It wasn't a terribly interesting film, but the building and surroundings were spectacular.

When I got back to London the following day, there was a postcard from my brother who'd been on holiday in Scotland. The photo on the card looked really familiar. Later on, I realised where I'd seen it before. It was the same ruined castle they'd used in the film in Madrid.

REVIEW OF UNIT 6

This exercise provides a reminder of one use of *wouldn't* with controlled practice, but the main task here is to produce likely or acceptable collocations. It can be done individually or in pairs. An additional task would be to see if pairs can go back to the beginning and complete each sentence with a second verb which is also acceptable in the context.

Answer key

Possible answers:

1. The waitress wouldn't serve me, so I left.
2. The telephonist wouldn't connect me, so I hung up.
3. The doctor wouldn't see/treat me, and I complained.
4. The plumber wouldn't repair the sink, but I managed to do it myself.
5. The surgeon wouldn't operate, and there was nothing we could do.
6. The dustman wouldn't collect our rubbish, so I had to get rid of it myself.
7. The scissors wouldn't cut.
8. The brakes wouldn't work.
9. The drawer wouldn't open/shut.
10. The car wouldn't start.
11. The lid of the jar wouldn't come off.
12. The rain wouldn't stop.

QUICK NOTES

This went well:

....

....

There was a problem with:

....

....

Things to think about:

....

....

8

ADDRESSING THE ISSUES

CONTENTS

Language focus:	*it's time* + past tense	
	textual cohesion	
	expressing willingness	
	political vocabulary	
	collocation: crime and the law	
Skills:	Speaking:	choosing a political candidate
		factors influencing voting habits
		censorship
	Listening:	people from different countries talk about voting habits
	Reading:	profiles of political candidates
		a text about TV censorship
	Writing:	expressing an opinion

SCANDAL

Introduction

The title of the lesson is *Scandal*, and some of the activities are about the willingness of people to support those in positions of power who may have been guilty of past misdemeanours or controversial actions. **If any of these subjects are likely to be sensitive in the culture where you are working, you may wish to omit this lesson.**

The lesson includes a number of lexical items connected with law and order, and ways of expressing willingness or reluctance. A reading text gives the background to a group of political candidates and the main speaking activity is discussing and selecting the best candidate for the post of mayor, councillor or local leader.

Suggested steps

1

Begin by checking that your learners understand the word *scandal*. Then put them in pairs and set the task. Let the pairs exchange information and discuss their case studies, then collect views from the whole group and finish by reinforcing some of the key lexis in the two texts, e.g. a*ccuse someone of something, reveal, charge someone with something, speeding*, etc. This lexical focus will lead in naturally to the next exercise.

2

Learners will need access to good dictionaries to complete this task, and even then they may find one or two pairs quite difficult to separate. If any learners are experiencing difficulty, tell them to concentrate on the

ones they can do, and you can clarify the other pairs of words with the whole group at the end (otherwise you may find yourself explaining the same thing five times to five different pairs). The second part of the exercise should be omitted if it is politically sensitive.

Answer key

1. *Charged with* drink driving means you must appear in court to face trial; *convicted of* drink driving means you have been found guilty of the offence in a court of law.
2. *Stopped for speeding* means physically stopped by the police; *fined for speeding* means you have to pay money for committing this crime.
3. *Pushing drugs* means selling drugs to others; *taking drugs* means consuming/using drugs oneself.
4. *Bribery* means offering money to someone so that they will help you in some way; *blackmail* is forcing someone to give you money otherwise you will reveal a secret about them (that they would not want to be revealed).
5. *Shoplifting* is stealing goods from a shop; *burglary* is illegally entering and stealing money or possessions from private property.
6. *Fraud* is a method of getting money from someone illegally, often through clever deception; *tax evasion* is illegally avoiding the payment of your tax.

3

Despite the vocabulary work in Exercise 2, the texts will still include a limited number of new items for some learners, e.g. *GP, eloquent, euthanasia, solicitor, wound, subsidies.* You could quickly pre-teach a few of these items to ease the load, or allow learners more time and the use of dictionaries. Be prepared to offer help if they need it before highlighting the language in the box below and proceeding with the speaking activity. If you feel the text may present a number of problems, use the option below.

Option

Ask the group to draw three columns in their notebooks – one for positive points, one for negative points, and a third column with a *?* for information which could be interpreted as positive or negative. Then tell the group to read the four texts and make notes by putting the information in the appropriate column. (You can monitor this while they work and assess how well they have understood the texts.) Then they can compare in pairs: one reads through their positive points; the other responds with the negative points, and together they discuss the third column. With this activity they are already engaging in the discussion to choose the best candidate, so don't let it go on too long.

When you are satisfied they have understood the texts clearly, talk through the target language for expressing willingness and reluctance and elicit some examples as controlled practice.

Put the class into small groups and ask them to discuss their willingness or reluctance to vote for each of the four candidates. Monitor the discussion and bring it to a close when you sense the group have said all they wish. Give some language feedback, remembering that this should include positive feedback as well as error correction, plus any new language that learners clearly wanted in the discussion.

Option

You could also try this activity as a roleplay. Divide the class into groups of four, and assign each person one of the characters in the election. It is their job to prepare a short speech (2–3 minutes) representing their character's opinions and best qualities. Start by grouping together all the learners representing each character, e.g. all the Dr Rennisons together. They can help each other to prepare the most convincing speech. Then the groups can re-form and each character, in turn, can give their short speech. At the end, if you like, each group can decide on the most effective speech.

4

If the discussion was quite heated with clear differences of opinion, finish the lesson with a secret ballot to find the most popular candidate. Each person should write a first and second choice on a piece of paper (without showing it to anyone). Collect them in and give out the result.

Personal Study Workbook

1: Can you commit murder?: collocation
2: Definitions: vocabulary

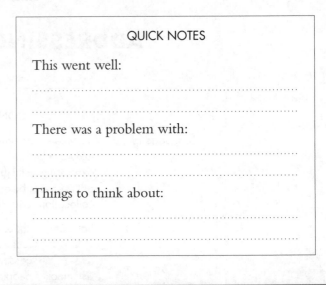

QUICK NOTES

This went well:

....

....

There was a problem with:

....

....

Things to think about:

....

....

POLITICAL ISSUES

Introduction

The lesson is largely concerned with the many different factors which influence people's voting habits, and includes listening, personalised speaking activities and a range of common collocations connected with the topic, e.g. *controversial issue*, *foreign policy*, etc. **If you or the group feel uneasy about discussing political issues in class, omit this lesson.**

Suggested steps

Option

If your class are particularly interested in politics, you could begin with Worksheet 8 on page 121, which starts with a brainstorming activity on political vocabulary and then goes on to discussion of a number of political topics. Much of this language will be relevant to this lesson on voting habits among people from different cultures.

1

You may wish to begin by asking the class for the last occasion when they had an opportunity to vote in an election, and what the outcome was of that election. You can then introduce the factors which influence people at elections and ask the group if they think the four factors in the list are significant. Afterwards, see if small groups can produce four more. Stress that the task is to think of factors which influence people in general, and not the learners themselves (that comes next). Conduct a brief feedback at the end by putting the ideas on the board, then compare them with the list on page 155 of the Class Book. Clarify any new vocabulary at the end, e.g. *spouse*, *record*.

2

Learners now have the opportunity to give their own view, although you should make it clear that **nobody is being asked (or should be asked) to reveal how**

they would vote in an election. Learners are free to divulge political affiliations if they wish, but this is not the purpose of the task. This activity may last five minutes or twenty-five minutes, so be prepared to adjust your timing for the rest of the lesson.

Option

If you work with a group from the same country, you could put these factors into context and talk about the last election in the country. Which specific factors did influence people in general in that election? Learners can also talk about the factors which influenced them if they wish.

3 ▭

By this stage, learners will have had a lot of ideas and vocabulary relevant to the topic, so the listening needs little introduction. Play the recording once and let learners compare their notes.

Answer key

Lynn:
She is English. She always votes for the same party because, in her words, they are 'the least of all the evils'. She is concerned about moral issues and is looking for politicians with integrity, honour and the ability to motivate people. She is very concerned about education.
Trude:
She is German. There are many centre parties in Germany, and she does not always vote for the same party. She is particularly concerned about environmental issues, and the party with the best policy on the environment will win her vote.
Jeff:
He is American. His family has always voted Republican, but he votes Democrat. When he was young he was influenced by the Vietnam War. He now supports the Democrats because he would like to see a better national health service, better education and better care for the poor.

Tapescript

LYNN: Well, I've always voted for the same party in Britain, not because I agree with all their policies, necessarily, but because when you look at all the parties, they're the least of all the evils. And the issues that concern me are largely centred around moral issues to do with, well, telling the truth. I don't think it's a crime to say you're sorry when you've got something wrong. Erm, I think it would be nice if people just had a bit more honour, and so I look for people with the integrity and who are prepared to tell the truth, even if it's not what we all want to hear. Erm, I'm not looking for strong leadership, because I think that actually lets people off the hook; it means that they don't have to be responsible for what happens in their environment, so I'm looking for people who motivate me and others to take action for themselves, and I'm very concerned about

education because I think it's the one thing that can help people move from one social class to another, and I think that the worst thing that dogs our country at the moment is a poverty of imagination.

TRUDE: Well, back in Germany, I have voted for different parties, because it's actually different from here, from England because we have quite a few parties that are middling, and so it always depends on who the politicians are, of the moment, really – what their outlook is, so that can change, so I was always flexible about this. For me the main issue is, erm, the current sort of attitude to environmental, erm, problems, and if a party shows that they are really concerned and they are, you know, about to do things that I think are very important, then, erm, I'm gonna give them my vote.

JEFF: Erm, I was brought up in the States by a family that always voted Republican. It was always party politics, we didn't even speak to Democrats. Erm, but then when I was growing up, the Vietnam War happened. I think people my age were allowed to think for themselves; the vote came down to a younger age, and I started voting – mostly Democrat – I think they care more about people. Certainly, Clinton now has tried very hard to introduce national health – which would be awfully nice. It makes sense in England; I don't know why it can't in the States. Erm, better education and better care for the poor, I think. Under the Republicans, the poor really suffer, and, erm, maybe we can finish with party politics and try to make society a little more equal.

4

Refer learners to the tapescript on page 155 of the Class Book, play the recording again, and see if they can complete the gaps. After you have checked their answers, allow a few minutes for learners to look up new words in the text and ask you questions. This is an important phase of the lesson because motivation will be high to understand a listening passage and learners are usually very keen to uncover new lexis in a listening text, particularly if the items seem useful or created comprehension problems for them when they listened.

Answer key

Lynn:
Gap 1: are largely centred around moral issues
Gap 2: a bit more honour
Gap 3: strong leadership
Gap 4: in their environment
Gap 5: a poverty of imagination
Trude:
Gap 1: current sort of attitude to environmental, erm,
Gap 2: gonna (going to) give them my vote

Jeff:
Gap 1: were allowed to think for themselves
Gap 2: better care for the poor
Gap 3: society a little more equal

5

You can make use of the definitions in the Class Book or explain the items yourself. Then move on to the table of adjectives, go through the examples, then set the rest of the task as pairwork. Check answers and clarify any problems.

Answer key

	issue	policy	leader
political	yes	no	yes
strong	no	yes	yes
economic	yes	yes	no
vital	yes	yes	no
global	yes	yes	no
trade union	yes	yes	yes
party	yes	yes	yes

6

This provides some practice of the vocabulary in Exercise 5 and is a more animated way to round off the lesson. Learners can do this individually then compare with a partner, or they can do it in pairs or small groups. It need not take more than five minutes.

Personal Study Workbook

4: Sounds and spelling: pronunciation
5: Politics in quotations: reading
8: Speaking partners

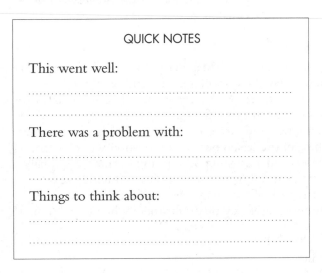

QUICK NOTES

This went well:

....

....

There was a problem with:

....

....

Things to think about:

....

....

TV CENSORSHIP

Introduction

The lesson makes use of an article about TV censorship to focus on and develop reading skills (the use of referencing words through a text), to highlight the use of *it's time* + past tense, and as a vehicle to promote class discussion. The lesson ends with an opportunity for learners to transfer some of their ideas into a piece of written English.

Suggested steps

1

In order to avoid the possibility of learners looking at the text, write the headline on the board and let pairs discuss it. You may need to provide a gloss for *sleaze* first (immoral behaviour, especially involving sex, dishonesty, and financial impropriety).

2

Continue working from the board. Highlight the use of *it's about time* followed by the past tense from the headline and see if anyone can explain the meaning and reason for the use of the past tense here. If not, explain yourself, and only then refer the class to the explanation in the Class Book. Follow with the pairwork task, and move round to check that the pairs have understood the meaning. Then form small groups to discuss the headlines created by the different pairs.

Answer key
Possible answers:
It's time we restricted the number of …
It's about time we prevented our children …

3

Learners should be allowed to use dictionaries while they are reading, but the focus of the task is reacting to the ideas expressed in the text. (Tell them not to worry about the highlighting of certain phrases at this stage.) Again, move round to see which ideas have been picked out by the group, and try to form groups where it is clear there is likely to be some difference of opinion. At the end, conduct feedback.

4

Now you can return to the highlighted phrases and use the examples to demonstrate how lexis in a text is constantly being used to refer back to points already made as well as anticipating ideas which are coming up. If learners are not making a mental note of these references as they proceed, they are unlikely to understand fully what the text is about. Let individuals compare with a partner when they have finished and discuss any differences; you can then focus on these differences when you go over the answers.

Answer key

it (line 10) refers to *terrestrial television*
which (line 14) refers to *The Good Sex Guide*
it (line 19) refers to *so-called entertainment (which The Good Sex Guide tries to be)*
those (line 22) refers to *our sensibilities and moral values*
then (line 33) refers to *at night*
it (line 36) refers to *what we put out*
that (line 39) refers to *our audience's*
it (line 41) refers to *our audience's trust*
this (line 47) refers to *a revolution in the way that moving images affect our lives*

5

You could, of course, give this final activity for homework, but if you decide to use it in class and get learners working together, don't try to cram it into a final ten minutes. Learners will need time to marshal their arguments and discuss the best order of points. From this, they can prepare their first draft. Afterwards, you could ask the pairs to move round, read each other's work and make suggested improvements. Many learners will read the efforts of others and see improvements they wish to make themselves. This is then followed by the second draft and final polishing of the language. This may seem like a very time-consuming process, but it is all concerned with learners' own ideas and their own language, so there is often a very high degree of motivation. If successful, you can adopt a similar approach for other writing tasks.

Personal Study Workbook

3: What's wrong with this?: grammar and vocabulary
6: Censorship on television: listening
7: In my opinion: writing

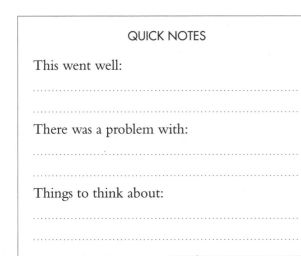

QUICK NOTES

This went well:

....

....

There was a problem with:

....

....

Things to think about:

....

....

REVIEW OF UNIT 6

1

Check the answers to the first part before the speaking activity, which can be done in pairs or as a mingling activity around the class in which learners ask one person two or three questions, then move on to another person.

Answer key

lie down; pick someone up; calm someone down; start up; two days off; sort out; see someone off; show someone round; give up; tell someone off

2

This exercise is simply to consolidate some of the concepts associated with different verb forms, with a final production exercise to see if the group can transfer the concepts to a new situation. You can always add further practice by asking learners to make up their own series of four sentences around a single verb, e.g. *live* or *have*.

Answer key

The train usually leaves at 6.15 every day.
The train will be leaving in a few minutes, so hurry up.
The train will leave as soon as the other one gets in.
I wear my blue hat on special occasions.
I'll wear my blue hat then you can borrow my other one.
I'll be wearing my blue hat, so you should be able to recognise me.
He works all the time.
He'll work if we need more staff next weekend.
He'll be working when you get back, so don't bother to ring.

Possible answers:
I spend a lot of time on my homework each week.
I'm spending a lot of time with my brother at the moment.
I'll spend a lot of time on this project if I don't get any help.
I'll be spending a lot of time at home, so don't ring me at work.

REVIEW OF UNIT 7

1

When the pairs have finished, they could move round the class and look at the sentences produced by others. Do they agree? Which sentence occurs the most? Which picture provokes the greatest number of different observations? etc.

Possible answers:

2. The boy looks guilty/ashamed. The boy looks like his father. The man looks as if he is angry / telling the boy off.
3. The man on the left looks suspicious. The man on the left looks like a thief. The shop assistant looks as if he is going to say something / stop the man taking the bag.
4. The young man at the front looks miserable. The paper on the noticeboard looks like a list of exam results. It looks as if the young man at the front has failed his exam.

2 ▭

Follow the instructions in the Class Book.

Tapescript

1. Can you make a jacket out of marble?
2. Is purple lighter than mauve?
3. Is beige a yellowish-brown?
4. Can you tell the difference between cotton and velvet just by looking at it?
5. If you're colour blind, can you tell the difference between red and green?
6. Would bright red, purple and pale lemon look nice together?
7. Would black and grey clash?
8. Is tartan the same as striped?
9. Is silk more fashionable than nylon?
10. If something fits you, does it mean you like it?
11. If you go window shopping, does it cost a lot?
12. If something doesn't suit you, should you try another size?

QUICK NOTES

This went well:

....

....

There was a problem with:

....

....

Things to think about:

....

....

MAKING THE MOST OF YOUR TIME

CONTENTS

Language focus: prepositions and adverbs
tense and time
nouns and adjectives + *-ing* or infinitive
non-defining relative clauses
time expressions

Skills: Speaking: discussing time management
doing a time quiz
giving a short talk
Listening: time management problems
a newsflash
Reading: nine rules of time management
Writing: writing and editing a news article

TIME MANAGEMENT

Introduction

A lesson on the topic of time management may be more interesting for people with jobs, although much of the advice will be relevant to learners who have to organise their study time. In the lesson, learners work on a reading text which contains not only useful tips on time management, but also some important language to make positive suggestions or give warnings. This language is highlighted before learners go on to practise it with reference to a range of different topics.

Suggested steps

1 🔲 🔳

It is often a good idea to start this kind of personalised activity with your own experience. Tell the group how you manage your time (self-censoring where necessary), then put them into pairs or groups to exchange ideas. Conduct a short feedback at the end, and put some of the ideas on the board if you wish. Play the appropriate version of the recording, and ask learners to note down the problems and solutions.

Answer key

Version 1:
Problem: She can't get down to her work and do what needs to be done because of constant interruptions.
Suggestions: 1. Her secretary should filter calls and only allow important ones to be put through. 2. She should delegate more so subordinates do some of her work.
Version 2:
Problem: Meetings are ineffective – they go on too long and nothing gets decided.

Suggestions: 1. Set a time limit for meetings – a time to start and a time to finish. 2. Reduce the numbers at each meeting.

Tapescript

Version 1

AISHA: My problem is that I really can't, I can't seem to get down to a decent day's work.

NEIL: Right.

AISHA: The phone goes constantly, (Hmm) I have people queuing at my desk, asking for information, bits of advice, and I actually can't achieve a proper day's work, I mean, do the big work that I really have to do.

NEIL: Right. Erm, I suggest that you get your secretary to filter all the calls; make sure she only lets through the most important ones, the most urgent ones. That way, you find your time is ... you'll have much, much more time to do things, er, on your own. The other thing I suggest is, er, I think you should delegate responsibility. I mean, don't do it all yourself. You have other people there to do things for you. Make sure that they do it! OK?

AISHA: Yes, you're right. It's easier said than done.

Version 2

LAUREN: I'm having some, er, problems with my meeting technique; the meetings that I, that I am conducting seem to go on too long, which I wouldn't mind if we were actually getting something done, (Hmm) but they go on a long time, and also I, I have trouble controlling the people attending the meeting. Everything seems to get out of hand, and everyone seems to have something to say, and I wondered if you had any feedback for me.

SION: Yes, I do know that these things can get out of hand, so my first suggestion would be that you set a very firm time limit for these meetings: absolutely specific, it will start at two o'clock, and it will finish at 2.45; don't let it run over any longer than that. And furthermore, I don't know how many people attend the meetings, but if it's possible for you to whittle the numbers down, have senior members of staff only, who can then relay to more junior personnel what has been discussed at the meeting, because the more people you have at a meeting, the more people will want to speak, and that's how these things get out of control.

LAUREN: Hmm. Thank you very much.

2

Some of the rules are self-explanatory while others are more obscure and will require greater powers of deduction. We would not advise giving too much help at this stage, but you could provide a quick explanation of *salami* (a strong-tasting sausage, eaten cold and usually sliced thinly) for some non-European learners, and also *curse*, e.g. that in this phrase it means the problem caused by perfectionism; and you might also offer a few hints for learners who are having difficulty, e.g. ask them to think about the main feature of elephants, and how they appear at a distance. Otherwise, just let them see how much they can guess or deduce, then conduct a feedback on their ideas.

3

Focus learners on the gist task, i.e. matching the headings with the correct explanation, and discourage any lengthy use of dictionaries at this stage. If necessary, you could introduce a time limit to encourage learners to skim the text rather than read every word carefully.

Answer key

1. C   2. F   3. H   4. B   5. E   6. D   7. I   8. G   9. A

When you have checked answers, you can then give learners a few minutes to look through the text again, look up new words or ask you questions.

4

Put learners into groups. You could then initiate the discussion yourself with one or two questions round the class, then let them carry on in their groups. Monitor the discussion and bring it to a close as soon as you sense the groups have said everything they want to say. You could ask one member of each group to provide a quick summary of the main points.

Option

Another way of organising a reaction to the text is by dividing the class into three groups:

Group A has to choose the best three rules.
Group B has to choose the three least useful rules.

Group C has to try to come up with more useful rules (possibly based on personal experience).
The groups can later re-form to exchange their ideas.

5

Most of the highlighted language is fairly transparent in meaning, although some of it will be new, e.g. *pointless* and *get into the habit of (doing something)*, and much of it may not be part of the learners' active vocabulary, e.g. *it's worth (doing something)*. Spend a few minutes going through the phrases, then choose a topic from which you can elicit some further examples from the class. For example, ask them to give advice and warnings for someone visiting their country for the first time (*it's worth going to the south coast, it's good if you get into the habit of using a few new phrases whenever you go out*, etc.). Then put them into groups and let them choose a topic to make up their own advice and warnings. Listen to some round the class at the end.

Personal Study Workbook

5: Take charge of your day: reading
6: The best time to do things: listening

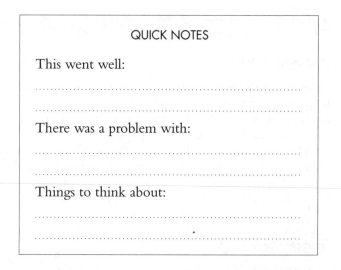

QUICK NOTES

This went well:

....
....

There was a problem with:

....
....

Things to think about:

....
....

TIME QUIZ

Introduction

The time quiz is a vehicle for teaching and testing a whole range of useful language connected with time, and while some of it will be revision, there is certainly something for everyone here. After learners have done the quiz and checked their answers, there is an intensive and personalised speaking activity to finish.

Suggested steps

1

This is just a warm-up to start the lesson, but it is surprising the number of learners who find it difficult to think of three ways of saying each time.

four forty-five; quarter to five; sixteen forty-five
twenty-one fifty-five; nine fifty-five; five to ten
six thirty; half past six; eighteen thirty, half six
(colloquial)

2

The time limit here is to spur the groups on, but you
can obviously adjust this if your learners find it fairly easy
or fairly difficult. And if one group finishes ahead of the
rest, refer them to the question at the end which requires
them to make up compounds – that will keep them busy
until the other groups finish. Move round and monitor
the different groups and provide help where necessary.
Check the answers at the end and clarify any problems.
The following *Language Points* may help with common
sources of confusion.

Language Points

1. *for* vs. *during*
Broadly speaking, *during* answers the question *when*
and *for* answers the question *how long*:
Examples: *He worked there during the summer.*
He worked there for three months.

2. *at last* vs. *eventually*
Eventually is a false friend for several nationalities,
and *at last* is commonly mis-used and over-used by
many speakers. When you want to say that
something was accomplished after a number of
difficulties or delays, it is usually safer to use
eventually:
Examples: *The traffic was terrible and there were roadworks
along the way, but eventually we got there.*
I found it eventually but it took me ages.
At last is similar but emphasises that a moment we
have been hoping for or waiting for has arrived:
Examples: *She sat nervously throughout the meal then
at last came the moment for her speech.*
*At last the train arrived in the station. It was
such a relief.*

3. *ex-* vs. *former*
Both words have the same meaning, but *ex-* tends to
be used only with reference to people, and in
particular to previous husbands or wives, boyfriends,
girlfriends, bosses or politicians. *Former* is used more
widely with reference to both people and places.
So, you could substitute *former* for *ex-* in Exercise 4,
question 1, but you could not use *ex-* in question 3.

For those who finish ahead of time ...
Examples: time lag, time bomb, timekeeper, flexi-time,
full time, part time, extra time, etc.

3

Make sure learners understand the topics in the list, and
give everyone time to make notes / prepare their ideas
on two or three different topics (if they only prepare
one, they may find someone else does it before they get
a chance to speak). When they are ready, be strict about
the time limit of one minute for each speaker – this not
only maintains the momentum, but also prevents one or
two people from monopolising the activity. Monitor
while the groups are working and collect examples of
appropriate and/or inaccurate language for feedback.

Option

You can add your own topics to the list in Exercise 3
based on your knowledge of the group, but try to ensure
that any new subjects will also include some items from
the quiz.

If your learners enjoy quizzes and competitions, you
could try a different type of time quiz in Worksheet 9 on
page 121. This time the quiz is about facts connected
with time. The answers are on page 53.

Personal Study Workbook

1: Put it right: prepositions and adverbs
2: Time: time expressions
3: Question and answer: tense revision
8: Speaking partners

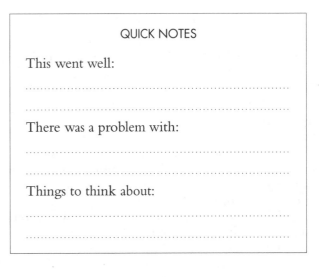

```
QUICK NOTES

This went well:
.............................................................
.............................................................

There was a problem with:
.............................................................
.............................................................

Things to think about:
.............................................................
.............................................................
```

Answer key

1. 1 b   2 d   3 f   4 c   5 e   6 a
2. 1 nowadays   2 long   3 afterwards   4 throughout
   5 meanwhile   6 eventually
3. 1 for   2 on time   3 until   4 in   5 current
   6 eventually
4. 1 ex-   2 previous   3 former   4 earlier   5 lately
   6 predecessor
5. 1 just in time   2 before my time   3 correct   4 for
   the time being   5 in your own time   6 correct

Introduction

This is a process writing lesson in which learners work collaboratively on a first draft of a newspaper article. They are then forced to make last minute cuts for final publication, which means some editing and rewriting. A listening passage provides the information for the article, and there is also a focus on non-defining relative clauses as they can be a very useful device in writing to incorporate additional information in a single sentence rather than using two sentences.

Suggested steps

1

The first exercise is a way into the topic and also a chance to teach/check the phrase *under pressure*. If everyone in the class thinks they work best under pressure, you might like to ask them why that should be the case.

2 ▭

Organise the pairs and give the group one minute to read the newsflash. Tell them to shut their books and tell each other what they remember. Elicit the information from the pairs, check/extend any new vocabulary, e.g. *seize* and *seizure*, then play the recording for more detailed information. Let the pairs compare, then elicit the answers. You could put these notes on the board or OHP, and learners can check using the tapescript on page 166 if they wish.

Tapescript

Late last night, Customs officials at Dover seized drugs – all of it thought to be cocaine – with an estimated street value of more than one and a half million pounds. This comes at a time when Customs officials have been particularly vigilant following the seizure in Rotterdam just six weeks ago of cocaine said to be worth over two million pounds, and there have been subsequent rumours of a large shipment of cocaine entering this country. Today's discovery resulted from a routine search on a van travelling from Ostend, containing mostly Belgian chocolate. Customs were suspicious because the van was unmarked, and at first they thought they had uncovered a shipment of stolen chocolates. However, they soon realised that they had made a much more significant and valuable discovery.

So far, the driver's identity hasn't been disclosed, but he was travelling alone and is thought to be in his twenties. He is now helping police and Customs officials with their enquiries.

This is the third major drugs haul by Customs officials this year and they believe they may have destroyed one of the largest drug smuggling rings operating in Europe. This is Pat Harman in Dover, and now back to the studio.

3

Non-defining clauses are more common in writing than everyday speech, and in a condensed news article learners will be able to incorporate additional information in their sentences without the need for new sentences. Go through the examples carefully and point out that the sentences would still be coherent without the clauses, but they allow the possibility of adding additional information to the sentence. You may want the group to read through the Language Reference now; alternatively make sure they read it at the end of the lesson.

When you are satisfied that they understand this type of clause, let them complete the other sentences and compare with a partner. Move round and monitor carefully, then elicit a few answers.

Answer key

Possible answers:

One of the witnesses, who only came forward with information recently, ...

The police van, which had been pelted with stones by the crowd when it arrived, ...

The policeman's dog, which was named Copper after its owner, ...

4

Ideally learners should only have enough time to write the story, but not enough for careful editing and refining. With this in mind, be ready to reduce or extend the deadline as you think appropriate, and don't let learners read the instructions for Exercise 5 at this stage. When time is up and the pairs move round to read different stories, make sure they note down different information, and also encourage them to suggest ways of including non-defining clauses if they are not included.

5

Now the pairs have to do some editing. Again, use your discretion with the timing: reduce it if they don't really need ten minutes, but extend it a little if they haven't finished after ten minutes. Remind them they can use the tapescript if necessary.

6

Adding a headline will give a more finished look to the stories. Pin them on the wall and other pairs can go round and read each other's.

Personal Study Workbook

4: Oh, by the way ...: relative clauses
7: Amazing but true: writing

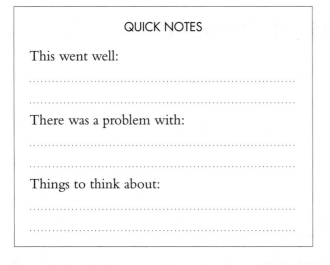

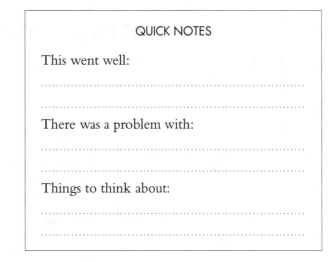

REVIEW AND DEVELOPMENT

REVIEW OF UNIT 7

1 ▭

This is really something of a 'mouth exercise'. You could play the poem first while your learners listen, then you could just point out one or two common features of connected speech:

1. The elision (sounds disappearing in certain circumstances) when the final consonant in *red* meets the first consonant in *jam*, producing /re dʒæm/; and when the final consonant in *black* meets the first consonant in *bread*, producing /blæ bred/.
2. The linking that takes place in the refrain: *spread͜ it, say͜ it, repeat͜ it, eat͜ it*.

After that, let learners practise on their own. Then they can say it at the same time as the recording and maintain the same rhythm.

2

You will probably be required to help the groups in finding the right language to express some of their consequences. When each group has finished, mix them up so they can exchange answers.

REVIEW OF UNIT 8

1

Follow the instructions in the Class Book.

Answer key

Possible answers:
2. blackmail, subsidies, a charity, bribery, tax evasion, pensions, burglary, fraud. (Burglary is usually linked with money as burglars commit the crime to obtain money.)
3. speeding, burglary, taking drugs
4. euthanasia, pensions

Worksheet 9 Answer key

1. b 2. c 3. c 4. a 5. b 6. c 7. a 8. b 9. b
10. b

TELLING STORIES IN ENGLISH

CONTENTS

Language focus:		linking spoken discourse, e.g. *actually*, *to be honest*
		attitude adverbs, e.g. *luckily*, *surprisingly*
		purpose clauses
		phrasal verbs and idioms
		crime vocabulary
Skills:	Speaking:	developing ideas for a story
		features of a good story
		is murder ever justifiable?
		meeting famous people
	Listening:	predicting parts of a story
		anecdotes about meeting famous people
		a short story (*Hobbyist* by Fredric Brown)
	Reading:	how to write a short story
	Writing:	writing a short story

YOU'LL NEVER GUESS WHO I MET ...

Introduction

The lesson helps learners to become more familiar with a range of different discourse linkers and attitude adverbs, and contains several activities which should demonstrate to learners how an understanding of these link words can assist comprehension. There are also several recordings of anecdotes for listening practice.

Suggested steps

1

If you wish, you could broaden the scope of the activity to include people living or dead. After the pairwork activity, share some of the ideas with the whole class.

2

You could write the first example on the board and try to elicit a logical answer. If you are successful, ask the group to explain how they were able to predict the second part of the sentence. If they seem unsure, do a second example as well. Then put them in pairs to finish the task, and conduct feedback.

Answer key

Possible answers:
and to be honest, I wasn't very keen to go.
So anyway, we just carried on eating and talking and then we went home.
– in fact, they earn very little compared with many professions.

eventually I got a reply.
for instance, Sylvester Stallone has got three bodyguards.

Language Point: link words in spoken English

Actually / in (actual) fact: These are used when we are saying what the facts/truth of a situation are/is, particularly when this is different from what is expected or thought.
Eventually: This is used to introduce the outcome of something after a long delay or series of difficulties.
For instance/example: These are used to introduce an example.
(So) anyway/anyhow: These are used when you want to get back to the main topic of conversation (after a digression), or to continue the thread of a story (also after a short digression from the main narrative).
To be (perfectly) honest: This is used when you are confiding in the listener and telling them your true feelings about something – and often this may involve feelings which will disappoint the listener – or are critical of others. We also use *frankly* and to *tell you the truth* in similar ways.

3 📼

As these link words are more common in spoken English, it makes sense for learners to hear them spoken. Here, they test their understanding by predicting what comes after each link word or phrase. Play the recording, pause after each one, get learners to write down their answer, listen to several examples, then go back and play the whole sentence/utterance again, and stop after the next link word; and so on. At the end, you could play the whole story through, and learners could follow the tapescript on page 166 or look at it afterwards.

Tapescript

A: Hi, Sue, how are you?
B: Oh, great; I've just come back from South Africa, actually.
A: No! What were you doing there?
B: I'm working on a project to do with primary schools, but I must tell you ...
A: What? Something happened to you?
B: Oh, yes. Actually, I met Nelson Mandela!
A: You're joking!
B: No, really.
A: Well, go on ...
B: Well, I was staying in a hotel in Johannesburg and I got friendly with a woman in the restaurant, and I saw her several mornings, so anyway ... one morning she said she was going to a big ceremony, and Nelson Mandela was going to be there, (Yeah) oh, and she'd got special seats in an enclosure with famous people, so of course I said 'Can I come?' (Yeah, I bet) and to be honest, ... I didn't expect her to say yes, but in fact ... surprisingly she did, so anyhow ... we went and eventually ... Mandela turned up, and I said hello to him. I just felt really privileged to have met him. (Yeah) He looked exactly as I expected.
A: Wow! That's amazing! Talking of famous people ... I was in my local coffee bar the other day and Mel Gibson and Tom Cruise walked in ...

4

It is asking quite a lot for learners to think up an interesting anecdote and successfully incorporate a range of link words, so don't press them too hard and certainly don't be too concerned if you don't hear all the link words being repeated back to you. This will come in time, and you should give praise (now and in the next few lessons) when you hear these link words and phrases being used appropriately. At the end, feed in any new language the learners obviously needed to complete the task, and let the whole class listen to one or two of the more interesting stories.

5 ▭ ▱

Play the appropriate version of the recording (or play both), then let learners compare answers before you check. Play it a second time if necessary and/or let learners look at the tapescript on page 166.

Answer key

Version 1:
Speaker 1
1. In a restaurant in London.
2. He was celebrating a special occasion.
3. Mick Jagger.
4. No.
5. No, because Mick Jagger's presence distracted his companion. However, the speaker didn't really have a negative feeling towards Mick Jagger.

Speaker 2
1. In Bath.
2. She was a student at the university.
3. Dustin Hoffman.
4. Yes (she interviewed him).
5. No.

Version 2:
Speaker 1
1. In southern Ireland.
2. She was on holiday.
3. Marlon Brando.
4. Yes (he spoke to her).
5. Yes.
Speaker 2
1. At his cousin's house.
2. He was at a wedding reception.
3. Winston Churchill's son (who is an MP).
4. Yes (they talked to each other).
5. Yes.

Tapescript

Version 1
1. Gareth
A friend of mine had just been offered a really wonderful job, and she rang me up and she said I'd like you to come and celebrate with me. I'm going to take you out for a terrific meal. And she'd chosen this restaurant in the west end of London, really smart restaurant where lots of, you know, starry people go. And we turned up and there were plenty of faces that you recognised and, er, we were being very cool about it, and then suddenly we saw over in the corner at a very discreet table was Mick Jagger. Well, of course we both stopped and stared at him, the thing that struck me I think was that, of course he's a man over 50 now and in my head I still see him as a, you know, a young rocker. Anyway, we sat down at the table and had this wonderful meal but I was furious with her because instead of looking at me throughout the meal, she was staring at Mick Jagger.
2. Lynne
Well, I was a student at Bath University at the end of the seventies and I had to write an interview for our student newspaper about Dustin Hoffman, (Right) because he was making a film in Bath or something. And so I had to go down and meet him, er, near the baths (Really?) and he was supposed to get out of his taxi and there were lots of TV people around, and when he did get out it was quite lovely 'cos he pushed all the TV people out of the way and came and talked to me and it was quite extraordinary really; he was much shorter than me, much shorter than I expected, and he had like a mug of tea with a dirty old tea bag in the bottom and he sort of gave that to his minder and then he had, he took out a razor and started shaving and just being incredibly silly and my impression of him was well ... he was ... I think I was giggling a lot as well 'cos I was quite young, but I think he was trying to wind me up really and I was just slightly disappointed.

Version 2
1. Marcella
It was about two years ago, and I was on holidays in the
very far south of Ireland, down in Kerry, and I was
driving back up to Dublin through the midlands, which
is not at all particularly interesting, it's not touristy or
anything, and I wanted to have some lunch, 'cos I was
starving, so I was passing through this very ordinary little
village, and I saw a pub, and, just an ordinary, small little
pub, and I went in, and, er, I was standing at the counter
and then I spotted a friend of mine who I hadn't seen for
ages, guy called Michael, over, er, at the window, and,
er, he'd been made redundant from his job, and I hadn't
seen him for ages, but I'd heard that he'd actually taken
up chauffeuring as part of, well, a new change of career,
and so I went flying over to him, 'cos we used to be such
good friends, and then we'd lost contact, and he was
sitting with this huge, large man. I couldn't believe it.
When he turned round, it was Marlon Brando. (Good
Lord!) And I have adored Marlon Brando since I've been
a kid. I mean, I was completely dumbstruck, and I'm
sure it was written all over me, you could see it, I, just
standing there, open mouthed, and I couldn't say
anything, and he was so nice, 'cos I'd say that that
happens to him all the time, and he was just so sweet and
charming. It turned out that he was looking for locations
for some film or other that he was going to do, but I was
just, I couldn't believe it ...
2. Jeff
My wife and I were invited to my cousin's wedding, my
cousin's daughter's wedding, and we arrived there and
we were a little bit surprised at the size of the house and
how many guests there were, but anyway we just carried
on – lovely reception, lots of Pimms, everybody was
feeling very convivial. And I got chatting to this guy, and
we had a perfectly normal sort of conversation, about
fifteen minutes. And I walked away and my wife pulled
me to one side, 'Do you know who that is?' I said 'No'.
'That's Winston Churchill's son.' I went, 'I was telling
him about, like, dogs and how I hate kids and he was
being very polite'. Anyway, I didn't talk to him again for
the rest of the wedding. (laughter)

6

These adverbs follow on very naturally from the link
words and phrases your learners have already covered in
the lesson, and the group will also now be familiar with
this type of task. If time is limited, this would be a very
suitable homework activity.

Answer key

Possible answers:
... unfortunately she got in the car and drove off at that
moment.
Surprisingly though, he got the part.
... so naturally, he looked exhausted.
Luckily, there was a cancellation and I managed to get a
couple.
Obviously, that may not be easy with my lack of
experience.

Personal Study Workbook
3: Being watched: punctuation and pronunciation
4: Make the connection: link words

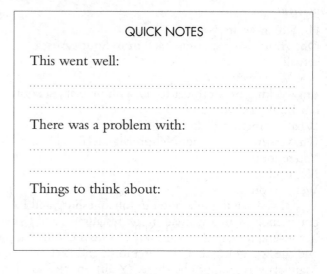

QUICK NOTES

This went well:

....
....

There was a problem with:

....
....

Things to think about:

....
....

WRITING SHORT STORIES THAT SELL

Introduction

As the focus is a text which offers advice on how to
write a short story, this lesson will probably be of
greatest interest to learners who enjoy literature. The
lesson also introduces and practises a range of phrasal
verbs and idioms, and offers several opportunities for
groups to develop their own short story and later
evaluate the ideas on which the story is based.

Suggested steps

1

Some learners may wish to do this on their own while
others will prefer the security of working with a partner,
so you could let the group decide for themselves how
they wish to tackle this activity. It shouldn't take up too
much of the lesson though, as the rest of the lesson is
designed to provide more help with thinking up a story,
and in any case, you won't finish the lesson if this first
activity takes too long.

2

It is probably easier and more logical for learners to find
the meaning of the new language and sequence the
activities at the same time. If dictionaries are in short
supply, you may have to put the learners in pairs or small
groups. When everyone has finished, give them two
minutes to memorise their sequence, then ask them to
tell a partner (or a new partner if they worked on the
sequencing in pairs or groups).

Answer key

Possible answer:
make up your mind to write a story
come up with an idea
decide who your characters will be
do any research necessary
work out the plot
do a first draft of your manuscript
get some feedback from a friend
go over it again and make revisions
think up a title (This could come earlier.)
send it off to a publisher or a magazine

3

You could ask the group to read the introduction, then try to predict the six guidelines to consider when writing a short story. Then divide the class, let them read their section of the text, and exchange ideas. Monitor as carefully as possible to assess their understanding of the text and their ability to summarise.

4

We have included this activity because learners will do it anyway. When the group has finished, conduct a feedback on the text. Do they agree with the guidelines? Are they impressed or surprised by any of them? Would they like to add any ideas of their own?

5

This final activity could last two minutes or twenty minutes, so it may be a good idea to have something up your sleeve if the lesson does not generate as much interest as you hoped. One possibility is Worksheet 10 on page 122 as it returns to the lexical area highlighted in the first part of the lesson but extends it by introducing further noun + verb or verb + noun collocations.

If the lesson did generate a lot of interest, follow up with Project 2 on page 79.

Personal Study Workbook

1: Work it out: phrasal verbs and idioms
2: Quizword: vocabulary
5: Writing competition: reading

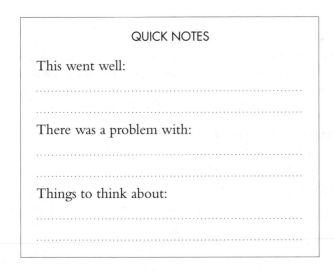

QUICK NOTES

This went well:

....

....

There was a problem with:

....

....

Things to think about:

....

....

A TALE OF POISON

Introduction

Learners have a chance to listen to a short story. It represents quite a long listening (just over five minutes), so we have divided it into two sections. But first, in preparation for the listening, learners work on key vocabulary from the story, they engage in some practice of purpose clauses, and they discuss moral issues which will later surface in the story. They are then ready to listen to the first part of the story, which is followed by some prediction of the second part. Finally, they listen to the second part and discuss it in groups.

Suggested steps

Option

Instead of following the route in the Class Book, you could begin with Exercise 2, then go back to the lexical items in Exercise 1 and ask your learners to look up the meanings and try to predict the story they are going to listen to. Then play the first part of the story, i.e. Exercise 4.

1

If your learners don't have dictionaries or you want to save time, you could pre-teach these items yourself. Pay special attention to *to bluff* and *to deserve something* – the concepts can be difficult for some learners. A good example to illustrate *bluff* is the following:

Someone breaks into your house – you catch them and say, 'If I push this button, the police will come.' Is this the truth or is it a bluff? In other words, a lie which deceives someone into believing that you are in a stronger position than you are.

To explain *deserve*, you could give these examples:
If you work hard all year, you deserve a holiday. (You should by rights have one.)
He earns $30,000 a year. Really? But he's such a good worker! He deserves more.

2

Learners will already be familiar with the concept of *in order to*, so your task here is simply to graft on one or two new constructions which will give learners more scope and variety in expressing a purpose or reason for doing something. Follow the models with the controlled activity for learners to test their understanding, and conduct a brief feedback.

Answer key
Possible answers:
1. get money from them
2. warn the police
3. convince the interviewer they are the best person for the job
4. start an investigation
5. get a lighter sentence
6. you get the best possible medicine

3

You could do this in small groups or as a class if it is not too big. If learners query whether the poison is deadly or not, you could ask them to consider the justification for administering a) a lethal poison, and b) a non-lethal poison.

4 ▭

Check answers carefully after you have played the first part as there is little point in playing the second part until your learners have understood the story so far. When you are satisfied that the group have understood the first part, put them in groups to predict the rest of the story. Conduct a feedback and put some of their ideas on the board.

Answer key

1. Sangstrom is a man who wants to buy poison to kill his wife.
2. 'I already have' means that he has already given Sangstrom the poison – in his coffee.

Tapescript

HOBBYIST

by Fredric Brown

'I heard a rumour,' Sangstrom said, 'to the effect that you ...' He turned his head and looked about him to make absolutely sure that he and the druggist were alone in the tiny prescription pharmacy. The druggist was a gnomelike, gnarled little man who could have been any age from fifty to a hundred. They were alone, but Sangstrom dropped his voice just the same. '... to the effect that you have a completely undetectable poison.'

The druggist nodded. He came around the counter and locked the front door of the shop, then walked toward a doorway behind the counter. 'I was about to take a coffee break,' he said. 'Come with me and have a cup.'

Sangstrom followed him around the counter and through the doorway to a back room ringed by shelves of bottles from floor to ceiling. The druggist plugged in an electric percolator, found two cups and put them on a table that had a chair on either side of it. He motioned Sangstrom to one of the chairs and took the other one himself.

'Now,' he said. 'Tell me. Whom do you want to kill, and why?'

'Does it matter?' Sangstrom asked. 'Isn't it enough that I pay for ...'

The druggist interrupted him with an upraised hand. 'Yes, it matters. I must be convinced that you deserve what I can give you. Otherwise ...' He shrugged.

'All right,' Sangstrom said. 'The *whom* is my wife. The *why* ...' He started the long story. Before he had quite finished, the percolator had finished its task and the druggist briefly interrupted to get the coffee for them. Sangstrom finished his story.

The little druggist nodded. 'Yes, I occasionally dispense an undetectable poison. I do so freely; I do not charge for it, if I think the case is deserving. I have helped many murderers.'

'Fine,' Sangstrom said. 'Please give it to me, then.'

The druggist smiled at him. 'I already have.'

5 ▭

Play the second part and put learners in pairs to retell it.

Answer key

The order of the pictures is: F, D, A, E, C, B.

Tapescript

The druggist smiled at him. 'I already have. By the time the coffee was ready, I had decided that you deserved it. It was, as I said, free. But there is a price to pay for the antidote.'

Sangstrom turned pale. But he had anticipated – not this, but the possibility of a double-cross or some form of blackmail. He pulled a pistol from his pocket.

The little druggist chuckled. 'You daren't use that. Can you find the antidote' – he waved at the shelves – 'among those thousands of bottles? Or would you find a faster, more virulent poison? Or if you think I'm bluffing, go ahead and shoot. You'll know the answer within three hours when the poison starts to work.'

'How much for the antidote?' Sangstrom growled.

'Quite reasonable. A thousand dollars. After all, a man must live. Even if his hobby is preventing murders, there's no reason why he shouldn't make money at it, is there?'

Sangstrom growled and put the pistol down, but within reach, and took out his wallet. Maybe after he had the antidote, he'd still use that pistol. He counted out a thousand dollars in hundred-dollar bills and put it on the table.

The druggist made no immediate move to pick it up. He said, 'And one other thing – for your wife's safety and mine. You will write a confession of your intention – your former intention, I trust – to murder your wife. Then you will wait till I go out and mail it to a friend of mine on the homicide detail. He'll keep it as evidence in case you ever *do* decide to kill your wife. Or me, for that matter.

When that is in the mail, it will be safe for me to return here and give you the antidote. I'll get you paper and pen ...'

'Oh, one other thing – although I do not absolutely insist on it. Please help spread the word about my undetectable poison, will you? One never knows, Mr Sangstrom. The life you save, if you have any enemies, just might be your own.'

6

If you haven't done the previous lesson, you can still ask groups to discuss whether they think *Hobbyist* is a good short story, and if so, why. The summary is an optional activity and would be very suitable for homework.

Personal Study Workbook

6: An Italian folk tale: listening
7: Cheating death: writing
8: Speaking partners

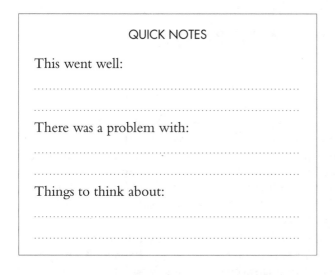

REVIEW AND DEVELOPMENT

REVIEW OF UNIT 8

1

Do the first one as an example or elicit the answer from the class, then let learners complete the rest of the slogans with a partner. Move round and help where necessary, and when the pairs have finished, put them in small groups to compare and discuss the slogans.

Answer key

Possible answers:

1. It's time we paid them a really good salary.
2. It's high time we banned all guns ...
3. It's about time newspapers stopped prying ...
4. It's time the government banned all private cars from city centres.
5. It's high time companies stopped using chemical additives in the food we buy.
6. It's about time we thought more about our free time than our work time.

2

Move round and listen carefully to the explanations but don't worry too much about grammatical accuracy – the main point is whether the learners are able to demonstrate that they understand the difference.

Answer key

1. An *issue* is a problem or subject that people discuss; a *policy* is a course of action that has been agreed upon by a company or organisation.
2. A *local* election is to elect someone for a small area, e.g. a town; a *general* election covers the whole country and elects people to serve the nation.
3. A police *investigation* is the official work they carry out to find the reason for a crime and the person who committed it; police *evidence* is facts or information which help the police to prove that something is true or false.

4. The *main* issue is the most important issue; a *minor* issue is an issue which is not very significant.
5. *Tax evasion* is illegally avoiding the payment of tax (or paying less than you should); a *tax exile* is a person who lives in another country in order to avoid paying high taxes in his or her own country.
6. A *parking* offence is a crime related to parking; a *driving* offence is a crime relating to driving in general (which would include parking offences).

REVIEW OF UNIT 9

1

There was probably quite a lot of new input for the group in the time quiz in Unit 9, so it should repay another look with the opportunity to revise the less familiar items. An alternative to the procedure in the Class Book is to divide the quiz in half so that Partner A can prepare questions on parts 1–3, while Partner B prepares questions on parts 4–6.

2

Look at the example together as a class, then give the pairs a few minutes to prepare their sentences (one learner works on 1, 3, 5 and 7; the other works on 2, 4, 6 and 8). Move round and listen, then elicit some examples from the group at the end. Discuss any problems together.

Answer key

Possible answers:
who usually looks like a tramp
who always wears those horrible baggy trousers
who drives that very old Ford Capri
who works for that second-hand garage
who was recently declared bankrupt
who has six children from three different wives
who never talks to any of the other neighbours
who often comes home drunk and shouting at the top of his voice

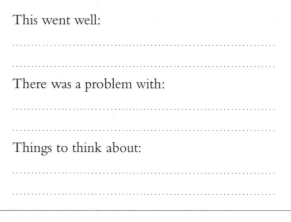

PROJECT: GROUP MAGAZINE

Introduction

This project is the ideal follow-up to Unit 10, and in particular, the lesson *Writing short stories that sell*. As the first activity makes clear, nothing is being imposed on the learners: they decide how they work (individually or in pairs), how long the stories should be, whether they are written in class time or at home, etc. Your job is simply to implement their decision-making and monitor their discussions and their first written drafts.

Suggested steps

1

This first activity is crucial, not only because it involves the whole class in the decision-making about the conditions and directions of the project, but also in helping to create an interest in the project – the first stage is often the most difficult as there will/may still be learners (and some teachers) who are not yet convinced it is going to work and be productive.

At the end of the group discussion and the feedback stage from the notetaker, you may feel it will be beneficial to rearrange the groups. For instance, if you have a large class, they can regroup according to the style of magazine they want to produce.

2

Refer the class back to the text on page 75 to reconsider the advice given. After that, learners have to start thinking about their actual stories. If the picture on page 73 of the Class Book helped to trigger some ideas, you could bring in some pictures or book covers of your own to provide a stimulus for those who need a bit of direction. But don't worry if the learners initially appear a bit slow off the mark – it is not a straightforward task to come up with a plot for a story. You might decide to let learners think about it at home and come back to the next lesson with one or two ideas to discuss.

3

After learners have read the text and answered the questions *written by the reader*, elicit their answers and ask for suggestions to improve the text. This is likely to include adding to the text, so ask learners to amend the text, then listen to some of their additions. After that, they can read the text on page 155 and compare it with their own suggestions.

Tell them to go back to their own draft and pretend to be a reader (similar to the one in Exercise 3). Are they left with unanswered questions about their own stories, which seem to suggest improvements can be made? If so, they should make them now.

4

Now get the learners to swap stories, and give the other person/pair feedback on their story. Make sure they think about the questions in the Class Book and try to balance any negative comments with positive feedback.

5

Individuals or pairs can now think about the suggestions and possibly incorporate them in the final draft of the story. You can then decide whether it is practical or desirable for you to collect them in and look at them (with a view to making a few corrections and suggestions of your own), but it would certainly help to improve the presentation if learners had access to computers/word processors in order to produce the final draft in preparation for the wall display or magazine. They could do this on school machines or at home, and this has the added bonus that it presents learners with another opportunity to correct, edit and refine their piece of work.

6

If the project has worked well and the class is pleased with the end result, you should at least try to make their work available for other classes to read. Would it be possible for you to run off additional copies of their magazine of short stories? Would an artistic learner like to produce an attractive cover for the magazine? You could even consider selling them for a small sum, perhaps to raise money for a local good cause.

EATING OUT

```
                        CONTENTS

Language focus:    reporting verbs
                   verb patterns
                   simile and metaphor
                   adjective suffix -y
                   partitives, e.g. a slice of bread
                   food and cooking vocabulary

        Skills:    Speaking:   discussing food, diet and recipes
                               restaurant experiences
                   Listening:  conversations overheard in a restaurant
                               definitions of food vocabulary
                   Reading:    restaurant reviews
                   Writing:    a restaurant review (using simile and metaphor)
                               reporting a dialogue
```

FOOD QUIZ

Introduction

The food quiz provides – we hope – a motivating, but also convenient way of tackling a wide range of lexical items that are both relevant and sometimes problematic for learners at this level. The personalised speaking activity that follows then gives learners the opportunity to discuss subjects connected with the topic and incorporate some of the new language. Food remains a motivating subject for most groups of learners, as does the appetite for new language in this area.

Suggested steps

1

You could start the discussion going with one or two ideas round the class, then allow smaller groups to continue with the topics that most interest them. Conduct a brief feedback (you can always return to these topics at the end of the lesson if you wish), and use it to teach any items that learners clearly needed to express their point of view.

2 🎞

Allow about fifteen minutes for the groups to complete the first six questions in the quiz, moving round to help where required, then play the recording for the group to complete question 7. At the end, go through the answers and deal with questions. If learners like the competitive nature of scoring in groups, get them to total their answers out of 50.

If they enjoy the quiz and are interested in food vocabulary, you could follow the lesson with Worksheet 11 on page 123, in which learners have a gapped menu for completion, followed by a short restaurant roleplay. The answers are on page 66.

Answer key

1. Check learners are aware of / can pronounce:
   the three syllables in *recipe*; the /ɔː/ in *prawns*; the /eə/ in *rare*; the /eɪ/ in *pastry*; the silent *p* and then collapsed syllable /brɪ/ in *raspberry*; the silent *l* in *salmon*; the /ɪ/ in the second syllable of *lettuce*; the /aɪ/ in *pie*; and the stress in *ingredients*.
2. Not included are:

broccoli   aubergines

3. Clockwise from top left: slice, grate, peel, carve, chop
   The odd one out is *simmer*, which means to cook something gently in water so that the water is just boiling.
4. a piece of cake/lemon/toast; a slice of lemon/toast/cake; a pinch of salt; a drop of milk (lemon juice would also be possible); a spoonful of sugar/salt; a squeeze of lemon

5. *Possible answers:*
   1. meat, fish, cheese
   2. most fruit and vegetables
   3. citrus fruits, e.g. oranges
   4. cakes, cream, sugar
   5. potato, rice, pasta
   6. coffee
6. 1. tender 2. sour 3. bland (or tasteless) 4. still
   5. heavy 6. fatty 7. stale 8. off (or weren't fresh)
7. 1. flour 2. vinaigrette 3. raw 4. a hangover
   5. the yolk 6. sweet or pudding 7. be sick
   8. aperitif

Tapescript

1. What's the name of the white stuff used to make bread?
2. What do you call the dressing made from oil and vinegar that you put on salad?
3. What do you call food when it isn't cooked?
4. What's the name of the condition you may experience the morning after you have drunk too much alcohol?
5. What do you call the yellow part of an egg?
6. What is another word for dessert?
7. What is another word or expression meaning *vomit*?
8. What's the general word for a drink you have before a meal?

3

It is a good idea to check that each pair or individual has a topic they are prepared to talk about. Try to ensure a good spread of learners for each topic, but don't worry too much if learners opt for just two or three of the topics. Give help where necessary while they prepare, and give them dictionaries if possible.

4

You could start by putting learners with the same topic together. As they give their talks, make notes on their performance, follow it up with some language feedback, then reorganise the groups so that learners are with people who have chosen different topics. Let them give their talks a second time to see if they can improve on their first effort.

Option

You could get learners to write their talk for homework, or make a recording of it. If they do the latter, they can listen to it and make a transcript, then make further corrections if possible, and finally give it to you for feedback. This is a lot of work for the learners, but very worthwhile, and there is a high degree of motivation for learners to transcribe their own speech.

Personal Study Workbook

2: The steak was tender: adjective + noun collocation
3: Do you want a piece?: partitives
5: Tasty treats for hungry cybernauts: reading

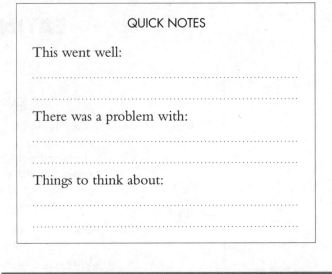

WHO'D BE A FOOD CRITIC?

Introduction

Learners have an opportunity to swap good and bad food experiences, then work quite intensively on some of the language contained in two authentic restaurant reviews, one positive and one negative. They focus on the use of simile and metaphor, and the use of the generative suffix -y used with adjectives. Finally, they have a chance to use some of the new language by rewriting one of the reviews.

Suggested steps

1

Starting with your own personal experience is often the best way to stimulate interest in a topic. When you listen to the group, see if they use any of the language from the previous lesson, and give praise if they do.

2

This may appear a strange mix of items, but they all appear in the later texts, and that is why they are here. It doesn't matter if learners don't know these words in English – the activity will give them practice in paraphrasing and explaining. In feedback, you can elicit or feed in the new vocabulary items.

Answer key

From left: stuffed squid fried in garlic; roast pheasant; scrambled eggs; steamed mussels; grilled trout (or similar fish); mashed potato

Before learners read, emphasise that they will have a chance later to study the new language in depth, so they should not worry too much at this stage – just focus on the meal, where it was eaten, and the writer's general impression of the meal. Monitor their spoken summaries of each text, then let them skim read the other text.

3

One problem learners may have with the task is in distinguishing between words used as adjectives which end in -*y*, and words used as adverbs ending in -*y* (e.g. *exactly*, *highly*, *early*, etc.). You may need to point out the difference to some learners when you go through the answers.

Answer key

-*y* (= with a certain quality)	-*y* (other examples)
leathery	tiny
greasy	soggy
rubbery	empty
spicy	high-quality (used here as
lumpy	an adjective)
creamy	
herby	
meaty	
lemony	

4

If you work with a monolingual group you may be able to embellish this list with one or two metaphors which are commonly used to describe food or dishes from the country you are in. (Is there, for example, a common metaphor used to describe badly-cooked rice in Japan, which translates easily into English?) Check the answers with the group before asking pairs to think up more examples of their own. Don't worry if they cannot produce many examples on the spot.

Answer key

Possible answers:
The coffee looked like washing-up water.
The peas were like bullets.
The pasta was like rubber.
The scrambled egg looked like a sponge.
The mashed potato was like cotton wool.
The pastry was like cardboard.
The steak was like leather.
The cheese smelt like old socks.
The wine tasted like vinegar.

5

You can obviously give learners some latitude in how closely they keep to the original text. Make this clear at the beginning, and emphasise that learners should be free to use lexical items and similes/metaphors that have already appeared in the lesson. When they have finished, let them go round and read the reviews written by other pairs. If you are short of time, they could just write part of the review, then finish it for homework.

Personal Study Workbook

4: You be the waiter: pronunciation
6: How was your meal?: listening
7: Make it interesting: writing

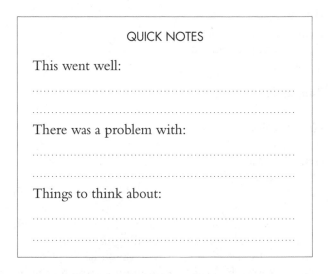

QUICK NOTES

This went well:

....

....

There was a problem with:

....

....

Things to think about:

....

....

WHO REFUSED TO DO WHAT?

Introduction

Learners have a listening passage which tests gist listening and more detailed understanding, and this then leads on to a close look at a number of reporting verbs and the syntactic patterns which accompany their use. Learners practise them in a controlled environment, then have a chance to use some of them in a freer and more personalised activity in which they predict a couple's conversation from a picture they are given.

Suggested steps

1

Pre-teach *to overhear* then follow the instructions in the Class Book.

2 ▭

You could play the recording without much introduction, but if you would like to give learners more help, you could do this option first.

Option

Ask pairs to think about the couples in the picture and answer these questions.
– How old are they?
– How are they dressed?
– What are they doing (if anything)?
– What is their relationship?
– Do they seem to be enjoying themselves?
– Have you any idea what they could be talking about?

Conduct a feedback without confirming or rejecting any answers at this stage, although you could ask the group which answers seem the most likely. Then play the recording.

After the recording, elicit answers with reasons. Discuss any problems.

Answer key

Conversation 1: table 4
Conversation 2: table 2
Conversation 3: table 1

Tapescript

1.

IAN: Oh dear, clumsy of me. Another dribble.

SHEILA: Filthy.

IAN: Pardon?

SHEILA: You're filthy.

IAN: No, no, no it's only a dribble. It won't notice in a minute. I suppose I'll have to have it cleaned if we're going to this wretched wedding, though.

SHEILA: You can't go to the wedding in that suit.

IAN: Why, what's wrong with this suit?

SHEILA: You've had it for years and it's absolutely filthy.

IAN: Well, if I have it cleaned it'll be as good as new.

SHEILA: No, no, no. You've absolutely got to buy a new one.

IAN: Buy one? Don't be so stupid!

SHEILA: What do you mean, stupid?

IAN: I'm not buying a new suit – it'd be a total waste of money.

SHEILA: Well, there'll be plenty of other opportunities for you to wear it.

IAN: When?

SHEILA: Well, we'll be invited to other weddings for one thing, and funerals I expect.

IAN: Well, I can have this one cleaned again, can't I?

SHEILA: No you can't. I mean, honestly, if you just see yourself. Have you looked in a mirror recently?

IAN: Well ... no, not particularly.

SHEILA: Well then do. Next time you go home, you have a look and see how shabby it looks. I mean is it fair on me?

IAN: Well, I mean, if it's cleaned, it'll be pressed, it'll be very very smart.

SHEILA: No it won't. It's gone, it's worn, you can see.

IAN: Oh for goodness' sake, I wish I'd never mentioned your wretched wedding.

2.

NIGEL: I had a word with George about, erm, getting next week off ...

KAREN: Yes?

NIGEL: Unfortunately, no can do.

KAREN: Oh!

NIGEL: I'm really sorry, a couple of days, he said, you know, Thursday and Friday, take a long weekend, but the whole week, no way. We've just got too much on at the moment at the office.

KAREN: Oh, but you know how much I've been looking forward to this week. I put the whole week aside.

NIGEL: I know. I'm really sorry. I thought, I thought he'd let me ... but just not possible.

KAREN: Well, couldn't you go down with the plague or something? Flu?

NIGEL: I can't, I can't.

KAREN: Chicken pox?

NIGEL: No, I really can't!

KAREN: Mumps.

NIGEL: You must understand. We've got to get this order finished by the end of February.

KAREN: Oh well, I'm terribly disappointed, you know. I really am.

NIGEL: Look. This will be all over in a couple of weeks. How about we go skiing in March?

KAREN: Yes, I could do that.

NIGEL: Come on!

KAREN: Oh, all right. I mean, I'll have to check it all out. Yes, all right.

3.

NICK: That was nice.

CAROL: Gorgeous.

NICK: Would you like a cappuccino?

CAROL: Love one.

NICK: I'll get the waiter's eye if I ... Oh, Carol, come on, that's the third this evening.

CAROL: What, you're counting now?

NICK: I thought you were giving up.

CAROL: I didn't say I was going to give up, I said I was going to cut down and try and save money for the flat.

NICK: So, that's cutting down, is it?

CAROL: Well I am trying to.

NICK: Well I think you're gonna have to cut down a bit more if you're gonna save any money.

CAROL: Oh, well, you talk about me cutting down a bit more. What about you?

NICK: What?

CAROL: Well, I think you could make a bit of an effort at saving some money.

NICK: I thought I was.

CAROL: What! What, with that new shirt you've bought?

NICK: This isn't a new shirt. What are you talking about? I don't spend money on clothes.

CAROL: Well, OK not clothes, then. What about the car?

NICK: Uh, uh, I've been promising myself that car.

CAROL: I let you have that car because I know, I knew you wanted it. Can't you let me do a few of the things that I'd like to do?

NICK: I admit the car is a luxury, and, er, you know, maybe I'll just keep it for the year, OK, and we'll talk about maybe getting something cheaper, but I don't spend money on clothes and I think that what you're doing, is, is ... if you added it up through the year it would be far more costly than a new wardrobe.

CAROL: Well, look I'm really trying, and as long as ... look, as long as we both try to save money, then, you know, I think that's, that's all we can do really, but we can't just cut everything out completely.

NICK: Well ...

CAROL: I'll try if you try.

NICK: Yeah, well, that's what I was going to say; a bit more effort on both sides, maybe.

CAROL: All right then.

3 📼

Before playing the recording a second time, go through the questions and make sure the meaning of the verbs is clear: you may need to explain *accuse* and *deny* (see *Language Point* below), and you should also point out that the question forms in each case show learners how they need to structure their answers. Pause the recording where necessary to give learners time to complete their answers (a minute at the end of each conversation may be sufficient), and play each conversation twice if necessary. Check answers at the end and be quite precise about correcting their sentence constructions.

> ### Language Point
>
> If you *accuse someone of something*, you state that you think they are guilty of doing something wrong or illegal. And if you accuse someone and they *deny* it, they are saying that it isn't true.
>
> If you *blame someone for something*, you are saying they are responsible overall. Compare:
>
> He *accused* the boy of stealing the money.
>
> He *blamed* the boy's parents for not teaching him the difference between right and wrong.

Answer key

1. The woman tried to persuade the man to buy a new suit.
2. The man refused to buy a new suit.
3. The man regrets mentioning the wedding/suit.
4. The woman encouraged the man to pretend he was ill.
5. The man suggested going skiing.
6. The woman agreed to go skiing.
7. The woman accused the man of wasting money.
8. The woman denied promising to give up smoking.
9. They both promised to economise and save money.

4

This is an opportunity for learners to test their knowledge of the patterns they have just been using, and then extend it with other verbs. Some of the verbs in the second list will be new, so you need to decide whether to pre-teach the meanings, or let learners look them up in a dictionary. The second option is preferable if the learners have access to good dictionaries, as they will uncover not only the meanings but also the sentence patterns used with them (you should, however, point out that dictionaries are likely to show that some of these verbs can be used with more than one pattern in this list).

Check the answers at the end and clarify any problems with the meanings of the verbs, then give learners time to study their lists before they test each other in pairs. In the testing activity, try to ensure the pairs maintain a good pace otherwise the activity loses its momentum and becomes very ponderous.

Answer key

verb + inf	verb + obj + inf	verb + -ing	verb + obj + prep
promise	encourage	regret	accuse
regret	persuade	suggest	thank
refuse	advise	deny	prevent
agree		avoid	
offer			
threaten			

5

This could be given for homework; alternatively you could ask learners to do it orally in class if you don't have much time. You may need to set them off in the appropriate tense. For example:
I think they're having a heated discussion and he's explaining something to her. Maybe she's trying to persuade him to …

Personal Study Workbook

1: She advised me to finish it later: reporting verbs
8: Speaking partners

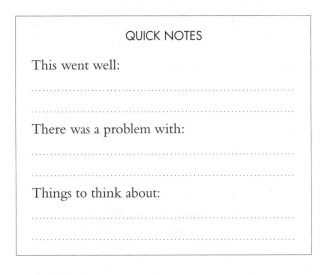

> QUICK NOTES
>
> This went well:
>
> ....
>
> ....
>
> There was a problem with:
>
> ....
>
> ....
>
> Things to think about:
>
> ....
>
> ....

REVIEW AND DEVELOPMENT

REVIEW OF UNIT 9

1

You could do one example topic with the class, eliciting answers and putting them on the board. Then give learners about five minutes to choose another topic and complete their sentences. When learners compare answers, with a partner or in small groups, emphasise that they should also evaluate the suggestions and discuss them.

2

Before learners begin, point out that the word *time* may be the first component in the compound or the second; and that the compound word may be a noun or an adjective. It is sometimes difficult to decide if a word is technically a compound or not, e.g. *overtime*, and so it may be easier to relax the instructions and just ask for any words or phrases which include *time*.

Answer key

There are many possible answers here, but these are some of the most common:
time limit; time bomb; timescale; time lag; time-consuming; time machine; full time (n); full-time (adj); half time; part-time; extra time; flexi-time; a waste of time (common phrase); in time; from time to time; for the time being; take/have time off; at times; all the time; at one time; at the time; in X days' time, etc.

3 ▭

This short exercise illustrates how meaning affects sentence stress, then provides an opportunity for some controlled practice. Go through the example to explain the principle, then let learners complete the exercise individually or in pairs. They can check their answers by listening to the recording, then practise the same dialogues in pairs.

Answer key

The words stressed in each dialogue are:
1. ex-   2. after   3. previous   4. earlier   5. predecessor
6. former   7. nowadays   8. lately

REVIEW OF UNIT 10

1

If you think it is necessary, you could give the class some questions to think about to stimulate their ideas. For example:
– Who is Barry?
– What type of office is it?
– Why might the police be visiting the office?
– If Barry 'froze', what does that suggest?
– What choices does Barry have in his next course of action?
etc.
After a few minutes' discussion, you could elicit some ideas and write them on the board. Play the recording and conduct a short feedback.

Then follow the instructions in the Class Book for parts C and D. At the end, elicit further ideas from the group for the way the story could continue.

Tapescript

Barry glanced out of his office window at the car park below. Two police officers were getting out of a car, making their way towards reception. Barry froze.
'... and I've had a lot of trouble with the computer this morning, so I'll type those letters later,' Gemma was saying.
'Pardon? Oh, fine, don't worry, Gemma,' Barry stuttered, trying to concentrate and think what to do.
The phone rang, screaming to be answered. Barry heard the receptionist's voice in his ear.
'Mr Gordon? There are two policemen at reception. They want to ask you about the computer.'
'Could you tell them I'm in a meeting and I'll be out in five minutes, please?'
Barry's blood ran cold.

Option

If the group enjoyed developing a plot round Barry and his exploits with the police, you could try to extend it yourself. Take one of the suggestions from the class that has potential for further development, then write the next stage yourself. If possible, ask another teacher to record it for you, so you can then play it in class as a listening and dictation task (as in parts B and C of the exercise above). After that, the class can then extend the plot further; and so on.

2

Follow the instructions in the Class Book. You could also introduce a time limit to make it more competitive if you wish.

Answer key

1. blackmail   2. rape   3. poisoning   4. arson
5. burglary   6. fraud   7. murder   8. drug dealing
9. theft   10. shoplifting   11. speeding   12. bribery
(The vertical word is *manslaughter*.)

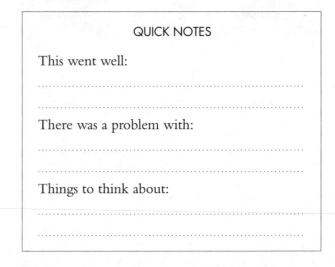

QUICK NOTES

This went well:
....
....

There was a problem with:
....
....

Things to think about:
....
....

Worksheet 11 Answer key

Thinly *sliced* tuna with ginger, lime and mayonnaise
Steamed mussels in white wine, *garlic* and parsley
Ravioli with wild *mushrooms*
Sautéed chicken livers in a sherry *vinegar* dressing
Half a dozen fresh *oysters*

Baked salmon on a bed of *spinach* with new potatoes
Grilled sea bass with stir-fried broccoli
Breast of chicken in a wine *sauce* with chopped carrot and *celery*
Roast *fillet* of Angus beef with glazed shallots
Leg of lamb with chargrilled aubergines and red *peppers*

Pear and almond *tart* with fresh *cream*
Lime or *raspberry* sorbet
Hot chocolate *sponge* with chocolate sauce
Selection of unpasteurised *cheeses*

THEATRICAL INTERLUDE

```
                    CONTENTS

Language focus:   question forms
                  vocabulary: personal interaction
                  adverbs of manner
                  adverbial phrases
                  pronunciation: accents
                  vocabulary: describing speech

        Skills:   Speaking:   pros and cons of living with parents
                              acting out a scene from a play
                              discussing accents and how to improve them
                              developing a scene from a play
                  Listening:  an extract from a Pinter play
                              listening to different accents
                              actors talk about learning different accents
                  Reading:    a scene from a Pinter play
                              a short sketch
                  Writing:    completing a scene from a play
```

A NIGHT OUT

Introduction

The language focus is the use of a range of more complex question forms (often ignored or assumed to be known at this level), e.g. negative interrogatives or ellipsis involving the omission of auxiliaries; and the material is a scene from a play by the well-known English writer, Harold Pinter. Not everyone is interested in literature, but the theme of the play is a compelling one, involving the tense relationship between a mother and grown-up son who is obviously now straining to become independent of her influence. Learners have a chance to both hear and read the excerpt from the play, and there are opportunities for speaking in both the practice of the questions forms, the reaction to the play, and the reading of part of the play.

Suggested steps

1

Explain the task and give learners several minutes to think about their answers. Then put them in groups for the discussion and conduct a short feedback. This is not just a warm-up task, but should also prepare them for the tension between the two central characters in the play.

Answer key

Possible advantages:
1. They can support each other.
2. They can provide comfort, security, love and affection for each other.
3. There may be financial benefits.

Possible disadvantages:
1. The son may find it difficult to break away, and may feel guilty if he tries to.
2. They might get on each other's nerves.
3. The son might feel he needs more freedom and privacy.

2 ▭

Again, allow time for the class to read the stage directions carefully. Then play the recording and ask learners to follow in their books. You will probably have to explain two or three idioms, e.g. *the bulb's gone* (i.e. it doesn't work); *I'll have to put the flag out* (i.e. it's a special occasion). At the end put them in groups for the task or let them work as a whole class.

3 ▭

While the pairs work on the vocabulary, move round to listen to them and clarify any problems. You can also encourage learner interaction if one pair clearly knows something another pair does not. Then play the rest of the recording and allow time for the class to complete the sentences. Check their answers.

Answer key

1. She (the example)   2. He   3. He; her   4. She; him
5. She; him   6. He; her   7. She; him   8. She; him
9. She; his   10. He; her

Tapescript

She goes over to the gas stove, examines the vegetables, opens the oven and looks into it.

MOTHER: (*gently*) Well, your dinner'll be ready soon. You can look for it afterwards. Lay the table, there's a good boy.

ALBERT: Why should I look for it afterwards? You know where it is now.

MOTHER: You've got five minutes. Go down to the cellar, Albert, get a bulb and put it in Grandma's room, go on.

ALBERT: (*irritably*) I don't know why you keep calling that room Grandma's room, she's been dead ten years.

MOTHER: Albert!

ALBERT: I mean, it's just a junk room, that's all it is.

MOTHER: Albert, that's no way to speak about your Grandma, you know that as well as I do.

ALBERT: I'm not saying a word against Grandma ...

MOTHER: You'll upset me in a minute, you go on like that.

ALBERT: I'm not going on about anything.

MOTHER: Yes, you are. Now why don't you go and put a bulb in Grandma's room and by the time you come down I'll have your dinner on the table.

ALBERT: I can't go down to the cellar, I've got my best trousers on, I've got a white shirt on.

MOTHER: You're dressing up tonight, aren't you? Dressing up, cleaning your shoes, anyone would think you were going to the Ritz.

ALBERT: I'm not going to the Ritz.

MOTHER: (*suspiciously*) What do you mean, you're not going to the Ritz?

ALBERT: What do you mean?

MOTHER: The way you said you're not going to the Ritz, it sounded like you were going somewhere else.

ALBERT: (*wearily*) I am.

MOTHER: (*shocked surprise*) You're going out?

ALBERT: You know I'm going out. I told you I was going out. I told you last week. I told you this morning. Look, where's my tie? I've got to have my tie. I'm late already. Come on, Mum, where'd you put it?

MOTHER: What about your dinner?

ALBERT: (*searching*) Look ... I told you ... I haven't got the ... wait a minute ... ah, here it is.

MOTHER: You can't wear that tie. I haven't pressed it.

ALBERT: You have. Look at it. Of course you have. It's beautifully pressed. It's fine.
He ties the tie.

MOTHER: Where are you going?

ALBERT: Mum, I've told you, honestly, three times. Honestly, I've told you three times I had to go out tonight.

MOTHER: No, you didn't. (*Albert exclaims and knots the tie.*) I thought you were joking.

ALBERT: I'm not going ... I'm just going to Mr King's. I've told you. You don't believe me.

MOTHER: You're going to Mr King's?

ALBERT: Mr Ryan's leaving. You know Ryan. He's leaving the firm. He's been there for years. So Mr King's giving a sort of party for him at his house ... well, not exactly a party, not a party, just a few ... you know ... anyway, we're all invited. I've got to go. Everyone else is going. I don't want to go, but I've got to.

MOTHER: (*bewildered, sitting*) Well, I don't know ...

ALBERT: (*with his arm round her*) I won't be late. I don't want to go. I'd much rather stay with you.

MOTHER: Would you?

ALBERT: You know I would. Who wants to go to Mr King's party?

MOTHER: We were going to have our game of cards.

ALBERT: Well, we can't have our game of cards. (*Pause*)

MOTHER: Put the bulb in Grandma's room, Albert.

ALBERT: I've told you, I'm not going down to the cellar in my white shirt. There's no light in the cellar either. I'll be pitch black in five minutes, looking for those bulbs.

MOTHER: I told you to put a light in the cellar. I told you yesterday.

ALBERT: Well, I can't do it now.

MOTHER: If we had a light in the cellar, you'd be able to see where those bulbs were. You don't expect me to go down to the cellar?

ALBERT: I don't know why we keep bulbs in the cellar!

MOTHER: Your father would turn in his grave if he heard you raise your voice to me. You're all I've got, Albert. I want you to remember that. I haven't got anyone else. I want you ... I want you to bear that in mind.

ALBERT: I'm sorry ... I raised my voice. (*He goes to the door.*) (*mumbling*) I've got to go.

MOTHER: (*following*) Albert!

ALBERT: What?

MOTHER: I want to ask you a question.

ALBERT: What?

MOTHER: Are you leading a clean life?

ALBERT: A clean life?

MOTHER: You're not leading an unclean life, are you?

ALBERT: What are you talking about?

MOTHER: You're not messing about with girls, are you? You're not going to go messing about with girls tonight?

ALBERT: Don't be so ridiculous.

MOTHER: Answer me, Albert. I'm your mother.

ALBERT: I don't know any girls.

MOTHER: If you're going to the firm's party, there'll be girls, there, won't there? Girls from the office?

ALBERT: I don't like them, any of them.

MOTHER: You promise?

ALBERT: Promise what?

MOTHER: That ... that you won't upset your father.

ALBERT: My father? How can I upset my father? You're always talking about upsetting people who are dead!

MOTHER: Oh, Albert, you don't know how you hurt me, you don't know the hurtful way you've got, speaking of your poor father like that.

ALBERT: But he is dead.

MOTHER: He's not! He's living! (*touching her breast*) In here! And this is his house!
(*Pause*)

ALBERT: Look, Mum, I won't be late ... and I won't ...

MOTHER: But what about your dinner? It's nearly ready.

ALBERT: Seeley and Kedge are waiting for me. I told you not to cook dinner this morning. (*He goes to the stairs.*) Just because you never listen ...
(*He runs up the stairs and disappears. She calls after him from the hall.*)

MOTHER: Well, what am I going to do while you're out? I can't go into Grandma's room because there's no light. I can't go down to the cellar in the dark; we were going to have a game of cards, it's Friday night, what about our game of rummy?

4

Emphasise that it is the *form* of the question that is the focus here; if in doubt, do one example to illustrate what you mean. Check the answers then move on to the second part. The purpose here is find out if your learners have recognised and understood that question forms may not simply be the innocent request for information that is superficially implied.

Answer key

1. Cleaning your shoes, Albert? You seen my tie?
   Both questions involve ellipsis; in this case the omission of auxiliary verbs (*are you* in the first and *have* in the second).
   In the first question the speaker knows the answer because she can see he is cleaning his shoes. Her real question is *Why are you cleaning your shoes?* In the second question, the speaker doesn't know the answer.

2. You're dressing up tonight, aren't you? There'll be girls there, won't there?
   Both questions have question tags. The speaker knows the answer to the first question (it's obvious he is dressing up, but why?). Notice that the intonation falls on both of the tags. She probably knows the answer to the second but wants to know Albert's attitude to the presence of girls.

3. What have you put your best trousers on for? What do you want your tie for?
   Both questions end with a preposition. The speaker partly knows the answer to each question (Albert is clearly going out), but his mother obviously wants to know more: What is special about tonight that Albert needs a tie and his best trousers?

4. You're going out? You're going to Mr King's?
   These are both affirmative sentences, but the question marks indicate they are clearly intended as questions and will therefore need to be said with rising intonation to signal that fact. Quite often, and in both of these examples, the speaker knows the answer to her questions, but is indicating shocked surprise at her discovery that a) Albert is going out, and b) he is going to Mr King's.

5. Didn't you hear me call you, Albert? Aren't those your best trousers?
   Both are negative questions – very common question forms and often avoided by foreign learners. They can be questions to which the speaker doesn't know the answer (in the first it is possible the mother is genuine in not knowing); but are also commonly used in a more accusatory way, i.e. those are your best trousers, so why are you wearing them; and also as a polite way of saying what should happen. For example: *Shouldn't we go now?* This question could be a polite way for the speaker to say *I think we should go now.*

Before moving on to the final activity, learners now need some intensive practice of these questions so that they can say them in a way that corresponds with their real meaning. For example, compare the casual and innocent *Seen my tie?* with the prying and suspicious *Cleaning your shoes, Albert?* Learners can have a lot of fun manipulating these questions and it is an opportunity to consider intonation in relation to meaning (and not just in relation to whether your voice rises or falls).

5

Allow learners to choose their own extracts, although you may want to guide them on the size of the extract, which in any case may be determined by the time available. Broadly speaking, we feel it is probably better that pairs are able to perform a small extract well rather than stumble through something quite lengthy.

Option

If you have several tape recorders and plenty of space, or access to a language lab, you could try 'shadowing'. Let pairs choose their extract and listen to it, then try reading it at the same time as the recording (this would be easier with the slow extract at the beginning). They do this a few times until they can do it without the tape.

Personal Study Workbook

3: Don't ask questions: question forms

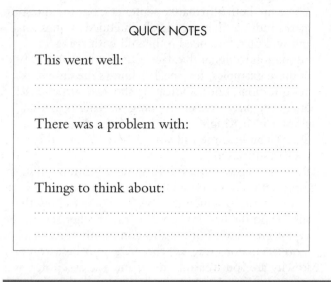

I LIKE YOUR ACCENT

Introduction

Learners are often fascinated by accents, and this lesson provides exposure to a number of different accents in English as well as a recording about how actors learn different accents. There is also personalised speaking as learners discuss accents in their own language, and the opportunity for learners to reflect on the relevance and value of strategies used by actors to master pronunciation. The lexical items needed to discuss these topics form the main language input.

Suggested steps

1 ▭▭

Ask the group to look through the questions, so they are clear about the task, then play the recording. Learners can discuss their answers in pairs or groups, then as a whole class.

Answer key

1. The first speaker is American (and comes from California), the second is Australian (and comes from Sydney), and the third is English (and speaks without any regional accent).
2. The most obvious differences are:
   a) the American speaker pronounces some words differently, e.g. new /nuː/, tomatoes /təmeɪdəʊz/, herbs /ɜːrbz/.
   b) The Australian has very different intonation, particularly in her rising intonation at the end of sentences.
   c) The letter *o* in b<u>o</u>ttom and b<u>ow</u>l is different for all three speakers.
   d) The American pronounces the double *t* differently from the other two; the Australian pronounces *it* differently from the other two.
3. The British speaker and, to a lesser extent, the American speaker.

2 ▭▭

Play one of the passages, then let learners try to copy the accent in pairs. If necessary, play the recording again, then listen round the class. Repeat for the other passages, then finish with some class discussion. In terms of pronunciation, the important point is that learners are not trying to reproduce a single sound or word, they are trying to recreate the essence of what they hear; in other words, a more holistic approach to pronunciation.

3

Check the meaning of the words in italics first and clarify where necessary, then put the learners in groups to discuss the questions. In our experience this discussion can last quite a long time. If this happens, and the group is clearly engaged in the activity, you could save the listening for the next lesson as it can also prompt a quite lengthy discussion afterwards.

4 ▭▭ ▭▭

As the listening is about actors learning accents, you could start by asking the class to write down some examples of actors who have employed particular accents in films or on TV (this should be quite easy with a monolingual group from the same country). Meryl Streep is a very good example as she has mastered a very wide range of different accents (e.g. British English in *The French Lieutenant's Woman*; Danish in *Out of Africa*, Polish in *Sophie's Choice* and Australian English in *A Cry in the Dark*). Do the class agree that the actors have copied the accent accurately?

When you are ready, play the appropriate version of the recording (or play both), let learners compare and then check answers. Play the recording a second time for the more detailed task, and again allow learners to compare before checking their answers. If there are still problems, you could play the recording one more time while learners look at the tapescript.

Option

If facilities permit, you could split the class in half, based roughly on their listening ability. The stronger half can listen to version 2 of the listening, while the others listen to version 1. They can then complete the task in pairs (a pair being one learner from each group), and exchange information about the actors they listened to.

Answer key

Version 1:
Speaker 1
1. He has to play an English-speaking Dutchman.
2. He has to master the pronunciation of the letter *s*, and the fact that Dutch people sound rather American.
Speaker 2
1. He has to learn a black South African accent.
2. He has to master the different rhythm.

Speaker 1
1. The actor has to learn a South London accent.
2. She has to learn to 'stretch her vowels' and imitate the glottal stop.

Speaker 2
1. She has to learn to speak English with an English accent (she is Australian).
2. This has meant a number of changes. Australians are quite slow speakers, and also quite lazy (they don't open their mouths much), and have rising intonation at the end of sentences. She has had to change all those things, and work hard on British English vowels and diphthongs.

Tapescript

Version 1

1. Ralph

RALPH: One of the most, um, difficult experiences as far as learning a new accent, er, was when I had to play an English-speaking Dutchman.

DENICA: Oh, gosh. That sounds difficult.

RALPH: Yeah, well, they speak very good English, as you know, but their accents are quite distinctive, and, er, one of the clues as to how to copy them was when I found out that they actually learn a lot of their English through American television, erm ...

DENICA: Right, yes.

RALPH: The older school learn it from sort of American tapes and things as well, so when they do speak English, they often have 'a slight American accent, you know,' you know, a lot of the sounds come through. Another thing about the Dutch is that the 's's are very strong (Oh?) The 's' is actually with an 'esch' ...

DENICA: Really? Is it?

RALPH: ... so that when they do speak, they sort of talk with American accents but a very strong 'esch' sound, (Aha) so it's quite, it's quite a weird combination, and, er, it's only through sort of finding out actually how they learn to speak English that I managed to copy, copy them.

DENICA: Cor, that's interesting.

2. James

Well, I once had to do a two-person play, erm, and this was in New York, a few years ago, erm, set in South Africa, and, er, luckily for me, I mean, I'd never done a South African accent before at all and, luckily for me, the guy who I was playing opposite was a genuine South African, living in New York, and he hadn't lost any, a trace of his accent, he was really strong South African. And, er, so I just attached myself to him, you know, everywhere he went, I went, and I just listened to him, which was quite difficult because he was a shy guy, but I got him talking, and, erm, I suppose the thing I tried to latch on to most of all, because we had very little time to rehearse, was the rhythm, because certainly African countries the rhythm when they speak is, is a very sort of strong characteristic, so, and I also listened to Nelson Mandela whenever he was on the television, which luckily at the time was quite often. So I suppose the things I would ... I got, I got a silly little phrase like, um, that he would come up with, like, 'the reason is this', and I would listen to, er, the rhythm of his speech and sometimes, and specially in South Africa, there's a kind of a strong, um, rhythm which is very often not an English smooth rhythm (Uhuh) but it sort of has its ... it's like a sort of wave-like rhythm, so it, for example, let me think of a line, like 'You look hot. What on earth have you been doing?' so it would, er ... I don't know, I suppose that you'd listen to a particular, you'd latch on to one thing like the rhythm, and you'd go with that.

Version 2

1. DeNica

Well, erm, I had to, er, play the part of a woman who had been 'inside', in prison for 17 years, and had come from a very poor area in London, and, er, living in London myself, I thought, 'Well, that's going to be pretty easy, I'll just listen to the accents around me,' but actually, there's so many different dialects of a London accent itself: you've got the north London accent, south London, west and east, (Oh, yes, yes) so having listened to all sorts of different London accents which I taped on my cassette player and then played back, I was getting very confused, so I actually enlisted the help of one of the voice coaches, erm, teachers that had taught me at drama school, (Right) and phoned her up and said, 'I want to make this character south London. What are the vowel sounds, and can you give them to me?' and she phonetically gave me the different vowel sounds, and that was really useful to me, and in fact then I worked on specific sounds, but oddly enough, I do find the London accent itself, and all the sort of 'Thames Estuary' quite difficult, just because there is so much variation in them, (Right) erm, and so, you know, the sounds that I was having to teach myself were, well, for instance to be less, erm, aware of the cons ..., my consonants, so you know, 'dustbin' became 'dusbin', and glottal stops, 'glo'l stops', actually it's quite an ugly sound if you sort of, lose the consonants, and sort of start putting in these 'glo'l stops', like 'bottle' becomes 'bo'ul', um, and also stretching and bending the vowel sounds, so that you get, you know, 'I was going deaauun the pub' instead of 'I was going down', 'I was going deaauun there', erm, 'eaut' instead of 'out', erm ...

2. Federay

Yeah, I came to England eight years ago from Australia to train as an actor, and had my full Australian accent when I came over, and I had to make a decision quite early on to learn to speak English, (Oh, right) with an English accent, which meant a change in vocabulary, in some cases as well as a new concentration on, on consonants and vowels I'd never paid any attention to before, because the normal Australian accent is really quite lazy, (Yeah) and we speak quite slowly, and it's quite kind of flat, and you don't use the mouth very much, (Hmm) and also have the tendency to go up at the end of sentences, so you make everything into a question, (Question, yeah) and, er, and that's not the English way at all: in fact they're quite the opposite, and they tend to fall off the end of sentences, (Hmm) and, um, so I had to learn really a new musicality, (Oh, right) and basically I had to become a whole lot more fit in the, in the mouth region, so that I could make the sounds that the English make and that Australians don't, and I suppose the mistakes I still make are in diphthong vowels, /aʊ/ and /əʊ/ and /aɪ/, and specially on tiny little words like 'it' and 'is' 'cos the English will pronounce them /ɪt/, and I'll say /ət/ (Yeah) and completely ignore it altogether, but it's been, it's been a very interesting experience, kind of learning a new way of speaking, yes, and I had to, to really take it on board in my everyday life, not just reserve it as a special voice for the stage. (Hm! Oh, right!)

5

Learners may or may not have ideas of their own to contribute at this stage, but if not, they can still talk about the strategies used by the different actors and whether they could make use of any of them to help with their English pronunciation. You could remind them of the 'shadowing' technique discussed in the notes to the previous lesson.

Personal Study Workbook

1: A serious mistake: collocation
4: What's your accent?: pronunciation
5: Speaking in tongues: reading
6: Learning accents: listening

QUICK NOTES

This went well:

....

....

There was a problem with:

....

....

Things to think about:

....

....

IT DEPENDS HOW YOU SAY IT

Introduction

The lesson opens with a quiz which tests learners' knowledge of the form of many adverbs of manner and also the meaning of some adverbs and adverbial phrases. It then goes on to further practice activities in which learners add the stage directions for a scene from a light-hearted play, then they develop the play in pairs and finish by acting it out. It affords a lot of opportunity for humour.

Suggested steps

1

Let learners work in pairs on the quiz, listen to their answers, then direct them to the Language Reference with a few hints about the questions which seem to have caused the most problems. Conduct a short feedback at the end to clarify any problems.

If you want more practice with adverbs of manner, you could try Worksheet 12 on page 124 after this lesson. The answers are on page 74.

Answer key

1. fast   2. softly   3. enthusiastically   4. correct
5. nervously   6. correct   7. gloomily   8. correct
9. in a friendly way/manner   10. wearily   11. correct
12. irritably   13. correct   14. with difficulty

2

If you illustrate the first example yourself, and elicit the next one from one of the class, you can then let them work in pairs while you monitor to check that their sentences accurately reflect the meaning of the adverb. Finish with a quick check round the class.

Option

For further practice of these adverbs, choose one target sentence. Then test the class by giving each learner an adverb or adverbial phrase in turn; they must then repeat the sentence in the style of the adverb, i.e. slowly, furiously, with difficulty, in a puzzled way, suspiciously, etc.

3

Explain the rubric carefully and make sure everyone reads 'The story so far' before starting work on the dialogue. You could do one or two examples together, and you should also point out that learners may want/need to go back and change some of their answers as they progress through the dialogue and see more obvious places for adverbs they have already used. At the end, discuss their answers. One possible interpretation is given below.

Answer key

Possible answers:
wearily (example), cheerfully, gloomily, in a puzzled way, irritably, sympathetically, suspiciously, nervously, tenderly, enthusiastically, surprised, whispering

4 ▭

Put learners in groups to act out the scene while the fourth member listens, then get them to change roles so that the fourth person can take a role. Finally, let the class listen and compare their interpretation with that of the actors.

5

If the group has enjoyed the lesson and you are now short of time, leave the final activity for another lesson, otherwise you will not get the most out of it. In this case, you could ask learners to think about an ending for homework, then write the ending the next time they meet together.

Personal Study Workbook

2: We studied happily: adverbs and adverbial phrases
7: What's going on?: writing a dialogue
8: Speaking partners

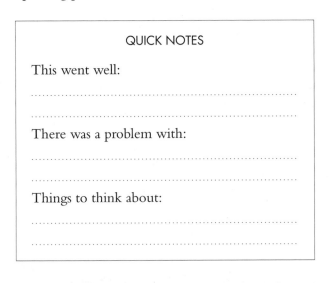

```
                    QUICK NOTES

  This went well:

  ...........................................................

  ...........................................................

  There was a problem with:

  ...........................................................

  ...........................................................

  Things to think about:

  ...........................................................

  ...........................................................
```

REVIEW AND DEVELOPMENT

REVIEW OF UNIT 10

1

Follow the instructions in the Class Book.

Answer key

Possible answers:
An author would need an original idea to write a successful novel.
A tourist might need an adapter★ in a foreign country so as to use their electrical appliances, e.g. a hairdryer.
A gambler would need a lot of luck in order to make a fortune.
An athlete might need determination to break a new record.
A hostage would need great courage in order to keep their spirits high.
A babyminder might need a dummy so as to stop a baby crying.
A mechanic might need a manual in order to fix a car.
A firefighter might need an axe in order to get into a building.
An employee might need a pass so as to gain entry to the building where they work.

★ This word can also be spelt *adaptor*. Most dictionaries give both spellings.

2

Explain the activity and ask learners to write down the correct answer for the example. Check and go over the example if anyone gets it wrong.

Answer key

The last sentence is the logical conclusion.

Then let learners complete the rest of the task and compare answers.

Answer key

Possible answers:
1. I crossed the road and stood next to him hoping I would also get the money.
2. I was in a terrible hurry and I couldn't stop to help her.
3. I didn't feel frightened at all.
4. It was approaching midnight, we were in the middle of nowhere, and we managed to get a puncture. Obviously, ...
5. The car spun several times then crashed into the wall with a sickening noise. Incredibly, ...
6. The ring must've come off while we were playing volleyball on the beach. Miraculously, ...

The final task is a challenging one, and it will take learners quite a long time to prepare their story then rehearse it carefully so that it takes exactly one minute to tell. Curiously, this wholly contrived time limit can sometimes make all the difference to the activity and give it a special purpose and focus.

REVIEW OF UNIT 11

1

We have used this type of activity throughout the course as it provides a quick and easy way to test grammar and/or vocabulary, provides intensive listening practice, then follows up with a controlled speaking activity which offers scope for pronunciation work on stress and rhythm. You can use this exercise type to revise all sorts of things.

Tapescript

1. Can you peel bananas?
2. Can you peel strawberries?
3. Can water simmer?
4. Is broccoli fattening?
5. Is an aubergine a vegetable?
6. Can you carve water?
7. Can you carve meat?
8. Do cookery books have recipes?
9. Do recipes include ingredients?
10. Does scrambled egg contain caffeine?
11. Can milk be grated?
12. Do raspberries taste salty?
13. Has a raw egg got a yolk?
14. Can lettuce be sliced?
15. Does fizzy water have a different flavour to still water?

2

Don't do this activity if you think your learners might feel uneasy about answering questions which may involve self-criticism. Alternatively, you could do the activity but restrict the questions to the work environment if your class are all adults with jobs.

If the class is happy to do the task, it can be very rewarding and lead to a lot of discussion, which often involves a natural use of the target verbs in order to explain or justify an answer.

```
QUICK NOTES

This went well:

...................................................................

...................................................................

There was a problem with:

...................................................................

...................................................................

Things to think about:

...................................................................

...................................................................
```

Worksheet 12 Answer key

1. politely   2. immediately   3. bitterly   4. casually
5. bravely   6. closely   7. gracefully   8. soundly
9. thoroughly   10. aggressively

ON THE JOB

CONTENTS

Language focus: expressing obligation, permission and entitlement
if ever/whenever
work vocabulary
adjective + noun collocation
adjectives for appearance
expressing probability

Skills: Speaking: discussing attitudes to work
talking about your own job
how to dress for an interview
evaluating job applicants
Listening: an argument about principles surrounding
redundancy
people describing the worst aspects of their jobs
Reading: professional people assess the clothes of
job applicants

Introduction

There is an extended speaking activity in which learners exchange opinions about a range of topics on the subject of work. Learners will require a lot of vocabulary for this discussion and so the first part of the lesson provides significant lexical input. The discussion also involves the use of different modal verbs and lexical items to express degrees of obligation, and after the discussion there is a chance for learners to reflect on this language and test their understanding of them. A listening activity provides further reinforcement and recycling of the target language.

Suggested steps

1

It is probably sensible to explain to the group that the initial vocabulary activity highlights language that they will see and need later on in the lesson. Begin by explaining the example, then create pairs for the rest of the activity. If the group do not have access to dictionaries, they will probably not be able to complete the task on their own and you will have to discuss any unknown words as a class.

Answer key

Go on strike is to refuse to work because of dissatisfaction with the conditions or terms of work; *get the sack* means to lose your job because the employer is unhappy with your work.

Be made redundant means to lose your job because there isn't enough work; *be dismissed* means to lose one's job because the employer is dissatisfied with your work. *Employ someone* is the same as *take someone on*. *Be promoted* means to get a job with more money and responsibility in the company; *be laid off* means the same as *be made redundant*. *Have to do something* means you are under an obligation to do something; *be forced to do something* means you are made to do something even though you don't want to. *Have the right to do something* means the same as *be entitled to do something*. *Be allowed to do something* means you have permission to do something; *be about to do something* means you are going to do something almost immediately. *Apply for a job* is a formal written request for a job; *give up a job* is to leave a job. *Maternity leave* is time off work for a woman while she has a baby; *paternity leave* is time off work for a father while his wife/partner has a baby. *Compulsory* means obligatory (you have to do something); *voluntary* means something is optional (you don't have to do it).

2

Asking learners to provide a snap response to the questions will give them a chance to ask about anything they don't understand (rather than have the discussion disrupted later on), and it also gives you a chance, by carefully monitoring the responses, to create groups where you know there will be some disagreement and hopefully more potential for engaging discussion.

3

Organise your groups where you can see clear lines of disagreement and monitor the discussion carefully, paying special attention to the way they use the different ways of talking about obligation. Our hope is that learners will use many of the constructions from the original questions, freely and accurately. If not, make a careful note, as this will be an area for greater attention in the next exercise. You may wish to go over these errors at this point, however, focusing particularly on the expressions of obligation.

4 ▢▢ ▣▢

Play the appropriate version of the recording, and ask learners to make notes while they listen. At the end they can exchange answers – in so doing, they should recycle more of the language used to describe obligation or lack of obligation – and you can see how much they have understood. As Exercise 5 involves listening to the recording one more time for a different reason, we would not recommend playing the tape twice at this stage, otherwise motivation and interest may start to wane.

Answer key

Version 1:
They are talking about question 7.
The man thinks people should be allowed to carry on working if they are fit. He also thinks people over retirement age still have a lot to offer.
The woman disagrees because there are younger people who will be unemployed if older people carry on working.

Version 2:
They are talking about question 4.
The man thinks the policy is both fair and clear.
The woman doesn't like it. She feels that redundancy should be voluntary first, and then it should be decided by people's individual circumstances, e.g. new people may be good and older people less efficient.

Tapescript

Version 1

JACQUI: Should people be forced to retire at 60 or 65, or should they have the right to carry on working if they wish? What do you think?

LINFORD: Well, I think if they're fit and healthy, I don't see any reason why they should be forced to retire. I mean, I think compulsory retirement is just a bit harsh, really, I think it should be voluntary.

JACQUI: Really? Why?

LINFORD: Well, you know, especially mature people are very experienced; they've got a lot to offer young people, you know, they've learnt a lot, they've had a lot of invaluable experience, and for them to have to go, I just think is too hard.

JACQUI: But if they stay on working until they're much, much older, what about the young people? There are far too many young people unemployed, and they need the chance to start work. I think basically people should be forced to retire at 60 or 65, whatever age, in order that young people can take over the jobs.

LINFORD: Yes, but I mean, to be forced to go, I think that's just too hard, you know, these people have been working all their lives and sometimes they have to work because their pensions are so low.

JACQUI: Oh, but I mean fixed age retirement should be compulsory. They have to think about the young people. I mean, if not, some people are going to carry on far too long, and then, you know, they're going to become less competent physically and mentally. I think they ought to think about young people, they ought to think about their retirement, what they can do when they stop working, you know, all the fun things they can do ...

Version 2

KATHERINE: When workers are made redundant, do you agree with the principle 'last in, first out'?

PAUL: Hmm, it's a difficult one (it is) particularly in the 90s when, you know, redundancy is so common. (Hmm) I think if, if you have to have a policy, erm, then 'last in first out' is a clear one, (Hmm) and it would work the same for everybody.

KATHERINE: I don't like it as a policy myself because it's so clear cut. I think the clarity of the policy is not necessarily in its favour. I think redundancy should be voluntary, and then I suppose if you don't get enough voluntary redundancies and it has to be a company decision, then maybe the company ought to look at people's individual circumstances.

PAUL: Hmm. Don't you think that people also should be rewarded for loyalty to a company? I mean how would you feel if you'd been working for somewhere for 40 years; somebody joined, six months, and redundancies came along and you were on the list and he wasn't?

KATHERINE: Well, that is a good point, and that's what I mean about taking into concern the individual, erm, so maybe that would come into your argument.

PAUL: That's why people say they have to have a clear policy and where 'last in, first out' works.

KATHERINE: But that's only one side of it. I think in that case you may end up, the company may have to actually get rid of people who are doing a very good job, they've just started, brought fresh blood into the company and you're having to get rid of them and keep on somebody who really is maybe past it, and only out of loyalty (hmm) you're, you're having to keep them on.

PAUL: So you'd like to see ...

5

This final gap-filling task allows an additional focus on language used to express obligation. After learners have compared answers, you can encourage them to discuss the meaning of the words and phrases picked out in the listening; perhaps by asking them to find synonyms or opposites in other parts of the lesson.

Answer key

Version 1:
should be forced to; compulsory retirement; should be voluntary; have to; should be compulsory; they ought to think about
Version 2:
should be voluntary; it has to be; ought to look at; should be rewarded; have to have a clear policy; may have to actually get rid of people

Option

If you wanted a round-up of much of the language used in the lesson to describe degrees of obligation, you could ask learners to complete this table.

have to	synonym = e.g. have got to
don't have to	....
obligatory	....
voluntary	....
should	....
be forced to	....
be permitted to	....
have a right to	....
do something	....

Answer key

don't have to = needn't; obligatory = compulsory; voluntary = optional; should = ought to; be forced to = be made to; be permitted to = be allowed to; have a right to do something = be entitled to do something

And if you still want further practice of either the work vocabulary from the unit or the focus on degrees of obligation (or both), try Worksheet 13 on page 124 or Review and development page 115, Exercise 1 of the Class Book.

Personal Study Workbook

2: Unfair dismissal?: obligation, prohibition, permission
4: Word stress: pronunciation

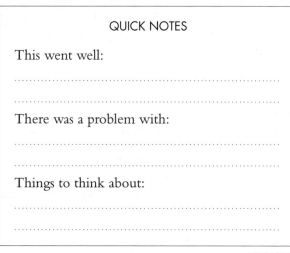

QUICK NOTES

This went well:

....

....

There was a problem with:

....

....

Things to think about:

....

....

Introduction

In this lesson learners have an opportunity to discover how a group of professional people evaluate the appearance of some prospective job applicants for jobs in their professions. Vocabulary work on adjectives describing clothes and character helps to prepare learners for the text, and language of probability and possibility is introduced to help learners talk about and analyse the text. There are also opportunities for the group to discuss the issue of dress for interviews as well as give their personal opinion of the job applicants pictured in the lesson.

Suggested steps

1

Most groups find this topic very easy to discuss (whether they have personal experience of interviews or not), and it obviously has enormous potential for cross-cultural discussion with a mixed nationality group. Even with monocultural groups there will be differences of opinion relating to sex, age and background. However, there is a lot of material in the lesson, so don't allow this first exercise to go on too long. You may also find that the opportunity arises to teach one or two of the lexical items that appear in the next exercise.

2

The activity will enable learners to get a reasonable understanding of the target vocabulary, but you will probably still need to reinforce the meaning with additional explanations and examples (see *Language Point* below), and you may be wise not to be too dogmatic about 'right' and 'wrong' answers to this exercise.

Answer key

Possible answers:

Positive	Negative	Positive and negative
smart	dreary	conservative
assertive	showy	fashion-conscious
daring		businesslike
quite stylish		provocative
adventurous		inoffensive
elegant		

Language Point

1. *Daring* and *adventurous* can both mean *willing to try new things and take risks*, and these words are often used positively because they may be used by people who do not take risks themselves and envy others who do. However, the same people may also view something or someone as *too daring* and *too adventurous*, and then the quality becomes a liability.
2. *Daring* can also mean new or unusual in a way that may shock people.
3. *Provocative* also has two meanings: *provocative remarks* are often intended to make people angry; *provocative clothes* (the meaning in this text) are intended to arouse some sexual excitement.

3

This is an opportunity for learners to practise the new vocabulary and acquaint themselves with the pictures which provide the raw material for the text that follows.

4

Before the group reads the text, go through the symbols and explanations, paying particular attention to the language in italics which illustrates the different degrees of probability and possibility – and which is the language you would like your learners to use in their interpretation of the text. Put them in pairs to complete the task, then create groups for the comparison and discussion. You can nudge them into using the target language, but don't pressurise them at this stage.

Answer key

Suggested answers (some disagreement is possible):

	Picture 1	2	3	4	5
Designer	★	★	?	??	?(?)
Banker	★★	??	X	★★	??
Head	X	?	X	X	★★
Doctor	★★	★	??	?	★

5

Learners can now exchange their own opinions freely. Monitor the discussion and make notes for the feedback session. When the discussion has run its course conduct the feedback with discussion of both the ideas discussed and language used (or not used).

6

This transfer activity allows for more personalisation. You could do the activity in the next lesson if you are short of time (it provides natural recycling of the language input from the lesson), and you could also change the job titles if you think there are more relevant jobs for your group to discuss.

Personal Study Workbook

3: Clothes and appearance: vocabulary
7: Arguing a case: writing

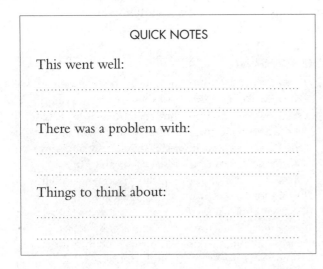

QUICK NOTES

This went well:

....
....

There was a problem with:

....
....

Things to think about:

....
....

Introduction

Learners begin by predicting the negative side of different jobs. This is followed by a vocabulary exercise on common adjective + noun collocations, and the two strands are then brought together as learners listen to people (in the jobs learners discussed in Exercise 1) as they talk about their jobs and use vocabulary from Exercise 2. The listening passage is used to highlight another common structure (*if ever/whenever*), and the lesson concludes with learners using this target language to talk about the negative side of some different jobs.

Suggested steps

1

You could begin with a brief description of the downside of being a teacher (make it fairly light-hearted if possible), then put the class into groups to discuss the jobs shown in the pictures. Conduct feedback at the end and put some of the ideas on the board (this will help learners later).

2

We would suggest learners find the collocations they are already familiar with, e.g. *embarrassing situation* should be an obvious one for most learners, then proceed by a process of elimination and dictionary use to search for both meaning and likely collocation. Check answers and then complete the second part of the task, which is really just a further check on meaning. You should first emphasise that some of the phrases might be used by people in more than one of the jobs.

Answer key

disruptive behaviour
complete stranger
abusive language
embarrassing situation
deprived background
physical violence
great patience
awkward customers

3 ▭

When you play the recording, ask learners to listen for some of the ideas they talked about in Exercise 1. In this way, their earlier predictions may make the ideas on the recording more familiar and thus easier to understand. Conduct a feedback at the end.

Tapescript

1. A nanny
Well, I find the most difficult things really, the things that are most likely to cause friction are money (Oh, yeah) and, um, well, time-keeping. If you never get a pay rise, or you don't get the baby-sitting money you're owed, then you begin to lose respect, you know, for the people you're working for. And, er, well, it's the same if they're always late back, oh, they always have some excuse, you

know, about the traffic or they forgot something or whatever. (Yes, yes, I know what you mean) And you can also find yourself in very embarrassing situations. If ever I walk in on a row, I just sing loudly, 'cos it can be awful, you know, so I sing so that they know I'm there. (That's a good idea!) Do you know, at one job I had, the phone rang and this woman at the other end, well, she thought I was the children's mother. So she said, 'I'm going to tell you everything. I'm having an affair with your husband (Oh, my God!) and he's too scared to tell you. And I've got some photos to prove it.' (Did she?) And she wouldn't listen to me, I tried to say you know, you're not talking to her, but she just said that and put the phone down. I didn't know what to say to her.

2. A public relations officer for a large travel agent

A: I handle customer relations at head office and I'd say, on average, I receive, oh, about 300 letters or calls a week. (Goodness!) The worst occasions are when people swear at you, abuse you or threaten you with newspapers and lawyers before you've even had time to speak. Inside you think, 'Well, go off and do it then', but, well, I mean, you have to maintain your calm. (Yes, of course) Having said that though, I do draw the line at abusive language. If someone comes on the line saying, 'I don't want to talk to a stupid little woman', or won't stop swearing at me, then I hang up.

B: Does that often happen?

A: Uh, I guess that's happened to me on two or three occasions since I've been in the job. Oh, and the other thing that can be difficult is insurance claims, because, well it's funny how most people buy their clothes from very ordinary shops, (Yes) but when a suitcase goes missing, they will say it was full of Armani suits and Vivienne Westwood dresses or stuff like that, you know. I mean, I suppose it's human nature, but it does make it very difficult for us to deal with those claims, When we know that people aren't actually telling the truth. (Hmm, of course)

3. A head teacher in a poor inner city area

A: Well, the stress starts first thing in the morning with the worry over whether I'm going to have a full complement of staff, I mean, because quite a lot ring in sick quite a lot of the time. And those phone calls start about, about 7 in the morning so I have to find teachers to deputise then at short notice; I do that over breakfast. (Not good for the digestion!) Not very good for the digestion! So I get to school, I'm usually, it's usually about 8.00 and the caretaker and I clean the playground because most of the area seems to use it as a rubbish dump. One morning I arrived to find £10,000-worth of computer equipment just gone. (God!) Completely gone.

Then the kids start to arrive about 5 to 9, and I check and see if they're all settled and starting to work. We have a number of pupils from deprived backgrounds, but our school's got a pretty good reputation and generally the kids are very well-behaved, but we do have a growing minority of students whose disruptive behaviour can be a real problem. (In the classroom?) In the classroom, yes. I have to deal with physical violence quite a lot in the classroom (Against teachers or against each other?) against each other and against teachers, yes. There's no difference these days. I mean, quite a lot of the kids just deliberately ignore the teachers, sit with their backs facing them, and there's nothing they can do.

Answer key

Nanny:
Two negative aspects are money (not getting a pay rise or being paid baby-sitting money) and time-keeping (parents going out and arriving back late).
It can also be embarrassing living so closely with others, e.g. if you come in when the parents are having a row.

Public relations officer:
Angry and abusive customers on the phone
Customers who lie

Head teacher:
Stress (sick teachers, vandalism to property)
Dealing with physical violence in the classroom and generally disruptive behaviour

4

Clarify the use of *if ever* and *whenever* and ask the questions in the Class Book. With the four sentences, tell students to justify their decisions.

Answer key

Possible answers:
1. head teacher or nanny
2. head teacher
3. public relations officer, head teacher
4. nanny

5

As the first part of the lesson has concentrated on the negative aspects of different jobs, you may wish to focus more on the positive side; or perhaps split the class and have one half working on negative aspects and the other half on positive points. At the end let pairs or groups exchange answers and conduct a feedback.

6

This final personalisation activity is an opportunity for learners to use language from the lesson to express their own ideas, but it may also create the need for additional words and phrases, so be prepared to move round and help where necessary. At the end, let pairs or groups exchange answers.

If you feel this activity is too similar to the previous one, you could omit one of the exercises – particularly if you are short of time – and return to the other exercise for revision at a later date.

Personal Study Workbook

1: Wordbuilding: vocabulary
5: Analysing a text: reading
6: A station announcer: listening
8: Speaking partners

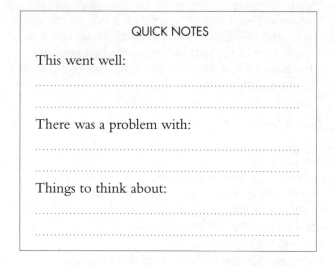

QUICK NOTES

This went well:

....

There was a problem with:

....

Things to think about:

....

....

REVIEW AND DEVELOPMENT

REVIEW OF UNIT 11

1

It makes sense for learners to underline *like* or *don't like* while they complete the sentences – this allows them to express their own views and not ones they may not share. When they have finished they can exchange answers and explain the reasons behind them.

2

This exercise picks up the food theme from Unit 11, but actually introduces some new language – idioms and fixed expressions relevant to the topic. After the dictionary work, elicit the meanings from the group to check their understanding, then move on to the memorisation task.

REVIEW OF UNIT 12

1

Part A just reviews the form and meaning of question tags (in case some of the group have forgotten), but you could elicit the answers from the class before turning to the book. Then do the completion exercise and check answers to ensure learners can produce the correct forms.

Answer key

1. doesn't she   2. have you   3. will it   4. shouldn't they
5. isn't it   6. hasn't he   7. doesn't he   8. didn't they

Part B gives learners a chance to see if they can use question tags appropriately and get the intonation right. Check answers at the end then give the pairs a chance to practise their completed dialogues.

Answer key

Any two tags from the following:
1.
A: What's up?
B: I haven't got any money in the bank.
A: Well, never mind. You get paid tomorrow, (don't you)? *fall or rise* (both are possible here)
B: Yes, but I'll be broke again next week, (won't I)? *fall*
A: You really need to win the lottery, (don't you)? *fall*
2.
C: They're very strange people, (aren't they)? *fall*
D: Oh, do you think so?
C: Well, they keep snakes, (don't they)? *fall* Anyone who keeps snakes has to be a bit unusual, (don't they)? *fall*
D: Oh, come on. There's nothing wrong with that. Uncle Donald used to have a snake, (didn't he)? *rise or fall*
C: Precisely. Uncle Donald wasn't exactly normal, (was he)? *fall*

QUICK NOTES

This went well:

....

....

There was a problem with:

....

Things to think about:

....

....

14

ACCIDENTS WILL HAPPEN

CONTENTS

Language focus:	present/past continuous (habits)	
	keep + -ing form	
	used to/would (past habits)	
	participle clauses	
	verbs, e.g. *spill, scratch, rip*	
	accidents and medical vocabulary	
Skills:	Speaking:	absent-minded or clumsy habits
		predicting a story from key words
	Listening:	people describing clumsy or absent-minded habits
		narrative about an emergency operation on an aircraft
	Reading:	a humorous text about driving
		first part of the story about the operation on an aircraft
	Writing:	an accident description/report

ARE YOU CLUMSY OR ABSENT-MINDED?

Introduction

The main lexical input is a group of verbs, most of which can be seen to have a connection with clumsy or absent-minded behaviour. That becomes the subject matter for the lesson as learners first process the verbs in relation to their meaning, then listen to people talking about their clumsy or absent-minded habits. This is followed by a second language focus on structures used to express irritating habits. After controlled practice and personalised speaking practice, the lesson finishes with another listening as more people describe their clumsy and absent-minded behaviour.

Suggested steps

1

Illustrate the meaning of *clumsy* and *absent-minded* (knock things over in the classroom, and build a situation to elucidate *absent-minded*) then let learners see the definitions in the Class Book before they go on to the task. Remind them that some sentences do not illustrate clumsy or absent-minded behaviour. Do the first few examples, then monitor, help where necessary, and check answers and check pronunciation on items such as *leapt* /lept/ and *bruised* /bruːzd/, and the other *-ed* endings which are pronounced /t/. You may also wish to elicit some of the verb forms, e.g. *creep/crept, mislay/mislaid, spill/spilt, leap/leapt.*

Answer key

Clumsy: 1, 2, 5, 7, 8, 12, 13
Absent-minded: 4, 9, 11, 14
Neither: 3, 6, 10

2

This is an opportunity for personalised practice, and you might like to start by talking about yourself. You might also need to help with lexis here if learners have different examples of clumsy or absent-minded behaviour they wish to describe. If you find some learners have no vices of this kind, encourage them to talk about friends or relatives who do.

3 ▭

Play the recording, allow an exchange of answers, then refer learners to the tapescript on page 170 to check their answers.

Tapescript

My problem is, I'm always mislaying things, important things, such as my front door key or my credit cards – that sort of stuff. And it's really irritating because I know they're important but I keep putting them down in different places in the house – I don't have one place, you see, where I keep these things – and within hours, minutes even, I can't remember where they are. My wife used to spend half her life looking for things I'd mislaid, but now she refuses to lift a finger to help me.

I remember as a teenager I used to be incredibly clumsy and my body was covered in bruises all the time where I kept bumping into things and falling over. And at home I was forever dropping plates and smashing glasses – my

---

mother would never let me do the washing-up or anything like that, and for a while it got so bad that she would actually hide anything of value so that I couldn't get my hands on it and break it.

4

Make it clear to the group that these questions all relate to the sections they completed in Exercise 3. When they think they have answered the questions, refer them to the Language Reference on pages 149–50. You can, of course, explain the answers yourself, but the aim here is to get learners into the habit of using their Language Reference as a personal resource.

Answer key

1. He uses the present continuous + *always*, and *keep* + *-ing* form.
2. These forms emphasise the fact that the actions are repeated again and again, and they also indicate to us the man's irritation that these things continue to happen.
3. She uses *used to* + verb, *keep* + *-ing* form, and the past continuous + *forever*.
4. *Used to* and *would* are interchangeable in the first text, and in the second example in the second text, because both examples refer to regularly repeated actions, i.e. 'looking for things' and 'hiding things'. *Used to* is not interchangeable with *would* in the sentence 'I used to be clumsy', because this refers to a state and not an event.

5

In order to stimulate interest, you could elicit more ways of finishing the example sentence. For example:
... looking for the most sensational stories.
... distorting the facts. (Learners won't know *distort*, but if they are clearly trying to express that concept, this is the perfect opportunity to teach them the word.)

Then give them a few minutes to complete the sentences before they exchange answers and discuss them in groups. Conduct a class feedback at the end.

6 ▭▭ ▭▭

Unusually the lesson ends with a listening, which you could save for another lesson or use for revision. If you play it now, choose the appropriate version, or play the first one, and then move on to version 2 if there are no problems.

Answer key

Version 1:
Speaker 1: She is absent-minded, e.g. she keeps forgetting where she has put something; and she goes into rooms to get something, then forgets what she is looking for.
Speaker 2: She used to be very clumsy and was always breaking things. The worst thing was when she broke a painted egg that her grandfather had had all his life and which had been given to him by his mother.

Version 2:
Speaker 1: He used to be absent-minded, e.g. he used to go into his bedroom and start getting undressed, then realise he had gone in there for a different reason.
Speaker 2: He is very clumsy, e.g. he used to catch one foot on the back of the other and trip over. He still does it occasionally, but sometimes now he does it as a joke.

Tapescript

Version 1
1.
DENICA: Well, more and more recently, erm, I keep forgetting where I've put something in my flat. (Right) It's just a habit that seems to be happening more and more, I used to know exactly where I kept everything and be very kind of tidy and (Yeah) what have you. But I keep losing things and ... (Why?) I don't know – perhaps because my life is, is ... I'm so busy these days, um, and I literally don't have time to, you know, tidy my desk or, you know, really keep things as much in order as, as I used to. (Yeah, I know what you mean) And also I tend to, um, go into rooms, um, looking for something and then I've forgotten what I'm looking for because my mind is on all sorts of other things, um, and so I stand in the room and look around and think 'oh no, now what was I looking for?' (Yeah) have to go back out.

2.
LORELEI: When I was younger, I used to be very clumsy, I was always breaking things. Whenever I'd handle anything, it would break, and the worst thing that ever happened because of this clumsiness was I broke an egg of my grandfather's. It was a blown-out egg that had been painted, that he had brought, his mother had given it to him when he was a little boy, he'd brought it from Yugoslavia. He'd had it his whole life – he was 80, and I dropped it, and I broke it. (Ooh, no!) I still choke up when I think about it. He forgave me.

Version 2
1.
WILLIE: I'm not very absent-minded now but when I was younger I think I was very absent-minded and it used to drive my mum and dad mad, I think. And I used to do that thing where in the middle of the day you go into a room, and like, I used to go into the bedroom and I'd suddenly find myself getting undressed, and I'd be in my pyjamas.
DENICA: Oh, really. Why?
WILLIE: Well, to ... 'cos I associated going into the bedroom with getting ready for bed.
DENICA: Of course, I see that.
WILLIE: I'd actually gone in for a different reason.
DENICA: Mmm.
WILLIE: But somehow the act of walking into the bedroom made me think, 'Oh, I must go to

bed.' And I'd put on my pyjamas, and halfway through I'd suddenly realise that I'd got it wrong.

DENICA: It was in the middle of the day or whatever.

WILLIE: That's right, and you'd snap back into doing whatever it was you were doing.

DENICA: Sounds very absent-minded to me. Are you better now?

WILLIE: Yeah. Yes, I am, thanks.

2.

NICK: I'm always tripping up. I don't know why, but, er, I used to do it when I was little, um, and my mum used to say I was lazy-footed. And, er, I'd be walking along and I'd catch one foot on the back of the other usually and trip up. And I tend to do it now, not as often, but what I've found myself doing is doing it as a joke, ha ha, so, um, I like doing it, um, if I'm on a walk and there's a lot of people coming the other way, and just as I'm getting up to them, er, I sort of pretend to trip and they all go 'Oh, oh, careful', and it's a very silly joke really, but the people that I'm with know that I'm going to do it, and they hold, hang their heads in despair really.

Personal Study Workbook

1: Annoying habits: present continuous; *keep* + *-ing* form
6: I remember ...: listening; *used to/would*

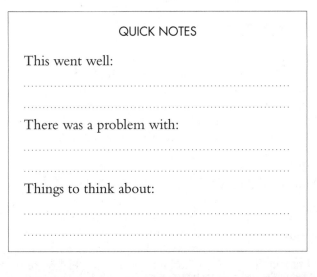

QUICK NOTES

This went well:

....

....

There was a problem with:

....

....

Things to think about:

....

....

UNUSUAL CLAIMS

Introduction

Superficially this may appear to be a rather downbeat subject, but the text is actually a very amusing account of some of the ridiculous excuses that drivers make to explain an accident. The language focus is on synonyms for *hit* (there are many), and some different ways that we use participle clauses. Skills work develops through reading, writing (describing an accident) and speaking (reacting to the text and paraphrasing what people intended to say).

Suggested steps

1

Follow the instructions in the Class Book.

Answer key

Possible answers:
1. The dog ran into the road.
2. The sharp bend. (The driver was going too fast.)
3. The fruit stall distracted the driver.

Option

If your learners respond to the picture by saying things like, *Maybe he ...* or *I'm sure the driver ...*, this might be a perfect opportunity to highlight the use of *might've* + past participle (for speculation) or *must've* + past participle (for deduction). You can put the forms on the board, check the concept, and then elicit further examples to explain the likely or possible causes of the accident.

2

One shouldn't be too heavy-handed when approaching an amusing text, but if you think your learners may struggle to see the humour in these accounts you could examine one or two with the class and ask them if a) they find them funny, and b) they can identify the source of the humour. Alternatively, you may feel the text will have more impact if you just allow the class to read it and discover the jokes for themselves. And when laughter builds from an unexpected source it can become quite infectious.

At the end, learners can form groups to give their reaction to the text – this is really more important than the task – and then think about how they could paraphrase one or two of the more confused accounts. Listen to answers round the class.

Answer key

The following clearly suggest the driver wasn't paying attention:
Arriving home ...
I pulled out from the side of the road ...
Approaching the junction ... (possibly)
Attempting to kill a fly ...
My car was legally parked ...
I had been driving for forty years ...

3

Look at the example carefully so learners understand the task. When you go through the answers you may need to clarify the differences between some of these partial synonyms.

Answer key

crash into; ran over; struck; back into; collide with
(See the *Language Point* on page 84.)

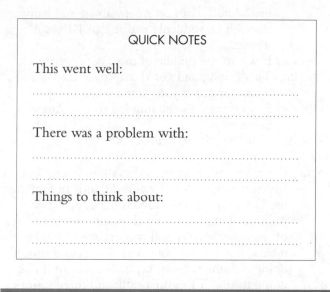

QUICK NOTES

This went well:

....

....

There was a problem with:

....

....

Things to think about:

....

....

DRAMA AT 9,000 METRES

Introduction

Through both a reading text and a listening text, the lesson recounts the dramatic true story of a life-saving operation that took place aboard a plane at 9,000 metres. The lesson opens with key vocabulary which learners use to try to predict the events, then the story unfolds through different skills activities, additional vocabulary input, and finally, a letter.

Suggested steps

1

As the box of words and phrases is limited, you could write them on the board and so avoid the danger that learners may start reading the text in Exercise 2. After five or ten minutes, elicit a few ideas from the different pairs and ask them to select the most likely story.

Option

You could do this activity with the whole class and approach it slightly differently. Write just two or three phrases on the board, e.g. *holiday romance*, *motorbike*, *injury*, and ask the class to predict a possible storyline. Then add more words or phrases, e.g. *jumbo jet to Heathrow*, *Hong Kong*, and let them either elaborate on or change their story. Finally, add one or two more, e.g. *surgeon on board*, *knocked Paula off*, and see how that changes the story. Basically, you can give learners as much or as little as you like, depending on their responses.

2

After they have read the text and talked to their partner, you may wish to talk about some of the vocabulary. Bear in mind that there is a vocabulary activity in Exercise 5 which concentrates on medical vocabulary and parts of the anatomy, so don't spend too long on it now. You should also ask for one or two learners to recap the story so you can be certain that everyone is clear about the facts so far (if they aren't, they won't have a chance of understanding the recording in the next exercise).

4

It may be more effective to illustrate these clauses on the board or with an OHT rather than have learners' heads buried in their books. The task itself is quite short and should not take more than a minute.

Answer key

Arriving home (second); approaching the junction (second); removing my hat (second); attempting to kill a fly (third); lorry coming in the opposite direction (first)

5

After the control and close text analysis of the previous two exercises, this is a chance for learners to operate much more freely. You can encourage the use of participle clauses and relevant vocabulary from the lesson, but we prefer not to box learners in with too many linguistic demands, otherwise the activity becomes very contrived. At the end, allow learners to move round and read the different accounts, and make suggestions for improvements.

The humour in the text may not be to everyone's taste, but if your learners enjoyed it, there are some more extracts in Worksheet 14 on page 125, with some different activities.

Personal Study Workbook

3: Synonyms: vocabulary
4: Men wearing strange uniforms: participle clauses
5: The safe tea cosy: reading
8: Speaking partners

3 🎧

Play the recording and then put the class back into pairs to tell each other what they understood. If learners find it difficult, play it again and refer them to the tapescript on page 171 with the specific task of underlining the parts of the story they couldn't grasp from the listening. This way, there is an opportunity to turn a problem into a learning experience.

If your monitoring of the pairs indicates they have understood the gist of the story, go on to Exercise 4.

Tapescript

So, the thing was, once they took off, Paula's arm was bandaged, and she was given pain killers. She settled back and listened to music on her Walkman and felt a lot better. Anyway, sometime later, she decided to take her shoes off, but when she bent down, she felt a terrible pain under her ribs. She was in agony and called for a steward. So, once again, the doctor came back. At first, apparently, he thought she may have fractured some ribs, but he soon saw that she was deteriorating fast. She was having breathing difficulties and turning blue. He suddenly realised that her lung must have collapsed! So, there was only one thing to do – they had to operate immediately – otherwise, she would die.
And with the help of, er, Tom Wong, Dr Wallace constructed this emergency operating theatre using the back seats of the plane. Apparently, there was some anaesthetic in the first aid kit that they used, but apart from that, they used the, some very basic instruments. They used a pair of scissors, a little water bottle, a coat hanger, a piece of plastic tubing, and a bottle of brandy that they used as disinfectant to clean the instruments. And with just those basic things, Dr Wallace carried out the life-saving operation. Unbelievably enough, Paula began to feel better almost immediately, and by the time they landed at Heathrow, she was cheerful and quite relaxed.
When they got off the plane she gave the doctor a very grateful kiss, and he received an award later for his work and (the doctor, this is, Dr Wallace) and he gave the money, £32,000, to his university medical school. (Wow!)

4 🎧

This gives the pairs a chance to test their understanding of certain details from the story. If they are unable to answer one or two of them, you may wish to play certain sections of the story again, but we do not feel it repays too much repetition, otherwise motivation may flag.

Answer key

1. She felt a terrible pain under her ribs.
2. He thought she had fractured some ribs.
3. When she had breathing difficulties and turned blue.
4. scissors, water bottle, brandy, coat hanger, plastic tube (from the oxygen mask)
5. She felt much better at once.
6. He received an award.

5

Many of these items will already have arisen in the lesson (in the reading text or the learners' summary of the recording in Exercise 3), so this exercise should not take too long. When you check the answers, you will need to check that your learners can pronounce these items, e.g. *bruised* /bruːzd/, *bandage* /bændɪdʒ/, *collapsed* /kəlæpst/, etc.

Answer key

Reading text: to be shaken; a bruised arm; a bandage; symptoms.
Listening text: painkillers; to be in agony; a fractured rib; breathing difficulties; a collapsed lung; an operating theatre; an anaesthetic; a first aid kit; instruments; life-saving.

6

You may not have time for the letter in class; if not, set it for homework and discuss it in the next class.

Personal Study Workbook

2: Personal injuries: vocabulary
7: Describing an accident: writing

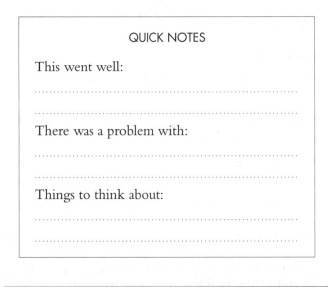

```
QUICK NOTES

This went well:
.............................................
.............................................

There was a problem with:
.............................................
.............................................

Things to think about:
.............................................
.............................................
```

REVIEW AND DEVELOPMENT

REVIEW OF UNIT 12

1

This returns to the main source of material in the unit, namely the theatre, only this time learners have an opportunity to talk about their attitudes to live theatre, and in particular it asks them to compare watching a play with reading one, watching TV and going to the cinema, etc. In this way, the activity should be just as relevant to non-theatregoers.

2

Look at the example carefully so that learners are clear they must provide adverbs or adverbial phrases of manner. Conduct a feedback at the end to find the most common answers, and, in the opinion of the group, the best answers.

Answer key

Possible answers:

Best	Worst
1. sympathetically	in a happy voice
2. politely	angrily/irritably
3. carefully	dangerously/fast
4. in a friendly way	angrily
5. quietly/softly	noisily/carelessly
6. instinctively	scientifically/cynically
7. confidently	nervously/gloomily

REVIEW OF UNIT 13

1 ▢▢

Follow the instructions in the Class Book. If your learners are able to remember the definitions from the recording, that's to their credit, but we imagine they will have to do some of the work themselves as well. You can slip in a few extra words of your own for them to define at the end of the activity.

Answer key

1. maternity leave   2. paternity leave   3. be made redundant   4. be sacked/dismissed/fired
5. retirement/retire   6. promotion/be promoted
7. resignation/resign   8. apply for a job.   9. take someone on   10. go on strike

Tapescript

1. It's when you take time off work to have a baby.
2. It's when a husband takes time off work to look after his wife and baby.
3. It means to lose your job because there isn't enough work.
4. It's when you lose your job because you're no good at it or you've done something wrong.
5. It's when you finally stop working, often at the age of 60 or 65.
6. It's when you get a better position in your company with more money and responsibility.
7. It's when you officially decide to leave a job.
8. It's to write formally for a job that you have probably seen advertised in a newspaper.
9. It's a phrasal verb, meaning to employ someone.
10. It's when you stop working for a time to protest about something, such as your pay or working conditions.

2

When the group has read the text, check their understanding with the questions before moving on to the speaking activity.

Answer key

1. Because of the new supermarket.
2. He has reduced his prices on some goods, and considered opening longer hours and cutting back on staff.
3. He is angry and resentful.

We hope the way the task is worded – using a range of modal verbs – will be enough to set the groups thinking along the same linguistic lines; if not, don't intervene, just listen and make notes on the language that is being used. At the end you can point out the accurate and effective use of modals, and also give examples where the absence of them impaired someone's ability to express an idea accurately and concisely.

QUICK NOTES

This went well:

....

....

There was a problem with:

....

....

Things to think about:

....

....

15

WAYS OF BEING BETTER OFF

```
                        CONTENTS

Language focus:   passives
                  expressing number/quantity
                  money vocabulary
                  use of whether
                  legal vocabulary
                  paraphrasing

        Skills   Speaking:   predicting results of an honesty survey
                             discussing legal cases
                             practice at haggling
                 Listening:  results of an honesty survey
                             a woman haggling in a shop
                 Reading:    a text about legal cases
                             a text about bargaining
                 Writing:    an article for a newspaper
```

HOW HONEST ARE WE?

Introduction

The lesson is based round a real experiment carried out in a number of different countries. Learners discuss how they would react if they found a wallet containing money, then they read about the real-life experiment carried out to discover the same thing. Language input includes ways of talking about number/quantity, and there are several opportunities for learners to use the target language. There is also a listening text which provides the results to the experiment, and a further speaking activity which is also an opportunity to practise the use of *whether*.

Suggested steps

1

Follow the instructions in the Class Book.

2

The short text should not present any real difficulty, but the task has been included just to check understanding, and as an opportunity for learners to learn and use some useful lexical input contained in the text (e.g. *carry out, drop, medium-sized, receipts*, etc.).

After learners have read and summarised the text, they can complete the language task. No pre-teaching is necessary, and learners should uncover the meaning of new items — using partners, a dictionary, or you — as they carry out the task. Check carefully when they have finished.

Answer key

Column 1	*Column 2*
nearly everyone	a huge difference
the vast majority	a big difference
quite a lot of people	a significant difference
a few people	a fairly significant difference
a handful of people	a slight difference
very few people	very little difference/hardly any
hardly anyone	difference

Language Point

1. *Few* vs. *a few*
   Few suggests not only a small number, but less than was expected. For example:
   A: How was the party?
   B: Few people came. (i.e. it wasn't a success)
   A: How was the meeting?
   B: Well, a few people came. (i.e. not many, but this does not necessarily imply disappointment)
2. *A few people* may be the same as *a handful of people*: it really depends on the total number that is possible, e.g. if *a few* came out of a total of 200, it would probably be more than *a handful*; but *a few* out of a total of 20 might well mean *a handful* (i.e. four or five).

3

Allow one or two minutes for individuals to read through the questions and think about answers, then form groups for the discussion. Pay attention to their use of the target vocabulary, but also listen for other language the learners might need in the discussion – you could feed it in after the activity, and they may be able to make use of it in the final activity.

4 ⟨⟩

Play the tape and check answers.

Answer key

1. b   2. yes, b   3. c   4. c   5. c   6. c

Tapescript

In Britain 52 out of the 80 wallets were returned – that's 65% overall. Now, in America and Europe the figures were a little bit different, but the difference wasn't really very significant. In America the return rate was 67%, which puts them a little bit above the UK. In Europe the figure was lower – 58% overall, although there were some really interesting fluctuations here, much more than in America and Britain. Two Scandinavian cities, for example, Odense and Oslo, recorded an astonishing 100% return rate, while Lausanne in Switzerland and Weimar in Germany recorded only a 20% return rate. Women were more likely to return the wallet than men: 72% compared with 60%; and people in medium-sized towns were slightly more honest than people in the cities: 67.5% against 62.5%. Now, maybe that's not as much of a difference as some people would've predicted. The response to the reward was interesting. One man refused it outright and most people were reluctant to accept it.

5 ⟨⟩ ⟨⟩

Again, learners can predict answers in pairs or groups, and you could elicit them and write them on the board before playing the appropriate version of the recording.

Answer key

Version 1:
1. They came from a religious background – they would feel guilty to have kept it.
2. They knew how they would feel if it happened to them.
3. One person returned it because it might contain something of sentimental value.
4. Some said it might belong to someone worse off than themselves.
5. They were brought up to be honest – it didn't occur to them to keep it. This was the most common reason.

Version 2:
1. They came from a religious background – they would feel guilty to have kept it.
2. They knew how they would feel if it had happened to them.
3. One person returned it because it might contain something of sentimental value.
4. One man returned it to the nearest police station without even opening it.
5. One man returned it because of the photos inside.
6. Some said it might belong to someone worse off than themselves.
7. A woman thought it belonged to a colleague of hers.
8. They were brought up to be honest – it never occurred to them to keep it. This was the most common reason.

Tapescript

Version 1
Why did people return the wallets? Here are the findings:
Several said they came from a religious background, and that it wouldn't be right, they would've felt guilty if they kept it.
Some returned it because, because they knew how, how it would feel if it happened to them.
One person returned it not because the wallet contained money but because he was afraid it might contain something of sentimental value to the owner.
And a number of people said they thought the wallet might belong to someone such as a pensioner or, or an unemployed person – in other words, someone who was worse off than themselves, someone who really needed the money.
But the most common reason people returned the wallet was that they said they had been brought up to be honest and it never even crossed their minds to keep it. They just returned the wallet instinctively.

Version 2
The reasons people gave for returning the wallets were, were numerous. Several people said that they came from a religious background. It would've been wrong to keep it, it would've been sinful and they, they would feel guilty if they'd kept it.
Several returned it because, um, they were empathetic; they knew they would've been very upset if it had happened to them. Er, one person returned it not because of the money but because maybe it would, would've contained something of sentimental value to the owner, something irreplaceable.
Er, one man returned the wallet to the nearest police station without even bothering to look inside. He said it never even crossed his mind to do anything else.
Another man was, was very touched by a photograph in the wallet, er, when he saw the picture of the woman and the two children he said he couldn't possibly have kept the wallet and the money – it would have been on his conscience for the rest of his life.
Some people said that they thought the wallet might belong to someone such as an older person, a pensioner or, or an unemployed person – in other words, someone

who was worse off than themselves who might really need that money.

One woman said she was sure the wallet belonged to a workmate and that's why she returned it.

But the most common reason why people returned the wallet was that they had been brought up to be honest and, and it never even occurred to them to keep it. They just returned the wallet instinctively.

6

The context provides a very natural opportunity to introduce and practise *whether*, and learners should be able to understand it and use it without any real explanation. After the discussion you can talk about the use of *if* and *whether*, and learners can confirm their guesses or find out the answers by reading the Language Reference on page 150.

Personal Study Workbook

1: Hardly anyone: expressing quantity
6: If I were better off ...: listening
7: Describing an experiment: writing

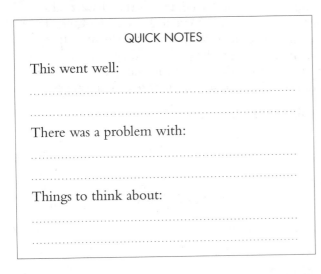

QUICK NOTES

This went well:

....

....

There was a problem with:

....

....

Things to think about:

....

....

JOIN THE RUSH TO SUE

Introduction

There is some quite specialised lexis in this lesson, but much of it appears quite frequently in newspaper articles and would obviously be very useful for learners studying law. The use of the passive is also very prominent in newspaper texts and it forms the main language input of the lesson. The criminal case studies also offer an intriguing source for different opinions and extensive personalised speaking; and the lesson ends with learners using notes to construct their own written texts around criminal cases of compensation.

Suggested steps

1

You should emphasise that this exercise is not concerned with finding a single correct solution, but with building correct collocations – in some cases there will be three or four nouns that collocate with each of the verbs on the left. Learners can do the exercise individually or in pairs, but if done individually we would still recommend that you allow them to consult with each other if they wish, and they really must have access to dictionaries as some items will be new. When you go through the answers, clarify the meaning of new lexis.

Answer key

reach a settlement/a decision/a verdict
ruin someone's reputation
settle out of court/a dispute
sue someone for damages/compensation/negligence/libel/£1m
appeal against a decision/a verdict

> ### Language Point
>
> 1. There are several synonyms for *dispute*, e.g. *argument, row, quarrel*. You may need to point out that *a dispute* is usually used to describe a serious disagreement between countries, political groups, large organisations, etc., and it is more common in written English than spoken English. It can also function as a verb, meaning to disagree with a fact, or question the validity of a decision, e.g. *Lawyers have disputed the claims made by the police*.
> 2. Point out that *damages* is a plural noun (and doesn't have the same meaning as *damage*), and is only used with this meaning in a legal context. It is synonymous with *compensation*, although the latter noun is used more widely and not restricted to a legal context, e.g. *We all had to work on Sunday, but the boss gave us Monday afternoon off in compensation*.

2 ▭▭

The brief listen and answer exercise tests the concepts of the target vocabulary from the previous exercise. If learners are unable to answer, play the tape again. You could even check a third time by reading out the questions yourself, but in a different order.

Answer key

1. yes   2. yes   3. no   4. yes   5. yes   6. no
7. yes, probably   8. no

Tapescript

1. Does a verdict give you an answer?
2. If you sue someone, will they be angry?
3. If you receive damages, do you have to pay the money back?
4. Does compensation make you better off?
5. If you settle a dispute, have you solved a problem?
6. If you ruin someone's life, will they thank you for it?
7. If you are awarded damages, will you be happy?
8. If you appeal against a decision, are you satisfied with it?

Option

If learners are finding these lexical items difficult to commit to memory, you could extend the activity by asking one partner to read out the questions while the other answers. They can then swap round and repeat the exercise.

3

After the pre-teaching of lexical items in Exercise 1, learners should now be able to cope with the text. Allow them ten minutes to read and choose the correct forms in the text, and also ask them to think about the amount of compensation in each case.

4

If too much time is spent on the language content of a text, the message of the text may be forgotten – for this reason learners have a chance to react to the text before returning to the use of passives in the text. However, you may wish to allow learners a few minutes to ask questions about the text before discussion.

When learners discuss the cases, you could ask each group to nominate a member to summarise the group's response to each case after the group discussion. Monitor their language while they talk and note down useful language (i.e. language that is used and language that is not used but clearly needed), in preparation for some feedback at the end, after the groups have reported back to the class.

Option

You may wish to focus on the passives exercise first and later return to the ideas in the text. This rules out an immediate response to the text but may encourage more thought about the use of passives in the later speaking activity.

5

After checking the answers, go through the explanation in the Class Book. This is probably best done by putting the reasons on the board; alternatively, try eliciting the answers from the group.

Answer key

The scalding apple pie: to be eaten; been injured
The burglary victim: was told; was jailed; sued
The stressed worker: was awarded; be treated
The rugby referee: ruled; was paralysed; collapsed

Learners can do the exercise on agents individually or in pairs, then you can check with the group.

Answer key

to be eaten by people in general (we don't know exactly who)
had been injured by a scalding apple pie
was told by the judge
was jailed by the judge
was awarded by the judge
be treated by employers in general
was paralysed by the combined weight of the players who collapsed on him

6

Ask learners to read through the different situations and explain any new vocabulary. Then go through the rubric carefully so they understand what they have to do. Encourage learners to look at the texts for guidance, but also encourage them to add new information if they wish. Be available to help pairs if they need it, but don't interfere if not required. At the end, pairs can move round the class comparing their text with others.

Personal Study Workbook

2: Written and spoken: active and passive; paraphrasing
4: Compensation: money and legal vocabulary

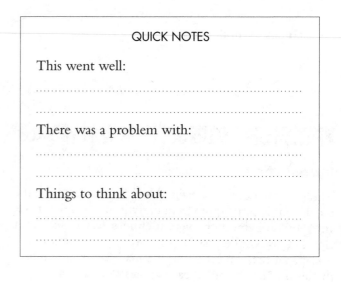

QUICK NOTES

This went well:

....

....

There was a problem with:

....

....

Things to think about:

....

....

WHAT'S YOUR BEST PRICE?

Introduction

Learners begin by discussing haggling in different types of shop, then read a text about strategies for negotiating a better price. The text is also used for contextual guesswork and paraphrase. The theme of the lesson returns with a listening activity (a recording of a person haggling in a shop), and concludes with a roleplay in which learners have to bargain in a similar context.

Suggested steps

1

With a multilingual group, this activity will be more interesting if you mix the nationalities. However, with a monolingual group you may actually find there is more disagreement and more heated discussion. If you come from a different country to your learners, you can tell the group how things would/might be in your own country.

2

Look at the two paraphrase examples in the text with the class, then let them read the text and complete the task. Put them in pairs at the end, then check the answers.

Answer key

knock something off = reduce the price
merchandise (formal) = the product(s)
in bulk = in large quantities
throw in = include
goes down well = is popular/successful
get rid of = remove/sell
bargains = good items at a low price
bear in mind = remember

Option

If you wish to make the text more interactive, you could divide the group into pairs or threes, and ask each person to read part of the text (three sections each for pairs, and two sections each for threes). Each member then explains their strategies to their partner or group. Everyone can then read the whole text at the end and complete the paraphrase exercise.

3

Put learners in groups to respond to the ideas in the text and share personal experiences. Conduct a class feedback at the end.

4 📼

Give learners a minute to refresh their memories of the different strategies used in the text, then play the recording. Play it twice if necessary. After checking the answers, you could allow learners several minutes to read through the tapescript on page 172 to find new words and phrases they want to learn.

Answer key

She uses these strategies:
5 (probably helped)
3 (not successful)
1 (successful)

Tapescript

CUSTOMER: Hello!

SHOP OWNER: Hi.

CUSTOMER: Um, I just think this shop's so lovely; I've come past here so many times …

SHOP OWNER: Thank you!

CUSTOMER: You've got lovely, really lovely things in the window, and, um, I just wonder, I'm looking for a present for my mother, um, and it's her 50th birthday, so it has to be something really, really special (Hmmm) and you've got a pair of earrings in the window, erm, they're sort of, I think they might be garnets or rubies?

SHOP OWNER: Oh, yeah, yeah, they just went in this week.

CUSTOMER: Hmm. I wondered if I could have a look at them.

SHOP OWNER: Yes, of course, of course. Well, there you are.

CUSTOMER: Oh, they really … you've got really lovely taste. They're beautiful!

SHOP OWNER: Well, actually, my wife does most of the buying, she got them at an auction last week. They've come in from France, in fact.

CUSTOMER: Oh, really?

SHOP OWNER: Yes, a clearance on an old, er, um, estate there, and they are rubies, encrusted in diamonds.

CUSTOMER: Could you, er, tell me the price?

SHOP OWNER: Well, these are quite old and in very, very good condition. The price is £150.

CUSTOMER: Oh, mm. That's just a bit more than, than I was thinking of.

SHOP OWNER: Oh, I see.

CUSTOMER: What a shame. They're so pretty. And, erm, that's, that's your final price?

SHOP OWNER: Well, I mean, I think you'll find that for what they are, they are quite reasonably priced. I mean, would you be interested in telling me what you would be prepared to pay for them?

CUSTOMER: Well, I'm sort of, I was really thinking about, you know, £130, about £20 less? I mean, if you look here, there's a sort of, it looks like they've been mended at some point. You wouldn't sort of …

SHOP OWNER: Really? Could you …?

CUSTOMER: Just here, look.

SHOP OWNER: Yes, well, obviously, I mean, they're quite old, and I'm sure, my wife priced it actually, I didn't do that so I'm sure she, that's reflected in the price already, but are you thinking of paying cash?

CUSTOMER: Er, yeah. Yes, I would pay cash.
SHOP OWNER: OK. Well how about a compromise of
             £135?
CUSTOMER: Well, I think that's great! Yes, thank you,
             I'll take them.
SHOP OWNER: OK.

5 and 6

After fixing a notional price for each object, pairs should
think of an object they wish to buy and discuss how they
might negotiate a better price. You can then divide the
class into shoppers and sales assistants and let them
roleplay the situation. Listen and make notes of language
which they might benefit from, then feed it in at the end
of the activity. You can then reverse the roles and do the
activity again. If it has been successful, you could even
do it a third time by putting 'shoppers' with different
'sales assistants', and asking the shoppers this time to buy
a different object. Repeating the activity in this way
ensures variety and a different outcome, but also the
opportunity to recycle language and improve on the first
performance. You could then talk to the group about the
roleplay and ask them if they felt they had performed
more effectively on the second occasion. Asking learners
to reflect on their performance in this way can be very
useful to you and them.

For further practice of paraphrasing (and revision of
various lexical items from the unit), you could do
Worksheet 15 on page 125 with the class. The answers
are on page 93.

Personal Study Workbook

3: It's got sentimental value: vocabulary
5: Money matters: reading
8: Speaking partners

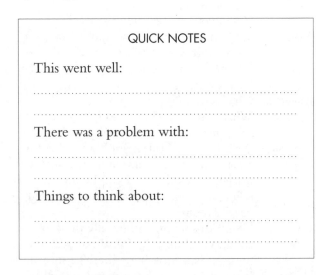

QUICK NOTES

This went well:

....

....

There was a problem with:

....

....

Things to think about:

....

....

REVIEW OF UNIT 13

1

Ask learners to read through the questionnaire and
complete section d) for each question. You can move
round and provide help where required. Then they
should pass the questionnaire to a partner who must
answer each question (they can underline as many
answers as they wish). Finally, they can discuss their
answers in groups and then report their findings to the
rest of the class.

2

Point out that the only errors involve the use of passives,
and that some of the sentences do not contain any
errors. After learners have compared with a partner,
check answers with the group.

Answer key

1. Airline pilots should be forced to retire at 50.
2. Correct
3. Children should be entitled to work ten hours a week
   from the age of 12.
4. If you are refused a job, you should have the right to
   know the reason.
5. If employees are given promotion, they should always
   get a higher salary.
6. Correct
7. If some workers in a company go on strike, they
   shouldn't be allowed to try to prevent other
   employees from going to work.

Now put the class into small groups to give their own
opinion on the corrected statements.

REVIEW OF UNIT 14

1

When learners have completed the sentences (you could
do the first one as an example if you wish), let them
move round the class and compare with others. You
could ask each learner to make their own selection of
the best sentence completion for each question, then as a
class you can collate the findings to select the best
sentences from the class as a whole.

Option

If you are feeling particularly ambitious, you could put
the class into small groups and see if they are able to
weave these sentences into a single narrative. The
sentences do have a common theme running through
them, so it is not as difficult as it may seem at first. One
change in the sentences you can allow is with articles,
i.e. they can change *a* to *the*, or vice versa.

2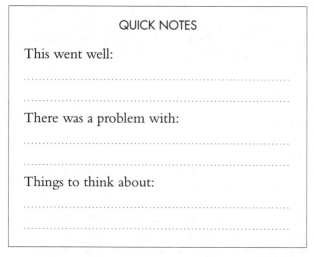

Go round and listen to the pairs working on the pronunciation, then check the words with the whole group. When you are satisfied, play the recording while the class writes down their answers. Play it a second time if necessary, then check. You can provide further controlled practice by following the instructions in the Class Book. You could even ask learners in groups to think up their own questions using these key words from the box. They then test another group on their questions. This is a simple but convenient way to test a wide range of lexical items and also provides some controlled practice in intensive listening, speaking and pronunciation.

Tapescript

1. Is disinfectant used in surgery?
2. Can you get a bruise by breathing?
3. Can a pedestrian collide with a vehicle?
4. If you injure yourself, might a bandage be useful?
5. If you deteriorate, is it a good sign?
6. Do you need an anaesthetic for surgery?
7. If you're in agony, will you definitely collapse?
8. Can you fracture your skull?
9. Do symptoms show that you have an illness?

QUICK NOTES

This went well:

....
....

There was a problem with:

....
....

Things to think about:

....
....

Worksheet 15 Answer key

1. reluctant   2. saved all of them   3. in large quantities
4. a discount / something knocked off   5. instinctively
6. apologetic   7. a great success   8. bother   9. crossed his mind

PROJECT: EDUCATION IN THE ADULT WORLD

Introduction

Learners everywhere seem to have heard of the Cambridge exams, but often they know little about them, and even less about what is involved in passing them. Other public exams, such as Oxford Higher or ARELS Higher, are often a complete mystery. This project gives learners more information about these exams (via a recording which gives them listening practice), and follows it with sample questions from the different exams. Obviously it cannot cover all the components of the different exams (this should be pointed out very clearly), but it is a taster for learners to get an idea of what is involved. It also provides varied language input and practice, and it concludes with an opportunity to discuss and assess the value of the different exercise types used. We feel it could be of interest to groups even if they have no intention of doing one of these exams.

Suggested steps

1

If your learners already know the answer to these questions because they have all studied with each other for years, you could start by asking them for their opinion of the exams they have taken, and/or their opinion of the value of taking exams in English.

2 ▭

You can obviously organise this activity as you wish, but if you split the task as suggested, it does create an additional speaking activity afterwards for which there is a high degree of interest and motivation. At the end, pairs can read the tapescript on pages 172–3 to make sure they haven't missed anything or got anything wrong.

Tapescript

The First Certificate in English – it's often known as FCE – is the most widely taken of the Cambridge examinations. Candidates for the exam come from a wide range of ages and backgrounds, although the majority are in their teens or early twenties, and perhaps surprisingly about two-thirds are female.

The exam was first introduced in 1939, but it's regularly updated and changes are made. But the basic aim of the exam remains the same – that is to assess general proficiency in English through a series of tests. There are five of these: three written papers which test extended writing, reading comprehension, vocabulary and grammar, then another test on listening, and finally a 15-minute interview to assess spoken English.

The Cambridge Advanced Exam in English – CAE for short – is the next exam up in terms of difficulty. It also has five papers like the FCE and each paper has the same sort of focus. But some of the exercises are a bit different, and of course, they're harder.

Some of the tasks in the Oxford Higher are similar to CAE, but the Oxford exam concentrates solely on reading and writing skills and there are just two papers. One important feature of the Oxford exam is that candidates have to read and write a lot in the time allowed for the two exams, and under such time pressure there is perhaps not quite the same emphasis on accuracy as in the Cambridge exams, and the main consideration is the successful completion of the task within the time limit. For example, in the reading tasks you need to understand the key information in the texts, select relevant information for the completion of the tasks, and be able to cope with difficult vocabulary. In the writing tasks you have to include relevant information and express it in a way that is appropriate for the person who will be reading it.

The fourth exam, the ARELS Higher, only tests the skills of speaking and listening. The exam takes place in a language laboratory and there are six different sections: you have to speak on a topic for two minutes, you have to tell a story from pictures – you have a few minutes to prepare both of these; you have to say how you would respond in a range of everyday social situations; there is also a little grammar test; you also have to read a passage in English as a test of pronunciation; and answer questions about various passages in English.

3 ▭

This will largely depend on time. Learners will probably want to do all of the exercises if time permits, and as the last exercise is on the recording, they will have to do this all together, at the same time. It may be sensible to play this first for the whole class, then let them work at their own speed on the other exercises. When they have finished, or you have run out of time, go through the answers or give them photocopies of the answer key below.

One word of warning. Make sure your learners read the instructions for each exercise carefully. If it says you cannot change the word given, it means just that.

Answer key

FCE
1. I'd rather not discuss …
2. Could you put me up for …
3. Paris is supposed to be a …
4. Rachel still hasn't sent/written (me) a reply.
5. I had a quick look through …
6. George asked Olga if she felt like going out …

CAE
31. and   32. of   33. for   34. an   35. to   36. ✓
37. the   38. about   39. ✓   40. for   41. not   42. ✓
43. ✓   44. them   45. the   46. being   47. finishing
48. himself

OXFORD Higher

Possible answers:

1.

Kathy,

I've just managed to get a couple of tickets for the Tina Turner concert next week. If you're free, I was wondering if you'd like to come with me. Let me know on Thursday.

Pat

2.

FOR SALE

Two tickets for Tina Turner concert
2nd December, City Arena, 8 p.m.
ONLY £25 each
Contact Pat in reception, or ring 699 3124.

ARELS Higher

Possible answers:

1. Yes, it was a shame.
2. Yes, there's a place just round the corner.
3. Oh, I am sorry.
4. No, thanks, not just now.
5. Never mind, I've got plenty of money on me.
6. No, me neither.
7. Have you got a room for the night?
8. Do you think it's a bit too smart?
9. I'm sorry, but I've got a terrible headache. You go on your own.
10. Could I have a packet of paracetamol, please?
11. Do you think you'll be able to get this oil stain out of these trousers?
12. Excuse me. I ordered chicken and salad about fifteen minutes ago. Will it be here soon?

Tapescript

The ARELS Higher exam

Part one

First you'll hear six remarks which might be made to you in various situations when you're using your English. Some are questions and some are comments. After each one, reply in a natural way. Here's an example to help you.

– Sorry to keep you waiting.
– That's all right. Don't worry.

Now are you ready? Here's the first.

1. We had a marvellous day on Saturday. What a pity you couldn't make it.
2. Is there anywhere round here where I can get my hair cut, do you know?
3. I'm sorry but I'm afraid I can't come with you tonight. I've got to go and visit my granddad. He's 84 and he's just had a stroke.
4. We've got half an hour before the next meeting. Fancy a quick drink?
5. Oh bother! I've left my money in my other coat.
6. I'm not sure I could eat horse meat. I mean, I know a lot of people do, but I don't think I'd fancy it somehow.

Part two

Now you'll hear some situations in which you might find yourself. Say what it seems natural to say in each situation. Ready?

7. You arrive at a hotel where you would like to stay the night. You haven't reserved a room in advance. What do you say to the receptionist?
8. You're out shopping with a friend and are trying on a coat. You think it's rather smart but you're not sure. What do you say to your friend?
9. You're on holiday with a friend. She wants to go sightseeing today, but you have a terrible headache. What do you say to her?
10. In the middle of the morning your headache is no better and you decide to go to the pharmacy to get something for it. What do you say to the assistant?
11. While sitting on a beach, you get some oil on a pair of trousers. You don't really think it'll be possible to clean them, but you take them to a dry cleaner's just in case. What do you say to the assistant?
12. You're in a restaurant. You ordered chicken and salad fifteen minutes ago, but nothing has arrived yet. What do you say to the waiter?

4

Learners may have a lot to say here, or very little. In addition to the issue of difficulty though, you could also ask them if they particularly enjoyed doing any of the tests.

5

If the class are not sure where to start on this question, you could help them by suggesting aspects of their English which might be assessed in a test. For example: grammar, vocabulary, pronunciation, speaking, listening, reading and writing. Which of these are most important? Are English exams useful? etc.

THAT'S A MATTER OF OPINION

CONTENTS

Language focus: conditional sentences: unreal past and present
expressing opinions
agreeing and disagreeing
words with different meanings
marriage vocabulary
military service vocabulary

Skills: Speaking: opinions on military service
discussing how you might have reacted in a
range of situations
should men still propose to women?
Listening: military service in Switzerland
people's responses to different situations
Reading: opinions about military service
a text about changing attitudes to proposals of
marriage
Writing: dictation

DO WE STILL NEED MILITARY SERVICE?

Introduction

Using the topic of military service (an old chestnut, but one which rarely fails to stimulate vigorous discussion), the lesson introduces a wide range of target language used to express opinions, and to express agreement or disagreement with other people's opinions. Following on from this there are activities which invite learners to express their own views using the target language. Additional skills development is provided through a listening activity which explains the Swiss system of military service, and an authentic reading text which shows the views of a cross-section of people from one canton in Switzerland towards military service.

Suggested steps

1

If you have any Swiss learners in your class, you should ask them to prepare a short explanation of the system of military service in their country. If not, then use the recording. Daniel is from Switzerland and has a Swiss-German accent, but he speaks clearly and is very coherent.

After learners have listened, made notes, and compared with a partner, they can check with the tapescript on page 173 to see if they have missed anything. Then put them in groups to discuss the system in their own country. With a multilingual group, mix the nationalities as much as possible, and at the end, ask certain learners to give a summary of the system in their own country. If

you work with a monolingual group, you might prefer to try this option.

Option

There may not be much point in learners from the same country talking about a system they are all familiar with. You could ask one half of the class to explain the system to the other half who pretend they know nothing about it; but if that seems very unnatural, divide the class into small groups, and ask each group to think of changes they would like to make to the current system. This might range from complete abolition (or restoration in the case of countries which have abolished it, e.g. Japan), to more modest changes involving the length of service, type of service that can be followed, etc. At the end, ask one person from each group to summarise the opinions of their group.

Tapescript

INTERVIEWER: OK, Daniel, then, could you just tell me a little bit about military service in Switzerland?

DANIEL: Yes, of course. I would like to start with the length of the military service we have in Switzerland. Er, usually, or it used to be that the basic training was about 17 weeks but now two years ago we had a kind of, er, military reform and it's now 15 weeks. And then you have to go every, or every year or every second year once to a, we call it a 'repetition' course, and this kind of course takes about, er, 2 or 3 weeks;

that depends on the troop. And all in all now at the moment you have to do at least 300 days.

INTERVIEWER: Right. So at what age do you actually finish?

DANIEL: Yeah, it's difficult to say. About 40.

INTERVIEWER: About 40?

DANIEL: Yeah, but then you have to go to the civil protection, but it's just one or two days a year.

INTERVIEWER: Women don't do it, do they?

DANIEL: For them it's voluntary. They can do it, but it's not compulsory for them.

INTERVIEWER: OK. And what about for men? Do you have to do it? Does everyone have to do it?

DANIEL: Yeah, if you're Swiss, you have to do it. Of course there are exceptions. If you are not able for medical reasons, you don't have to do it, but usually everybody has to do it.

INTERVIEWER: OK. And people don't all start at the same level, then. People go in at different levels.

DANIEL: Everybody starts with the basic ... with this kind of basic education, so you can start a career as an officer. You have to do the same thing at the beginning, everybody is equal, and then after a while you or your officers have to decide whether you have to continue or not.

INTERVIEWER: Right. And do you have to spend more time doing military service if you are an officer?

DANIEL: Yeah, absolutely, then you have to go every year. And they start usually 3 or 4 days earlier than, than the normal soldiers. And they have also some kind of instruction courses, technical courses during the year.

INTERVIEWER: Yeah?

DANIEL: Yeah.

2

Learners can do this in pairs, checking the pronunciation and meaning for each word as they proceed. These items all appear in the reading text which follows, so check and clarify the meaning and pronunciation with the group at the end.

Answer key

to abolish/abolition
voluntary
a deterrent/to deter
to provide security
basic training
self-defence
well-equipped
to eradicate

All the words would be useful to talk about military service, with the possible exception of *roots* (which actually occurs in the text in its figurative meaning, i.e. *origin*).

3

Before reading the text, go through the phrases in the list below, highlighting the use of *in favour of, mixed feelings about, against (something)* and *strongly opposed to (something)*. Emphasise also that there is not necessarily a clear-cut answer in every case – the important thing is that learners are able to use the text to justify their answers. For example, the difference between being *against* something and being *strongly opposed to* something is just a matter of degree, so beware of being too prescriptive when you elicit answers from the group.

Answer key

These are the most likely answers in our view:
In favour of: Carlo Lorusso; Gianni Quanchi; David Baumann
Mixed feelings: Paula Laudi (you could also make a case for Gianni Quanchi)
Against: Rosalia Albisetti; Nadia Castelli
Strongly opposed: Agnela Carletti; Enrico Giorgetti

4

Talk the group through the phrases in the book, or better still put them on the board and explain how they cover most shades of agreement and disagreement. Pay special attention to *tend to*, which is a very common verb to express generalisations. Learners may want to spend several minutes practising these phrases and committing them to memory, and in the final personalised speaking activity you may find some learners who keep quite strictly to the controlled use of the target language, while others tend to forget it in their desire to express their own views. To some extent this is simply a reflection of the different aims and demands of the individuals in the group and we would suggest allowing learners a measure of freedom in deciding how they approach the task. You can obviously direct the group towards a more controlled or more expansive response as you see fit. Monitor and give feedback at the end.

Personal Study Workbook

5: The end of military service?: reading
6: Do you agree with me?: listening/writing

QUICK NOTES

This went well:
....
....

There was a problem with:
....
....

Things to think about:
....
....

SO WHAT WOULD *YOU* HAVE DONE?

Introduction

The main focus of the lesson is conditional structures, with particular emphasis on past conditional structures. The lesson begins by highlighting different conditional structures; this is then followed by some language analysis. In the second half of the lesson, the target language is incorporated into several situations and listening passages, so learners have a chance to hear the structures being used naturally and have an opportunity to use the structures themselves in several personalised speaking activities.

Suggested steps

1

This would work well on an OHT or on the board, and you will need to give learners quite a bit of time to construct different sentences. Give the example first and make it clear that learners can use the same word from the wordpool in different sentences and can use the same word twice within one sentence if they wish.

When they have clearly done as much as they can, refer them to the sentences on page 157 to check and go on to Exercise 2.

2

Give each pair a few minutes to think about the four questions and move round the class to listen to their conversations (but don't get involved at this stage unless it is to prompt learners in a way that may push them further in their hypothesis about different constructions). Conduct a feedback with the group. The two mixed conditional sentences (7 and 8) are not the main focus of this particular lesson, but it is important that learners at this level are aware of the fact that conditional structures are not limited to three types as many learners believe.

Answer key

a. Sentence 1 is saying that a new manager is a possibility; sentence 2 suggests it is a certainty.
b. Sentence 2 is a hypothetical situation about the present; sentence 3 is hypothesising about the past and imagining how things might have been different if she had resigned (but she didn't).
c. In sentence 3 the woman did not resign; in sentence 5 she did.
d. Sentence 6 is talking about a situation in the past; sentence 7 is talking about the possible present implication of a hypothetical action in the past, i.e. If she had resigned last week (or last month), we would need a new manager now.

3 ▭▭

When the class has read through the situation, check that they understand vocabulary that may be new, e.g. *amber, sped away, narrowly missing, spilt,* etc. Then play the recording and ask learners to complete the tapescript in the Class Book. Play it twice if necessary, then they can compare with the completed tapescript on page 173 of the Class Book.

Tapescript

GARETH: I would've just sworn and driven on, I think. I mean you can get yourself into terrible trouble with, you know, people who drive like that. It says something about their personalities, doesn't it? You know, the fact that they're, they're capable of behaving like that.

MARCELLA: Yes, but they shouldn't be allowed to get away with it. I mean I'd have gone to the police station and reported it. I know it seems like a small thing and they'd probably tell me to just go away. What can you do? But ...

IAN: You'd have taken the number.

MARCELLA: I would've taken his number, yeah, and reported it. I'd have done that definitely.

IAN: I wouldn't have wanted to go after him but if ... depending on how I felt, I would've probably said something.

4

Allow learners some time to practise the completed sentences using the contracted forms. You could also put the class into pairs and let them practise the dialogue.

You could initiate the discussion stage with the whole class, then put them into smaller groups; or go straight into smaller groups. Remember that the class is now familiar with the situation, so they do not need to worry about the *if* clause – they only need to say what they *would've done* or *might've done* in that situation.

5

Learners now move on to a new situation. Once again, check that they understand the situation clearly, then put them in groups for their response. Monitor the discussions and make notes on effective language use, useful language you could introduce after the activity and any important errors you think are worth talking about. At the end, groups can report back on their ideas and you can put them on the board in preparation for the listening to follow.

6 ▭

Finish the lesson by playing the recording. The listening task can be to note down if the responses on the board are also mentioned on the recording. Elicit their response to the speakers, and if there is time, let the class look at the tapescript on page 173 for examples of conditional structures and any new vocabulary that interests them. If you have run out of time after Exercise 5, the listening passage would make very effective revision in the next lesson or even later.

Tapescript

IAN: I wouldn't have done just what she did, would you? I mean …

MARCELLA: No, I wouldn't have.

IAN: I'd've gone to find somebody from the store. I mean, it's not my responsibility. I mean, I would've found a store detective or failing that an assistant.

MARCELLA: That's exactly what I would've done. I think it's very risky to do what she did. I think I would've … well, it's hard to spot a store detective, so I'd have probably gone to a cashier or somebody else in uniform who looked like they were part of …

GARETH: It's difficult to know when to act, isn't it? I think I would've, perhaps once I'd seen them behaving suspiciously alerted somebody in the store, you know, I would've said, erm, 'There's a couple over there behaving rather strangely' …

IAN: A pre-emptive strike, sort of thing?

GARETH: Yeah.

If the class seem to enjoy exchanging opinions and you would also like to give them a further opportunity to exploit past conditional clauses, you could move on to Worksheet 16 on page 126.

Personal Study Workbook

2: I wouldn't have believed it ..: if sentences
3: … would you?: pronunciation

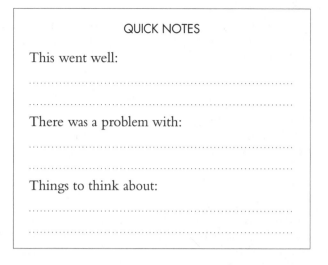

> ### QUICK NOTES
>
> This went well:
>
> ....
>
> ....
>
> There was a problem with:
>
> ....
>
> ....
>
> Things to think about:
>
> ....
>
> ....

HE'S AGREED TO MARRY ME!

Introduction

The lesson opens with a warm-up activity which teaches/revises vocabulary items connected with marriage, then proceeds with several activities to develop the reading skill: using cohesion to organise the paragraphs in a text; then an activity choosing synonyms for words in the text. The topic of the text itself is attitudes to proposals of marriage, and learners have several opportunities to give their own opinions as well as a final light-hearted speaking activity in which they evaluate the most glamorous way to make a proposal of marriage.

Suggested steps

1

Check the pronunciation of the lexical items then let learners do the task in pairs or small groups.

Answer key

The first event is the *proposal*, which lasts as long as it takes to say *Will you marry me?* Traditionally couples saw themselves as being engaged, and this *engagement* might typically last anything from a few months to a year. Nowadays, engagements (at least among British couples) are becoming less common. The *stag/hen night* takes place the night before or a few nights before the wedding and occupies the whole evening. Nowadays these occasions are also less common than in the past. The actual *wedding ceremony* lasts about half an hour and is followed by the *reception* which normally lasts three to four hours. The *honeymoon* is typically a week or two weeks, and starts immediately after the reception. The *anniversary* takes place every year and marks the fact that exactly one year has elapsed since the wedding, or the previous anniversary. Such anniversaries are sometimes celebrated with a party or dinner, especially the 1st, 10th, 25th and 50th.

2

Follow the instructions in the Class Book then check the answers with the group. At this stage don't worry about the underlined words in the text.

Answer key

The right order is:
Para 1: It all started ...   Para 2: The law was dropped ...
Para 3: But, according to a survey ...   Para 4: It is perhaps surprising ...   Para 5: Consider for example ...

3

The first reading task involved the ability to recognise cohesive devices; here we are concerned with the learners' reactions to the text. Put the class into small groups after they have completed the text. If necessary, provide a quick gloss for any words or phrases which are new, but don't spend long as the next activity develops the lexis in the text. At the end of the discussion conduct a brief feedback, allowing learners to find out the views of other members of the class.

4

It may be more logical for learners to start with the activity on choosing synonyms from the box for words/phrases in the text. When they have done that and you have checked their answers, you can then explain that words have different meanings, so a synonym for a word in one context will be inappropriate in another. The examples of *propose* and *single* in the Class Book will make this point clearly, and you can then move on to the next activity.

Answer key

reject = turn down
part = ingredient
penalty = fine
abolish/stop = drop
consent/say yes = agree
when you consider = given
amount = deal
basis = foundation

5

Point out that the word may be used as a different part of speech, e.g. *given* which learners will now be using as a part participle. When the pairs have finished, they can move round the class and compare their answers, and you can conduct feedback on any words which present problems.

Answer key

Possible answers:
Could you turn down the radio, please?
What are the ingredients for that recipe?
I feel fine.
He threw it over the fence but I dropped it, I'm afraid.
I don't agree with many of his ideas.
Have you given it to them?

I think the company got a good deal on that contract.
Since its foundation one hundred years ago, the school has expanded greatly.

6

Returning to the subject of marriage proposals, this is a light-hearted way to finish the lesson. Explain any new vocabulary items, e.g. *banner, neon lights*, etc., then create groups for the discussion. At the end, bring the class together and elicit a few of their ideas.

Personal Study Workbook

1: Words with different meanings: vocabulary
4: All's fair in love and war: figurative meaning
7: Speaking partners

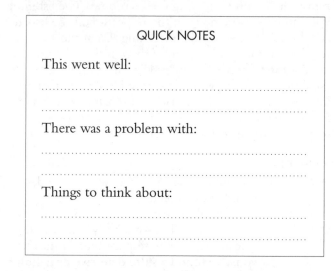

```
QUICK NOTES

This went well:
..............................................................
..............................................................

There was a problem with:
..............................................................
..............................................................

Things to think about:
..............................................................
..............................................................
```

REVIEW AND DEVELOPMENT

REVIEW OF UNIT 14

1

First, ask the group to match the verbs in the box with the objects in the photos (using each verb and object once only), and then they can write their sentences. At the end, let them move round and compare answers.

Answer key

Possible answers:
I bumped into the table.
He bruised his arm.
She spilt her orange juice.
I ripped my shirt.
I've mislaid my glasses.
He tripped over the bottom step.
She scratched the door with her keys.
I've smashed a wine glass.
He leapt over the fence.

2

You could do one as an example if you wish, then let the group complete the rest of the exercise individually, before comparing in pairs.

Answer key

Possible answers:
1. ... he kept spilling food over the customers.
2. ... she was always being rude to clients.
3. ... he kept giving people the wrong amount of money.
4. ... she was always getting the forecast wrong.
5. ... kept falling asleep during the night.
6. ... was always letting the animals escape.

REVIEW OF UNIT 15

1

This activity obviously depends on the class knowing each other quite well, and feeling comfortable with each other (to the extent that class members feel comfortable about predicting the opinions of others). If either is absent, you may be advised to omit this activity.

Option

If you are worried about class members referring to the opinions of individuals in the class, you could restrict the sentences to those that refer to the whole class or the majority of the class, i.e. 1, 2, 4 and 5.

2

Get rid of has appeared a number of times in the material; this is simply an opportunity to bring together some of its many meanings and draw attention to this important verb phrase.

Answer key

1. sell   2. throw away   3. remove/take away   4. sacked
5. lay off   6. lose   7. abolish   8. dispose of

QUICK NOTES

This went well:

....

....

There was a problem with:

....

....

Things to think about:

....

....

MANNERS

```
                          CONTENTS

Language focus:  functional language: surprise, requests, enquiries, apologies
                 and excuses
                 describing change
                 past tenses for distancing
                 vocabulary: money and manners
                 letter writing: style and layout

        Skills:  Speaking:   acting out everyday situations
                             evaluating one's own character
                             discussing manners in society
                 Listening:  people in everyday situations
                             how to lay out a formal letter
                 Reading:    a text on changing manners in our society
                             a letter
                 Writing:    writing a letter to a celebrity
```

EXCUSE ME, WOULD YOU MIND ...?

Introduction

The lesson provides language input and guided practice
in a range of everyday social situations – requesting
information, apologising, asking people to do things
politely, making excuses, showing surprise and so on.
Learners have an opportunity to talk about how they
would feel in a range of situations, then they listen to
native speakers operating in these situations and analyse
some of the language used – including structures such as
embedded questions, conditional clauses and verb +
-ing. Finally, they practise a parallel series of situations
themselves.

Suggested steps

1

It is important that your learners understand the
situations clearly, so check or pre-teach any new
vocabulary, e.g. *dash, prescription, be fined, mad about
(someone/something), involved in, a write-off,* etc. Then
initiate some class discussion about how individuals
might feel in the first situation. After this, pairs can
discuss how they would feel in the other situations. This
may be an opportune time to add several other items of
vocabulary if learners don't know them, such as *relieved,
upset, furious, fed up,* etc.

2

Keeping the class in pairs, ask them to think about how
they would react in each situation and what they might
say. It will help if they actually write down key phrases
or sentences, then they can compare with the speakers in
the recording which follows.

3 ▢

Play the recording but pause after each situation to give
learners time to write down their answers.

Answer key

Situation 1: 1. Yes.
Situation 2: 1. A woman. 2. Go straight on, left at the
lights, and Jones Street is the second on the right.
Situation 3: 1. The man braked on some ice and swerved
across the junction and got hit by another car coming
from the left. 2. The woman is very sympathetic
Situation 4: 1. No. 2. No.

After you have checked the answers, direct learners to
the tapescript on pages 157–8. They can have a go at
completing the tapescript either from memory or by a
process of deduction, then you can play the recording
again for them to check/fill in the answers. You may
only need to play those parts of the recording around the
blank spaces; otherwise it may make heavy weather of
the lesson.

1.

DRIVER: Oh, excuse me, no, er, is it too late? I ...

TRAFFIC WARDEN: Yes, it is too late, I'm sorry.

DRIVER: I'm really sorry, I *didn't mean to park here*. I had to go to the pharmacy. I've got some urgent medication that I needed to get, and I was literally there for two minutes. Is there any chance of just letting me off? I mean it was a ...

TRAFFIC WARDEN: It doesn't actually make any difference. I'm sorry, you were parking on a double yellow line, you've got a ticket.

DRIVER: I *didn't realise you couldn't park here*. I didn't see the line.

TRAFFIC WARDEN: Well, it says very clearly up on the lamppost here that er ...

DRIVER: Yeah, but have some heart! I mean, I had to go into the pharmacy. I mean it was a ...

TRAFFIC WARDEN: I'm terribly sorry, but it's a dangerous place to park. There are many accidents that occur because you've parked right on the corner here on a double yellow line.

DRIVER: Where on earth am I supposed to park, then?

TRAFFIC WARDEN: I've got to, er, I've got to move on.

DRIVER: No, excuse me, look, my explanation is quite valid, and I think that you, the least you can do is let me off this. I mean, it doesn't take much to ...

TRAFFIC WARDEN: Well, if you want to put it down in writing and complain to the, er ...

DRIVER: No, I don't want to put it down in writing, I want to sort it out right here! I think you just ...

TRAFFIC WARDEN: I'm terribly sorry, there's nothing I can do.

DRIVER: Oh, that's ridiculous!

TRAFFIC WARDEN: Yes, if you pay it within 21 days, thank you.

DRIVER: You're enjoying this, aren't you!

2.

WOMAN 1: Oh, excuse me, er, *do you happen to know where the nearest post office* is?

MAN: Oh, yeah, I think, erm, I think there's one on Palmerston Road. That's ...

WOMAN 1: Yeah?

MAN: Let's ... just get my bearings straight, OK. Right over here, that's Queens Road, right over here on the left. (yeah) OK, you go down Queens Road, and you go two blocks down, right and you'll turn left on, I think it's Berwick Avenue (yes) turn right there and ...

WOMAN 1: It sounds far!

MAN: Well, it's not that ... it's not really that far. Darn! No, I'm not really sure if that's really the right way ... You're asking an American!

WOMAN 1: I know!

MAN: Oh, wait, wait! Excuse me, *do you have any idea if there's a post office round here?*

WOMAN 2: Oh, yeah, erm, let me think. There used to be one on Palmerston Road, but that one's closed down. They built another one, though, on Jones Street, yeah, Jones Street. If you just go straight down here, take a left at the lights, and second on the right. That's Jones Street.

WOMAN 1: Yes, I think I remember now. OK, thanks very much.

MAN: OK, bye. Thanks!

3.

WOMAN: Sam, hi! You're walking to work – I don't believe it? Getting some exercise at long last!

SAM: Yeah, right. My car, you must have heard about my car.

WOMAN: No.

SAM: Oh, last week. I had an accident, just over by the pub.

WOMAN: Oh! Oh, my God. *What on earth happened?*

SAM: Oh, it's a complete right-off now. I was just going, going to the pub. You know the intersection just before it?

WOMAN: Yeah.

SAM: Well, I put the brake on, there was some black ice on the road, and just the car went straight through the intersection.

WOMAN: Oh, no, and smashed into that fence?

SAM: No, no I didn't ... a car was coming from the left going through the intersection and hit me on the side, through the passenger side so luckily I was OK, well, a bit of whiplash ...

WOMAN: Oh, *how on earth did you survive?*

SAM: Yes, well, I mean as I said, it hit the passenger's door, so I was OK. Yeah.

WOMAN: Wow!

SAM: But it's, er, I can't believe it, you know. Just had the car done up.

WOMAN: Such a beautiful car as well, oh, I'm really sorry to hear that, Sam.

SAM: Yes, well, that's what happens ...

4.

NEEMA: Hi, Michèle.

MICHÈLE: Oh, hi, good morning. Slept OK?

NEEMA: Yeah, yeah, fine. Um, I was wondering if I could have a bit of a word with you ...

MICHÈLE: Oh, yes, yes, certainly.

NEEMA: Last night when you came in, I think you left the door open.

MICHÈLE: Did I?

NEEMA: The front door, yes. Anyone could have, you know, come in and stolen whatever they liked.

MICHÈLE: Oh, I'm sure I closed it behind me.

NEEMA: Oh, yes, I know, but it was open this morning. *Would you mind checking that the door is locked* when you come in at night?

MICHÈLE: Yeah, I'm often ... you know, I'm going out a lot and I always check behind me, because obviously I know it's important to close doors behind you, specially not in your house ... you know, is your lock working OK?

NEEMA: Yes, the lock is working fine. *I'd just be really grateful if you could check* when you come in, because it was only you that came in last night. I locked it behind me.

MICHÈLE: Are you sure? There's nobody who came after me or anything like that?

NEEMA: No, Michèle ... it was only you.

MICHÈLE: Well, I really don't understand.

NEEMA: Well, the door was open – how do you explain that, then?

MICHÈLE: Well, I don't – maybe there is something wrong with your door, because I took the handle, I pulled it, I heard the click, and I thought, 'right, I'm in.'

NEEMA: Well, the door was open this morning, Michèle, so if you could just check it when you come in at night, and maybe this won't happen again, yeah?

MICHÈLE: Well, I will double check but you know, I was pretty sure I closed it.

NEEMA: Right, OK, well, I'll see you later.

4

Follow the instructions in the Class Book. This exercise checks whether the learners have fully assimilated the correct forms of the phrases they completed in the tapescript in Exercise 3, and they can refer back to that tapescript to check their answers.

Answer key

1. Do you happen to know where the nearest post office is?
2. Correct (The American speaker on the previous recording says *do you have any idea ...* – both forms are correct.)
3. Correct
4. Correct
5. Sorry I didn't realise there were parking restrictions.
6. Correct
7. I'd be really grateful if you could give me a hand.
8. Would you mind shutting the window when you go out?

Option

Learners often have problems with word order in embedded questions. You may need to highlight this word order on the board, and if you feel further practice is required, you could do the exercise *Polite enquiries* in the Review and development section of Unit 18.

5

This is a further opportunity for some controlled practice in which learners simply have to transfer the target language to a parallel situation.

Answer key

Possible answers:
1. Do you know when / Have you any idea when the film starts?
2. Why on earth do you want to do that?
3. I'm really sorry – I didn't mean to. / I'm really sorry, I didn't realise the iron was still on.
4. I'd be really grateful if you could get our order to us by the end of the week.

6

This time learners have to construct the whole conversation for themselves, and we think that rehearsal time is very valuable here, so don't rush them. Encourage them to try the conversations more than once, so that they can evaluate their performance, make improvements and develop both in confidence and fluency. You can monitor their conversations and note down things they are doing well, and things they need to work on. At the end, you could ask one or two pairs to act out their situation for the whole class and then conduct some feedback with the group. And if they haven't used some of the language from the lesson, this would be a good point to ask them in which situations the language could have been used.

Option

You can easily return to these situations in a later lesson and add more of your own which incorporate the same functions and possibly mix them. Use them for a bit of quick speaking practice at the beginning or end of a lesson, or to give the learners variety in the middle of a long lesson.

Personal Study Workbook

2: I really need to ask you something: requests
3: How on earth ...?: emphatic questions
6: What should I say?: listening and speaking

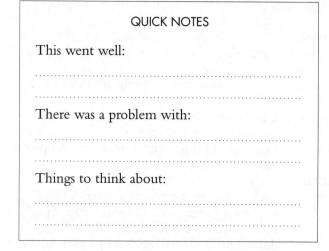

QUICK NOTES

This went well:

....

....

There was a problem with:

....

....

Things to think about:

....

....

THE WAR ON MANNERS

Introduction

A text on the changing attitude to manners in our society forms the core of the lesson, both in terms of topic and language input. The language focus is on ways of describing change, through both grammar and lexis, and learners have several opportunities to discuss the changes that are taking place in all areas of life in their countries. A wordbuilding activity opens the lesson, and gives learners a chance to focus on lexis used to describe people (*rude, courteous, a cheat*, etc.), and then practise it by talking about their own personalities.

Suggested steps

1

First ask learners to fill in the missing words and look up any new words in a dictionary. You can clarify the meaning if necessary when you check the answers. You will also need to check their pronunciation of items such as *swear* and *courteous*.

Answer key

untidiness: adj = untidy
swearing: verb = swear
rudeness: adj = rude
aggression: adj = aggressive
cheating: verb = cheat
respect for older people: verb = respect older people / have respect for older people

The speaking activity is an opportunity to personalise the items and internalise the meaning, and it is also important that learners are very familiar with them as they occur in the reading passage which follows. Go through the example carefully, not only to show learners *what* to do, but also to illustrate that if they follow the same way of doing the exercise, they will naturally incorporate both forms of each target item (e.g. *swearing* and *swear*, *courtesy* and *courteous*) when they speak.

2

Elicit ideas from the group on the meaning of the headline. If they don't have much idea, it is still worth pursuing because an understanding of the title may really help them to get a quick grasp of the text and what it is saying.

Answer key

A paraphrase of the title might be: If we continue to attack and neglect manners, it could have a negative effect on all of us.

3

Some teachers may be surprised by the absence of a string of comprehension questions, but the two questions are designed to focus the learners on a reaction to the ideas in the text and an evaluation of the ideas. This is the most natural, and ultimately the most

effective way of finding out what learners have understood, and by asking them to put *yes* and *no* next to the ideas they agree with or disagree with, you also have a very concrete way of knowing which parts of the text they find difficult to understand. (You can move round to see where they have indicated their agreement and disagreement.) Listening to them in groups will give you further evidence of what they have understood in the text, and afterwards you may wish to go back and look at certain stretches of the text which you think they have misunderstood or passed over without comment.

4

You could do this exercise with the whole class if you wish. Either way, check their answers carefully, clarifying the meaning of any new words, e.g. *widespread*, and highlighting aspects of form such as the use of *in* after decline, and *on* in the phrase *on the increase*. At this stage one should not expect learners to find it easy to incorporate this language while talking about the topics in the box, so give them time to consider the topics and prepare a few sentences including the target language. They can then exchange ideas and talk more freely without being under pressure to include specific words or phrases.

Answer key

The phrases demonstrate the use of grammar (in particular the use of the present continuous) and lexis (words such as *gradually* and phrases such as *on the increase*) to indicate a state in the process of movement and change.

5

You could omit this final activity if you are short of time, or ask the class to prepare some ideas on one of the topics for the next lesson.

Personal Study Workbook

4: How do you say it?: pronunciation of *ea*
5: Do we need good manners?: reading

QUICK NOTES

This went well:

....
....

There was a problem with:

....
....

Things to think about:

....
....

LETTERS

Introduction

Letter layout is a familiar subject for learners studying for Cambridge exams; this lesson takes the slightly different approach of introducing the various conventions used through a listening passage. Learners follow the instructions on the recording to complete a letter in their Class Book. The letter is then analysed for its organisation and the use of past tenses for polite distancing. There is a lexical focus on language connected with charities, then learners have to form their own charity and compose a letter to a celebrity who they would like to help them.

Suggested steps

1 ▭

It is not a good idea to encourage the group to read the letter yet, otherwise you may get bogged down discussing the new vocabulary; there are opportunities to look at the letter later.

Explain that the purpose of the passage they are going to hear is information about letter layout, both formal and informal, and it is important that they do carry out the instructions they are given. If necessary, stop the recording to ensure they follow these instructions. After you have played the recording (it is quite long so it is probably better not to play it twice), let learners compare their letters. If there is a difference, someone has misunderstood the instructions. Check answers carefully.

Answer key

```
                                    2 Barley Avenue
                                    West Ealing
                                    London W5 6RJ

                                    10 August

Dear Mr Connery

We are a newly formed charity and our aim is to
promote good manners among young children.

Our activities include visiting schools and playgroups,
giving lectures and putting on plays, pantomimes and
puppet shows. In order to raise funds, we have often
organised sponsored walks and swims. We have also
received generous donations from organisations and
private individuals.

Our most prestigious event is the annual competition to
find the boy and girl with the best manners in the
country, and this year we were hoping to find a
celebrity from the world of showbusiness to support us.
We appreciate that you are very busy, but we thought
this cause would appeal to you. We were therefore
wondering whether you would be available to give out
the awards at the next prize-giving ceremony in London
to be held on 10 April.

I would be grateful if you could give me an answer by
the end of the month to allow us time to make the
necessary arrangements.

I look forward to hearing from you.

Yours sincerely

ℱ Jones
```

Tapescript

OK, now the letter in front of you has been typed by an individual, not a company, and it's quite formal. But as we go through, I'm going to tell you a few things about informal letters as well – you might want to note this information down on a separate piece of paper. OK, the first thing is to write the sender's address in the top right-hand corner, OK. This has a set order with the number of the house or flat followed by the name of the street; and then underneath that, perhaps the district if it's a big town, then under that the name of the town or city, with the postcode. And it's now common, quite acceptable, to write all this without any punctuation at all. And the address – please write it now in the top right-hand corner – is 12 Barley Avenue (that's B-A-R-L-E-Y) Barley Avenue.

And the next line is West Ealing (that's E-A-L-I-N-G). Next line: London W5 – then a small gap – 6RJ. London W5 6RJ.

Now leave a line, and then write the date directly underneath the address. Now you can do this in several different ways. You can put 10 August, or August 10, or just 10 dot 8 dot 98. So use one of these methods and put today's date in the correct place.

And now, if you want, you could write the address of the person you are writing to. If you do that, you put it on the left-hand side of the paper, and you would usually start the address at roughly about the, the same level as the date which is on the right-hand side. For this letter though, we're not going to do that. Our letter is to Sean Connery, and we begin Dear Mr Connery – please note exactly where it goes.

Now, if you don't know the person's name you just put Dear Sir, or Dear Madam, or Dear Sir or Madam. In an informal letter you still use 'Dear' but you start with the person's first name – for example, Dear Maria or Dear Stephen or whatever.

And at the end of the letter you sign off 'Yours sincerely' – capital Y, but small 's'. So could you write that now at the end of the letter, leaving a line first? The spelling of 'sincerely' is S-I-N-C-E-R-E-L-Y.

Now, we put 'sincerely' if we know the name of the person that we are writing to. But if you don't know the name, the traditional ending is 'Yours faithfully'. Now, this is the custom in Britain, although it is true to say that not everyone keeps to it, and I think in America they use different endings – for example, they may finish a letter 'Truly yours'.

OK, if you are writing to a friend, then it's usually something like 'best wishes', or often 'love' if it's a member of your family or a very close friend, but not so common between two friends who are men. After the ending, in this case 'Yours sincerely', leave a line, and then put your signature directly underneath. So do that now – write your signature at the end of the letter. And that's it.

2

See how much the pairs can remember about informal letters, then refer them to the tapescript on page 174 to check their answers and unearth any additional information.

Answer key

We learn the following about informal letters:
1. You start with *Dear* but use the person's first name.
2. You finish the letter with *Best wishes*, or *Love* if it is to a member of your family or a very close friend (but not usually between two men).

3

Now turn your attention to the letter itself. You could pre-teach a few lexical items if you wish, e.g. *manners, pantomime, puppets, raise funds, sponsored walks, donations,* etc., or you could encourage learners to look up new lexis while they are doing the task. Check answers and clarify the meaning of new vocabulary at the end.

Answer key

Paragraph 1: The writer introduces the charity, i.e. the type of charity.
Paragraph 2: The writer describes the activities of the charity.
Paragraph 3: The real reason for writing the letter, i.e. the request for the reader to present awards at their most important function.
Paragraph 4: The writer outlines the action required of the reader.

4

Elicit answers from the group or put them in pairs to think about the question. With a monolingual group you could think about the learners' first language – does something similar happen there?

Answer key

The use of past tenses here is to be polite: the writer does not wish to impose on the reader, and certainly does not want to give the impression that they assume the reader will feel under an obligation to agree to their request. For most British native speakers of English, this distancing use of the past tense would be appreciated as an indication that the writer is not trying to pressurise the reader into saying *yes*.

5

Learners should now be familiar with most of this lexis (it is all from the letter), but this is a further chance to highlight items or clarify their meaning.

6

With a monolingual group from the same country you could suggest that their organisation/charity is a local one. This may help them to establish very clear aims, e.g. building a playground on the waste land behind the school for children from a local estate who have nowhere

to play. They might then be able to think of a celebrity who would be a very suitable person to write to for support, e.g. a sportsman/woman from a very poor background. With any type of group though, the activity will probably work more effectively if the celebrity is someone they all know and someone who has a tangible link with the organisation or charity they have formed.

If you would like a further free speaking activity which also practises vocabulary from this lesson and the previous one, use Worksheet 17 on page 127.

Personal Study Workbook

1: Untidy letters: vocabulary
7: He'll never agree to do it: writing
8: Speaking partners

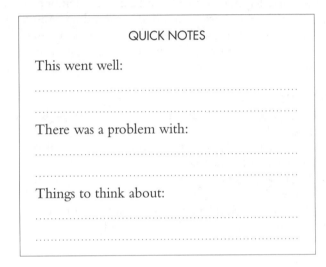

QUICK NOTES

This went well:

....

....

There was a problem with:

....

....

Things to think about:

....

....

REVIEW AND DEVELOPMENT

REVIEW OF UNIT 15

1

This refers back to the experiment to find out how honest people are. If your learners enjoyed that lesson, you may wish to try your own experiment on the same lines. The ideas here are just suggestions – you may be able to think of more interesting and relevant situations for your own particular environment. The important thing is to establish a clear procedure for the experiment, and to encourage learners to put their findings on paper and then prepare an oral report which they should rehearse at home before delivering to the group. If at all possible, record some of the reports.

2

Follow the instructions in the Class Book.

Answer key

1. were awarded   2. damages   3. were pestered
4. sued   5. were awarded   6. verdict   7. force   8. be held   9. protect

REVIEW OF UNIT 16

1 ⫿

When the group has completed the sentences, play the recording. Learners should only write down sentences which are different from their own, and then use these sentences for the pronunciation practice. Do one or two examples with the class, checking that they are producing the contracted forms and weak forms. To do the latter, it might be worth asking the class to think about the stressed words in the sentence which carry the main information. Then they can continue practising, either individually (some learners like to repeat things on their own at their own pace) or in pairs.

The final part involves some memorisation. In our experience, learners not only find this a challenging activity, they also enjoy it and find it rewarding. And if they can produce their sentences without looking in their books, it helps to give added momentum to the exchange.

Tapescript

1. If your teacher hadn't come to class today, would you have had a lesson?
2. If your school decided to put on a show, would you be prepared to take part?
3. Would you have come to class today if you hadn't felt very well?
4. If nobody in class had done the last piece of homework, what would've happened?
5. If you could ask your teacher any question you liked, what would it be?
6. How would you have felt if, last week, the students in your class had gone out for dinner without inviting you?

QUICK NOTES

This went well:

....

....

There was a problem with:

....

....

Things to think about:

....

....

18

WHAT ARE THE ODDS?

```
                          CONTENTS

Language focus:    expressing degrees of possibility and probability
                   future continuous and future perfect
                   revision of will for prediction
                   revision of grammar and vocabulary

        Skills:    Speaking:   discussing the probability of events,
                                 e.g. having twins
                                predicting your own future;
                                odds and evens quiz
                   Listening:   facts about the probability of events,
                                 e.g. being burgled
                                dialogue completion
                   Reading:     extract from The probability factors of life
                                questionnaire
                   Writing:     completing a dialogue and questionnaire
```

THE PROBABILITY FACTORS OF LIFE

Introduction

Learners are introduced to ways of expressing probability, then they have a chance for further personalised practice by evaluating a number of statements which may or may not be true. There is also a listening passage for skills development.

Suggested steps

1

Write the sentence in the speech bubble on the board, ask if it is true, then write up the four possible answers, a–d. You will also need to give a gloss for each one or elicit what they mean, i.e. the phrases in brackets after the sentences, but you shouldn't have to write these on the board. (If someone forgets, remind them.) They should complete their guess with a reason.

Answer key

Not true.

2

If learners think some of the statements could/might be true, then they may be reluctant to put *true* or *false* next to them. That is perfectly reasonable, so you should perhaps begin by making that clear. While the pairs are working together, you may also want to move round and clarify new vocabulary if it is causing any problems, e.g. *poisoned* and *strangled*. Conduct a feedback at the end, eliciting answers and commenting on their use (or misuse) of the target language, then give them the answers for Britain. Are they surprised at any of them?

Answer key

1. true   2. false   3. false   4. true   5. false   6. true
7. true   8. true

3 ⊡

As the group will be very familiar with the topic, go straight into the recording and elicit further information at the end. If they have failed to uncover some of the facts, play it again.

Answer key

We learn more information about the following statements:
1: The chances of having triplets are 1 in 3,360.
4: 65% of murdered people knew the person who murdered them.
5: The more people living in a house, the more likely it is that someone will leave a door or window open, and that increases the likelihood of being burgled.

Tapescript

A: Hm, that was interesting that, er, for pregnant women, the chances of having twins was, er ...
B: 2%! 2% is incredible, isn't it?
A: I know. I thought it was higher.
B: Did you?
A: But apparently, er, for triplets it's, it's actually lower than 2%.
B: Is it much lower? What is it?
A: Hm. It's one in 3,360. And that's going to change in the future with all the fertility treatment going on ...
B: The statistics go up and up, yeah.
A: So it'll be much more likely for people to have multiple births.

B: Yeah, yeah.

A: What else did we do here? Oh, yes, this was interesting, um, it was the likelihood of getting strangled, or shot or poisoned.

B: And it being in December, which I thought was interesting, at that time of year, when, you know, one thinks of things, as you say, like Christmas or New Year and festivities, parties and things ...

A: Yeah, I know.

B: Strange, isn't it?

A: And also apparently, it's got here that, er, it's, er, really quite likely that you will know the person who murders you.

B: Really? I mean, what, statistically ...

A: 65% of victims know the person who ...

B: 65%?

A: Yeah, knew the person who shot them, strangled them or poisoned them.

B: ... poisoned them, whatever. And as I say, it's likely to happen in December too. How strange. What was the other one? Burglary. I thought this was, this was really quite strange, that for some reason, the risk of, er, the risk of burglary goes up if there are more people living in a house.

A: Well, that's strange too. I thought because with more people coming in and out, you'd have thought a burglar would be put off, but apparently, no, because, you know, they're more likely to leave windows, doors open, etc., (Oh, right) thinking that somebody else has closed them ...

B: ... is going to be coming in later or whatever.

A: Yeah, or yes.

B: And so consequently, they get in, more chances of getting burgled. That's remarkable.

4

The meaning of most of these structures is fairly transparent (and had there been a problem of understanding it would have arisen before now), so the main focus is really to highlight the forms, and to provide contexts for some further practice and consolidation. In some cases, incorporating the structures involves quite lengthy sentences, so don't hurry the pairs at this stage. Move round and monitor their sentences and help where necessary.

When they have finished, split the pairs and create new groups of three or four: learners can read out their sentences to the rest of the group and then they can discuss them for some freer speaking.

Personal Study Workbook

2: Finish the definition: vocabulary
3: It's more than likely: probability

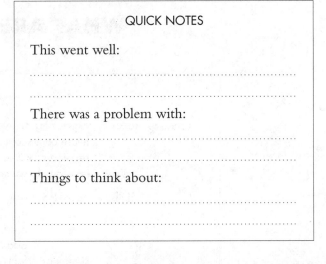

```
QUICK NOTES

This went well:

........................................................
........................................................

There was a problem with:

........................................................
........................................................

Things to think about:

........................................................
........................................................
```

WHAT WILL YOU BE DOING?

Introduction

This is a straightforward lesson with the main focus on the revision of *will* + infinitive, consolidation of the future continuous (introduced earlier in the book, but now recycled with a different use), and the introduction of the future perfect. The approach is contrastive, with learners having an opportunity to analyse the structures and form their own hypothesis about meaning, and then consolidate their understanding and familiarity with a questionnaire that promotes fairly intensive but quite natural use.

Suggested steps

1

When you elicit answers, make sure the learners can make a clear connection between the tense used in the sentence and what is going on in the picture.

Answer key

A When I leave class, I'm sure it will be raining.
B When I leave class, I'm sure it will have stopped raining.
C When I leave class, I'm sure it will rain.

2 ▭

The recording and subsequent task reinforce the concepts of the different structures, but with the added bonus of checking that learners can clearly distinguish between these closely related forms in spoken English. Learners can check their answers using the tapescript on page 174, then carry on to discuss why the different forms are used. They should be helped in this by referring to the previous examples in the pictures, and the language that you will have used to describe them, e.g. the continuous form indicates that the rain will be in progress before we leave, and is likely to be temporary; the future perfect refers to a point in the future when an action/event (in this case rain) will be finished. If necessary, refer to the Language Reference on pages 151–2.

1.

A: Oh, Betty, by the way, could *you give me a ring as soon as you get home* tonight – just to confirm things for tomorrow?

B: Well, actually my flatmate *will have made the dinner by the time I get in*, so can I give you a ring when we've eaten?

A: Yeah, OK then.

2.

C: Do want me to pop round this evening to pick up those samples?

D: Yes, could you?

C: Yes, sure – what time?

D: Sevenish.

C: Fine.

D: No, actually, could you make it a bit later? My *husband will be making dinner* and he gets really irritable if people turn up when he's in the middle of cooking.

C: [giggle] No problem – I'll come at about 8, then.

D: Great.

3.

E: Oh dear, *I don't really want to go round to* Sue and Mike's tonight – not after the last time. That meal Sue served up was absolutely dreadful.

F: *Don't worry, I bet Mike'll make the dinner* – he was a bit embarrassed about that last meal and he's not working at the moment.

E: Oh, well, that's a relief.

3

Some verbs are not usually used in the continuous form, and for some learners/nationalities this is not a point that needs to be laboured; for others it is a likely error. You will be the best judge of this for your own group. If you do not think it is an important issue, do the exercise orally round the class. You will need to highlight the time expressions common with these forms, e.g. *in a week's/year's time*; *(by) this time next week/year*.

Answer key

1. incorrect (I'll know) 2. correct 3. correct
4. incorrect (I'll never believe) 5. incorrect (I'll have)
6. correct

4

Check any new vocabulary, e.g. *to lose touch with someone*, then give the group about ten minutes to complete their questions. Check carefully before you continue, otherwise mistakes will be carried through to the next activity and repeated.

Answer key

will still be studying
will have got
will have
will be living
will have lost touch with
will have
will be working

will still have
will have changed
will still be living
will like
will still be doing
will be

Now follow up with the personalised interview. If it goes well, they could repeat it with a different person. At this stage, encourage learners to follow up the questions with further questions, e.g. if someone thinks they will have changed a lot in ten years' time, how will they have changed, and why? If you hear some interesting answers, you could tell other members of the class and initiate some whole group discussion.

5

This final extension provides further practice of the target forms, but adds a creative element for the group and also introduces some useful expressions that they can use in their replies. Go over those first, then give the pairs time to think up their questions.

If you want further controlled practice using these different forms, try Worksheet 18A on page 127.

Personal Study Workbook

1: Will you be working?: future simple, perfect or continuous
6: I can see into the future: listening
8: Speaking partners

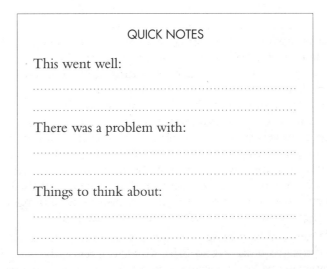

QUICK NOTES

This went well:

....

....

There was a problem with:

....

....

Things to think about:

....

....

ODDS AND EVENS

Introduction

This is a language game which occupies the whole lesson. Learners work in pairs and compete against other pairs to get to the end of the board. In order to do so they have to roll a dice, but can only move by the number on the dice if it takes them to the correct square (*odd* squares for pair A and *even* squares for pair B), *and* they correctly answer a language question which involves transforming a sentence by incorporating a new word or phrase but without changing the meaning.

Suggested steps

The question cards you need for this game are all on Worksheet 18B on pages 128–129. The best thing would be to photocopy the pages on to card (tougher and longer lasting than paper), then cut the questions out carefully, so you have sets of cards which you can use and then re-use with another class.

For the game itself, remember that you need a dice and counters for *each group* of four (you can also play in threes or fives if you have odd numbers, but a threesome will mean one learner working on their own). You should allow about half an hour for the game, but first you will probably need about ten minutes to ensure the learners know what to do, and what the objective is. The best way to do that is to throw the dice and then, if a move is possible, go through the examples carefully, and illustrate what would happen with a right or wrong answer. Demonstrate by reading aloud a sample sentence plus prompt word, and tell learners to give you the sentence using the prompt, e.g.
I saw him last Saturday.
SINCE
I haven't seen him since Saturday.

Impress upon the class that they should not shout out answers until they have conferred with their partner; should not write anything on the cards; should not show the cards to the other pair (but must read them out very clearly); and most important of all, should not argue with your decision.

There are obviously potential problems with a number of groups playing, e.g. one group may overhear an answer from another group, which they may then use to their advantage later in their own game. In this case, make sure you shuffle each set of cards so the questions come in a very different order from group to group. There is also likely to be a need for you to adjudicate on the accuracy of several answers at once (learners may give answers which they think are correct in addition to the given answer). Finally, there is the noise level, which may be annoying if pairs often feel they cannot hear the other pair read out the question. If you fear any of these problems, you could investigate the possibility of using a bigger room or a second room for the activity.

When you have played the game, you could give out the completed sentences so that learners can revise the language points by testing each other again (or in groups, or even with the whole group). Given a reasonable interval of time, you could also repeat the game with the same group.

Another possible extension is to add your own cards with examples you have collected during the course. If these build up to an impressive level, you could not only repeat the game with the class, but also make it available for them to play and repeat in their free time (provided they don't lose or deface any of your cards).

If you find the game is not lasting very long, you could also introduce this added difficulty to prolong the finish. When they are approaching the finish, tell learners that if they throw the dice and don't land exactly on *Finish*, they have to go back to *Start*.

Personal Study Workbook

4: Consonant clusters: pronunciation
5: Are you likely to forget?: reading
7: Say it another way: writing; transformations

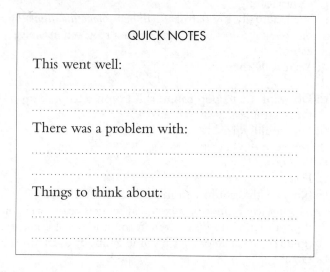

QUICK NOTES

This went well:

....

....

There was a problem with:

....

....

Things to think about:

....

....

REVIEW AND DEVELOPMENT

REVIEW OF UNIT 16

Part A of the exercise appears to focus on word order, but collocation is also very important in some of these sentences, e.g. we often use *strongly* before *opposed to*, and we often use *rather* before *mixed feelings*, etc. When you go through the answers, point this out to the class, and encourage them to learn these words and record them together – and use them in the next part of the exercise.

Answer key

I'm very much in favour of
I've got rather mixed feelings about ...
Generally speaking I'm against ...
I've always been very much against ...
I'm not at all in favour of ...
On the whole I'm not very keen on the idea of ...
(The phrase *on the whole* is interchangeable with *generally speaking* in most contexts.)
I've got particularly strong views on ...

In part B, make sure learners do understand all the items in the box and make clear they can write their sentences about any of the topics (one sentence per topic).

The phrases in part C will be useful for learners to register their agreement or disagreement with the opinions expressed in part B by other members of the class. Monitor the discussions and give feedback afterwards on effective use of language, any important errors, and language that was clearly needed/wanted but was not available or not known.

REVIEW OF UNIT 17

Take the first three stages fairly carefully as they test the learners' knowledge of form, style and meaning. For the final part though, allow them much more freedom and don't interfere or correct at this stage. You can always comment afterwards on their use of language, but the main aim here is to be as spontaneous as possible, with learners using any of the situations and including the actual sentences if they wish; their unsuspecting partner has to be prepared to produce a logical reply instantly, and bring the conversation to a satisfactory conclusion. The phrases at the end are a few more fixed phrases learners may wish to include in their answers.

Answer key

You could easily use *do you happen to know* and *have you any idea* with a stranger, as there is an assumption here that they may well not know the answer. These forms would be unlikely with a person in the information office (they ought to have some idea), but you would use *could you tell me* or perhaps *do you know.*

The next two questions are different in grammar as they are direct questions without the same word order as the embedded questions. The style is different in being more direct; it is designed to elicit a simple yes or no answer.

Possible answers:

1. Do you know when the Cambridge train arrives?
2. Have you any idea how much it costs to leave a suitcase here?
3. Do you happen to know if there are any snack bars around here?
4. Could you tell me where the ladies' lavatory is?
5. Do you know how long it takes to get to Dover?
6. Could you tell me when the next train to Brussels is?

QUICK NOTES

This went well:

....

....

There was a problem with:

....

....

Things to think about:

....

....

WORKSHEETS

What I want is a good dictionary!

1. Complete the questionnaire in small groups.

DO YOU USE A MONOLINGUAL DICTIONARY FOR THE FOLLOWING?

	Yes, often	Yes, occasionally	No
1 to look up the meaning of a word or phrase during lessons.	☐	☐	☐
2 to look up the meaning of a word or phrase outside the classroom.	☐	☐	☐
3 to find out how to pronounce a word or phrase.	☐	☐	☐
4 to find out information about the grammar of a word (e.g. the past tense of an irregular verb, or if a noun is countable or uncountable).	☐	☐	☐
5 to check the spelling of a word.	☐	☐	☐
6 to find out how to use a particular word or phrase in a sentence.	☐	☐	☐

DO YOU:

7 use the pictures in dictionaries to expand your vocabulary?	☐	☐	☐
8 use your dictionary to try to learn new words, or learn new meanings of familiar words?	☐	☐	☐
9 use the study notes, usage notes and tables that many dictionaries provide (e.g. the grammar of phrasal verbs)?	☐	☐	☐
10 understand and make use of the symbols and keys in dictionaries?	☐	☐	☐

Find out the answers of the other groups and enter them in your table. What are the most interesting answers?

2. From your own results to the questionnaire, you might like to ask yourself the following questions, and then discuss them in groups.

1. If your answers to 1–6 were mostly 'yes', then clearly you make use of dictionaries and therefore need a good one (in addition to a bilingual dictionary). Have you got a good dictionary? If not, get one.
2. If your answers to 1–6 were mostly 'no', why is that? Are you making enough effort to expand your vocabulary both inside and outside the classroom? If you think you are making that effort, why do you think a dictionary cannot help you very much?
3. If your answers to 7–10 were mostly 'yes', which are the most important, and why?
4. If your answers to 7–10 were mostly 'no', are you making the best use of your dictionary? Is your dictionary good enough? Find a dictionary with the features described in 7–10 and see if you can make use of them in a positive way.

1. Complete the boxes below with appropriate words and phrases. Use the vocabulary on pages 14–15 to help you.

THINGS YOU DO BEFORE GOING TO SLEEP	THINGS YOU DO DURING SLEEP
Example: yawn	Example: lie still
....	....
....	....
....	....
....	....
....	....

GOOD SLEEP AND BAD SLEEP
Example: sleep like a log
....
....
....

2. What are the opposites of the following words and phrases? The answers are all in Unit 2.

Example: to solve problems – *to create problems*   young people – *elderly people*

1. a soft bed ....
2. to stay awake ....
3. a recurrent nightmare ....
4. available ....
5. to sleep like a log ....

6. bland food ....
7. to let someone sleep ....
8. a little-known comedian ....
9. few of the visitors ....
10. to jump out of bed ....

3. Complete the table below, as in the example.

Ailments	Symptoms	Possible causes	Cures
asthma	difficulty in breathing	air pollution	an inhaler
sunburn	....	....	....
	....	....	....
cold sores	....	....	....
	....	....	....
cramp	....	....	....
	....	....	....
a hangover	....	....	....
	....	....	....
dandruff	....	....	....
	....	....	....
constipation	....	....	....
	....	....	....

1. The first letter is to a friend who has just had good news; the second is to a different friend who has just received bad news. Read them and answer the questions below.

Dear Jim,

I'm just writing to congratulate you on being promoted to Deputy Manager. I was really pleased that you got the job because I know how hard you've worked over the past two years, and I think you deserved it.

I imagine it'll mean a lot more work, but it'll be more challenging, so I really think it's a step in the right direction. I shall be away for most of the summer trying to sort out the problems in our Scottish office, but I hope to see you when I get back in September. Until then, give my regards to the rest of the family and enjoy your promotion.

Best wishes,

Carole

Dear Louise,

I'm just writing to say how sorry I am that you didn't get the job in Newport. It's such a shame because you were the ideal person for the job, and I imagine it must be particularly disappointing after being invited back for a second interview.

Anyway, you mustn't let it get you down. There are plenty more jobs to apply for, and with your experience and qualifications, I'm sure you'll get something soon. I'm looking forward to our lunch on Friday week, but until then, take care and good luck with any new applications.

Best wishes,
Carole

Cover the letters and try to answer these questions from memory.

1. What preposition follows *congratulate* in the first letter?
2. What is Jim's good news?
3. Why did he deserve it?
4. What is the best thing about the new job?
5. In the second letter why does Carole think it's *such a shame* that Louise didn't get the job?
6. And why is it *particularly disappointing* for Louise?
7. Why does Carole think that Louise will soon get a job?
8. What is Carole looking forward to?

2. Now look at the letters, check your answers, and underline any phrases you remember from the letters in Unit 3 of the Class Book on page 22.

3. Write your own letter based on either of these situations.

a. A friend of yours spent three months in England and took an exam at the end of her stay. You have just heard that she passed the exam, and you are going to surprise her by writing a letter to her in English.
b. You stayed in England last year and became friends with an English family. The daughter, the same age as you, was hoping to come and work in your country for six months, but unfortunately her company has now decided not to send her. You have just heard the news from another English friend and would like to write to her.

WORKSHEET 4

1. Imagine you are going to a country where you don't speak the language (except for *hello*, *goodbye*, *please* and *thank you*). You are going for a one-week holiday, travelling alone on public transport, moving from town to town and staying in small hotels.
Make a list of ten phrases you would need, then compare with a partner and agree on the ten you think are most useful. Now compare with another pair. Who has the best selection?

2. Here is a selection of phrases taken from a phrasebook for English speakers in a French-speaking country. Can you translate each of the English phrases into your own language?

Just a minute ....

Can you show me on the map? ....

Is it completely full? ....

Could you let me know when we get to ...? ....

I'm not sure how long I'm staying. ....

Is service included in the bill? ....

I'm just looking. ....

I'd like a film for this camera. ....

Do you mind if I smoke? ....

Can you write down the price? ....

3. How many of these expressions would help you a lot on your one-week holiday? Discuss in small groups.

TRUE TO LIFE UPPER-INTERMEDIATE   © Cambridge University Press 1998

WORKSHEET 5

1. A large number of compound nouns are based on phrasal verbs. Usually the particle goes at the end, but sometimes it goes at the beginning. For example:

*When I've finished the document, I'll **print** it **out**. (verb)*
*I'll do a **printout** of this when I've finished. (noun)*

*Another war could **break out** very easily in that region. (verb)*
*There could easily be another **outbreak** of war in that region. (noun)*

Note:

1. Sometimes the compound is written as one word, e.g. *outbreak*, and sometimes there is a hyphen, e.g. *hold-up*. (This can mean a robbery or a delay. Most nouns ending with *up* have a hyphen.)

2. To form a plural, you add *s* at the end, e.g. *printouts*, *hold-ups*.

2. Complete the sentences below using a word from the left-hand box (usually a verb), and a word from the right-hand box (usually a particle). Use a dictionary to help you.

take cut out break write sell check cover		through come off in up over back out

1. The company is spending too much, so we'll have to make .... somewhere, otherwise we'll be in real trouble.

2. After the accident the car was a complete ....

3. I went to the .... as soon as I got to the airport.

4. Nobody wants to try to predict the result of the election, so we'll just have to wait for the .... next Thursday.

5. The response to tickets was fantastic – it was a .... in days.

6. Doctors have made a real .... in recent years in the treatment of certain kinds of cancer.

7. They've bought two companies recently, but some analysts think there could be another .... before the end of the year.

8. There were strong rumours of a scandal, but nothing appeared in the papers, so there must've been a ....

Compare your answers with a partner and your teacher.

3. Now do the same exercise with these two groups of words, only this time you must write suitable sentences for another pair to complete.

turn break check take hold out		over out off put down up

WORKSHEET 6

1. Make a list of ten things a tour rep might have to do in the course of a normal day's work.

Example: *go off to the airport*
       pick up tourists who have just arrived

1. ....
2. ....
3. ....
4. ....
5. ....
6. ....
7. ....
8. ....
9. ....
10. ....

When you have finished, compare your list with the ideas in the text on page 49 in your Class Book.

2. Now make a list of ten things that people might do during a long flight.

Example: *take their shoes off and maybe put some slippers on*
       have a nap

1. ....
2. ....
3. ....
4. ....
5. ....
6. ....
7. ....
8. ....
9. ....
10. ....

3. Use a dictionary to sort these idioms into two categories and copy them in the table.

It made me jump.   It gave me a shock.   It drove me round the bend.   It bothered me.
I found it troublesome.   I was astonished.   It was a real eye-opener.   It drove me mad.
I was taken aback.   I was astounded.   It got on my nerves.   I was staggered.

Annoyance/irritation	*Surprise*
....	....
....	....
....	....
....	....
....	....
....	....
....	....

WORKSHEET 7A

Work in small groups. If you couldn't tell the difference between red and green, how would it affect your daily life? Use the language in the box to help you to construct different sentences.

It would be	(absolutely) impossible to ...
It might be	(very) difficult to ...
	(quite) hard to ...
It wouldn't be	(very) easy to ...
I couldn't	buy ...
I wouldn't be able to	tell the difference between ...
I wouldn't be allowed to	work ...

Tell other groups your list. Which group has the most interesting list?

TRUE TO LIFE UPPER-INTERMEDIATE   © Cambridge University Press 1998

WORKSHEET 7B

1. Look at the italicised words and phrases in the dialogues. What do they mean? Work with a partner and use a dictionary to help you.

A: How did he get that *black eye*?

B: ....

A: Do you *go brown* very easily in the sun?

B: ....

A: What kind of people vote for the *Green Party*?

B: ....

A: Why did she *go red*?

B: ....

A: They didn't arrive at your house *out of the blue*, did they?

B: ....

A: Are you still *in the red*?

B: ....

2. Work with a different partner. Take it in turns to explain the meanings to each other.

3. Practise the phrases in short dialogues. Read a sentence in turn, and see if your partner can give you a logical reply. Keep practising until you provide answers without hesitation.

TRUE TO LIFE UPPER-INTERMEDIATE   © Cambridge University Press 1998

WORKSHEET 8

Politics round the world

1. How many words can you add to each column below? Discuss in small groups, using a dictionary if necessary. Mark the stress on each word, as shown in the examples.

Individuals in politics
Prime Minister

Groups/bodies in politics
parliament
political parties

Political philosophies and movements
democratic socialism

2. Read the statements and decide whether they are generally true of your country. Compare your answers with a partner.

a. Most people are not very interested in politics.
b. Important political issues are sometimes decided by referendum.
c. The electoral system is based on PR (proportional representation).
d. The head of state is elected by the people.
e. The political situation is quite stable at the moment.

WORKSHEET 9

Divide into small groups and then try to answer these questions.

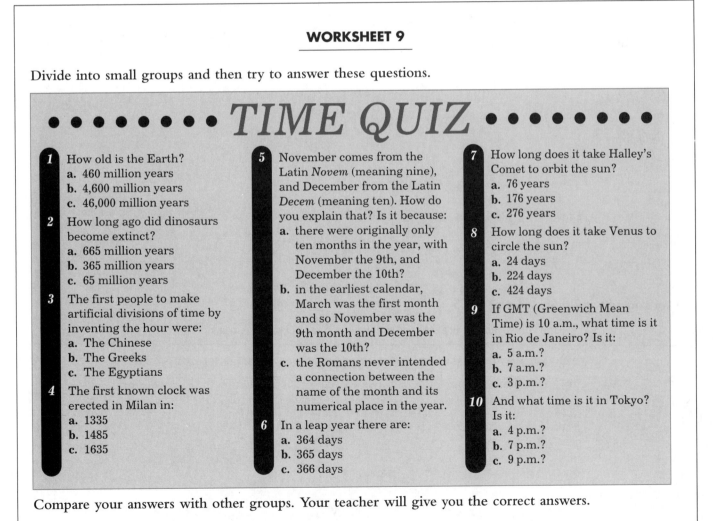

TIME QUIZ

1 How old is the Earth?
a. 460 million years
b. 4,600 million years
c. 46,000 million years

2 How long ago did dinosaurs become extinct?
a. 665 million years
b. 365 million years
c. 65 million years

3 The first people to make artificial divisions of time by inventing the hour were:
a. The Chinese
b. The Greeks
c. The Egyptians

4 The first known clock was erected in Milan in:
a. 1335
b. 1485
c. 1635

5 November comes from the Latin *Novem* (meaning nine), and December from the Latin *Decem* (meaning ten). How do you explain that? Is it because:
a. there were originally only ten months in the year, with November the 9th, and December the 10th?
b. in the earliest calendar, March was the first month and so November was the 9th month and December was the 10th?
c. the Romans never intended a connection between the name of the month and its numerical place in the year.

6 In a leap year there are:
a. 364 days
b. 365 days
c. 366 days

7 How long does it take Halley's Comet to orbit the sun?
a. 76 years
b. 176 years
c. 276 years

8 How long does it take Venus to circle the sun?
a. 24 days
b. 224 days
c. 424 days

9 If GMT (Greenwich Mean Time) is 10 a.m., what time is it in Rio de Janeiro? Is it:
a. 5 a.m.?
b. 7 a.m.?
c. 3 p.m.?

10 And what time is it in Tokyo? Is it:
a. 4 p.m.?
b. 7 p.m.?
c. 9 p.m.?

Compare your answers with other groups. Your teacher will give you the correct answers.

WORKSHEET 10

Complete the table using a dictionary. (For some crimes you will not find a special word for the criminal or the verb.)

Crime	Meaning/Translation	Criminal	Verb
arson	....	....	....
assault	....	....	....
blackmail	....	....	....
bribery	....	....	....
burglary	....	....	....
drug dealing	....	....	....
fraud	....	....	....
hijacking	....	....	....
kidnapping	....	....	....
manslaughter	....	....	....
murder	....	....	....
mugging	....	....	....
rape	....	....	....
shoplifting	....	....	....
smuggling	....	....	....
terrorism	....	....	....
theft	....	....	....
vandalism	....	....	....
....	....	....	....
....	....	....	....
....	....	....	....
....	....	....	....
....	....	....	....

Can you add any more crimes?

TRUE TO LIFE UPPER-INTERMEDIATE © Cambridge University Press 1998

1. Complete the menu below with suitable words from the box. Work with a partner.

cream   mushrooms   steamed   sauce   cheeses   fillet   peppers   raspberry   spinach   sliced
vinegar   garlic   tart   sponge   oysters   celery   grilled

MENU

Thinly .... tuna with ginger, lime and mayonnaise

.... mussels in white wine, ... and parsley

Ravioli with wild ....

Sautéed chicken livers in a sherry .... dressing

Half a dozen fresh ....

Baked salmon on a bed of .... with new potatoes

.... sea bass with stir-fried broccoli

Breast of chicken in a wine .... with chopped carrot and ....

Roast .... of Angus beef with glazed shallots

Leg of lamb with chargrilled aubergines and red ....

Pear and almond .... with fresh ....

Lime or .... sorbet

Hot chocolate .... with chocolate sauce

Selection of unpasteurised ....

2. Divide into groups of four. Two of you are waiters, the other two are diners. The diners must give their orders to the waiters, but for each of the courses, they must try to add information, make a request, or ask for further information. For example:
Where do your oysters come from?
I'll have the fillet of beef medium-rare, please.
Could I have the hot chocolate sponge without the chocolate sauce?

Waiters must be prepared to invent suitable answers in each case. When you have finished, you can change groups, change roles and repeat the activity. (In addition, you can order an aperitif, wine, water or anything else you want.)

WORKSHEET 12

1. Find a suitable adverb on the right-hand side to complete each of the sentences on the left. Use all the adverbs once only. Work with a partner.

1. They shook hands ....   a. immediately

2. At the end of the match the crowd left ....   b. closely

3. She complained .... about her experience.   c. politely

4. They strolled .... past the house.   d. gracefully

5. He struggled .... against his illness.   e. soundly

6. The police will watch him .... from now on.   f. aggressively

7. They danced so ....; it was wonderful.   g. casually

8. We slept .... in spite of the storm.   h. bravely

9. I always clean the flat .... at the weekend.   i. bitterly

10. I'm beginning to worry because he plays so .... with other children.   j. thoroughly

2. Now can you think of other words or phrases that could be used to complete the sentences above? They can be synonyms of the adverbs you have already used, or words with a completely different meaning, but they must be logical. Work with a partner, then compare your answers with another pair.

TRUE TO LIFE UPPER-INTERMEDIATE   © Cambridge University Press 1998

WORKSHEET 13

1. Put the following in the most logical order.

She was promoted.   ☐

She had an interview.   ☐

The company started losing business.   ☐

She applied for the job.   ☐

She was made redundant.   ☐

She saw the advertisement for the job in a national newspaper.   ☐

She was offered the job.   ☐

The company decided it would have to make cutbacks.   ☐

She accepted the job.   ☐

She was shortlisted for the job.   ☐

She did very well.   ☐

2. Find the pairs of similar jobs (or ways of making a living) in the box.

> doctor designer builder surgeon solicitor playwright accountant barrister teacher
> sculptor novelist bricklayer architect lecturer artist economist

For each pair of jobs, can you explain how they are different? Use a dictionary to help you, if necessary.

TRUE TO LIFE UPPER-INTERMEDIATE   © Cambridge University Press 1998

WORKSHEET 14

1. Here are some more accounts of accidents, as produced by drivers for their insurance companies. Read them, and then decide, with a partner, why each account is illogical or absurd.

```
An invisible car came from nowhere,        The other car collided with mine without
struck my car and vanished.                giving any warning of its intention.

I collided with a stationary lorry         To avoid crashing into the car in front,
coming the other way.                      I struck the pedestrian.

The guy was all over the road. I had to    I saw a slow-moving, sad-faced gentleman
swerve a number of times before I hit him. as he bounced off the roof of my car.
```

From The Bloomsbury Guide to Letter Writing

2. Work with another pair. Take it in turns to explain why each account is illogical or absurd.

TRUE TO LIFE UPPER-INTERMEDIATE   © Cambridge University Press 1998

WORKSHEET 15

1. Work with a partner. Confirm the information in each of these questions without repeating the underlined word or phrase, as in the example.

Example: A: Were the streets <u>completely empty</u>?
　　　　　 B: Yes, they were *deserted* .

1. A: Was he really <u>unwilling</u> to help?

   B: Yes, he was very ....

2. A: Did they manage to <u>rescue</u> the boys who were trapped?

   B: Yes, they ....

3. A: Do you always buy <u>in bulk</u>?

   B: Yes, we usually buy ....

4. A: Will they give me a <u>reduction</u> if I buy more than one?

   B: Yes, you should get ....

5. A: He just jumped in after her <u>without thinking</u>?

   B: Yes, he did it ....

6. A: Did she <u>say she was sorry</u>?

   B: Yes, she was very ....

7. A: Did the lesson <u>go down well</u>?

   B: Yes, it was ....

8. A: Didn't he <u>take the trouble</u> to ask her?

   B: No, he didn't ....

9. A: You mean it <u>didn't occur to him</u> that the shops would be closed?

   B: No, it never ....

Compare your answers with another pair, then with your teacher.

2. Now practise the dialogues with a different partner. Take it in turns to read the questions, and see if your partner can respond accurately without looking at the answers in their book.

TRUE TO LIFE UPPER-INTERMEDIATE   © Cambridge University Press 1998

WORKSHEET 16

Do attitudes change?

1. Read through the situations in the list. How would you react in each one? What would you do, say or think? Discuss in small groups and make a note of your answers.

1. Someone next to you in a public park is playing a radio and it is very loud.
2. You are walking along the street and a man spits into the gutter right in front of you.
3. You are in the cinema and there are two women in the row behind you who keep talking.
4. You are walking along the street and a dog owner allows his dog to foul the pavement. He makes no effort to stop the dog or pick up the mess.
5. You are on a bus and a young couple next to you start kissing each other quite passionately.
6. A middle-aged man lights a cigarette in a non-smoking compartment of a train.
7. You are sitting on a bus and a young mother next to you starts hitting her young son in order to stop him shouting.
8. While you are having a meal in a restaurant, the man at the table next to you keeps receiving calls on his mobile phone.

2. Now think back to ten years ago. Look at the situations again. Would you have reacted differently? If so, is that because you have changed, or is it because attitudes in society have changed?

3. Are there some things that *never* change, or can you think of other attitudes or customs that have changed in the last few years?

Exchange opinions in groups, using the topics in the box as a starting point.

bringing up children   eating habits   shopping habits   religious festivals   letter writing politeness: thanking, greeting, apologising, etc.   wearing particular clothes for certain occasions attitudes to money   education

Example: *Where I come from, things have changed a lot about bringing up children. For instance, parents let their children stay out much later than when I was a child.*

TRUE TO LIFE UPPER-INTERMEDIATE © Cambridge University Press 1998

WORKSHEET 17

1. With a partner, look at the words in the box and check that you remember what they mean.

> to cheat   to respect someone   to sponsor someone   to swear   to give a lecture   to put on a play
> to be involved in an accident   to support a charity   to make a donation   to be rude   to raise funds
> to attend a ceremony   to enter a competition   to be tidy/untidy   to be mad about something

You are going to interview other members of the group. With your partner, make up at least six questions using the words and phrases in the box.

Examples: *Have you ever been rude to someone and regretted it later?*
What do you think of people who cheat in exams?
When did you last attend a ceremony, and what was it like?

Find two new people to interview. They should speak for as long as possible about each question.

Go back and tell your original partner what you learnt.

TRUE TO LIFE UPPER-INTERMEDIATE   © Cambridge University Press 1998

WORKSHEET 18A

I'm afraid I can't ...

Using the future simple, future continuous or future perfect, think of a suitable negative response to the requests below. Try to use a range of different verbs in your answer.

Example: *Could you speak to them at five o'clock?*
    No, I'm sorry, I'll be driving back to the airport by then.
    or
    No, I'm sorry, I'll be on my way to the airport by then.
    or
    No, I'm sorry, I'll have left by then.

1. Could you give me a hand tomorrow afternoon?

....

2. Shall I give you a ring about 8 o'clock?

....

3. Can you start the new project next month?

....

4. Will you be free tomorrow evening?

....

5. When you're in Spain will you be able to visit that company in Seville?

....

Practise the situations with a partner and bring each one to a logical conclusion.

TRUE TO LIFE UPPER-INTERMEDIATE   © Cambridge University Press 1998

I don't like ironing.

KEEN

Answer: I'm not very keen on ironing.

I think it's going to rain.

LOOKS

Answer: It looks as if it's going to rain.

The wedding has been cancelled.

CALLED

Answer: The wedding has been called off.

Is his work related to insurance?
DO
Answer: Is his work to do with insurance?
or
Has his work got anything to do with insurance?

He's reluctant to go to the ceremony.

WILLING

Answer: He isn't willing to go to the ceremony.

She hasn't been there for ten years.

SINCE

Answer: She hasn't been there since (1988, 1989, etc.)

I'm sorry I didn't see Paul last night.

WISH

Answer: I wish I had seen Paul last night.

I find his attitude irritating.

ANNOYS

Answer: His attitude annoys me.

My grandparents would give me sweets every Saturday.
USED
Answer: My grandparents used to give me sweets every Saturday.

Although it was noisy, I slept quite well.

IN SPITE OF

Answer: In spite of the noise, I slept quite well.

They made us stay there till midnight.

FORCED

Answer: They forced us to stay there till midnight.

They rejected my offer.

TURNED

Answer: They turned my offer down. / They turned down my offer.

Most people in the group voted for Simon.

MAJORITY

Answer: The majority (of people in the group) voted for Simon.

Could you possibly open the window?

MIND

Answer: Would you mind opening the window?

I'm against capital punishment.

OPPOSED

Answer: I'm opposed to capital punishment.

Do you happen to know where he lives?

IDEA

Answer: Have you any idea where he lives?

TRUE TO LIFE UPPER-INTERMEDIATE © Cambridge University Press 1998

I support longer prison sentences for robbery.

IN FAVOUR

Answer: I'm in favour of longer prison sentences for robbery.

The trip was so successful we repeated it.

SUCH

Answer: It was such a successful trip that we repeated it.

She said she was sorry that she was so late.

APOLOGISED

Answer: She apologised for being so late.

Do I have to wear a uniform in this job?

COMPULSORY

Answer: Is a uniform compulsory in this job?

I agree with them to a large extent.

TEND

Answer: I tend to agree with them.

He didn't know anything about the changes.

AWARE

Answer: He wasn't aware of the changes.

They can't come this evening.

MAKE

Answer: They can't make it this evening.

John and I have never done anything illegal.
NEITHER
Answer: Neither of us has/have ever done anything illegal.
or
Neither John nor I have ever done anything illegal.

I sure he overslept.

MUST

Answer: He must have overslept.

He got stuck in terrible traffic.

HELD

Answer: He got held up in terrible traffic.

The jacket looks good with the trousers.

GOES

Answer: The jacket goes well with the trousers.

I came here in order to improve my English.

SO THAT

Answer: I came here so that I could improve my English.

He's unlikely to come now.

DOUBT

Answer: I doubt if he'll come now.

You should forget about her.

OUGHT

Answer: You ought to forget about her.

Thinking I would be late, I took a taxi.

BECAUSE

Answer: Because I thought I would be late, I took a taxi.

He's sleeping soundly.

FAST

Answer: He's fast asleep.

TRUE TO LIFE UPPER-INTERMEDIATE   © Cambridge University Press 1998

TESTS

TEST 1 UNITS 1–5

1 Sleep vocabulary   8 marks
Fill the gaps with a single word.

1. I forgot to .... the alarm clock and I overslept.

2. I often have a short .... after lunch if I'm tired.

3. I sat down and .... asleep on the sofa.

4. My husband .... in his sleep and it often wakes me up.

5. If I don't have to get up, I often have a ....-in.

6. Don't wake the children; they're still .... asleep.

7. I used to suffer from ...., but now I sleep much better.

8. I was really tired and I slept like a ....

2 Present perfect simple vs. continuous   8 marks
Underline the correct verb form in brackets. If both forms are correct, underline both forms.

1. She (*has seen/has been seeing*) him three times this month.
2. He's exhausted because he (*has worked/has been working*).
3. I (*have lived/have been living*) here for almost a year.
4. Both men (*have drunk/have been drinking*) for hours.
5. How long (*have you known/have you been knowing*) him?
6. I (*have finished/have been finishing*) the living room, so I decided to start the kitchen.
7. Oh look, it (*has rained/has been raining*).
8. I (*have seen/have been seeing*) an osteopath about my back for a couple of months now, and I really feel it is doing me good.

3 Wordbuilding   8 marks
Complete the following tables.

Adjective	Noun	Adjective	Noun
poor	....	....	sincerity
corrupt	....	....	hypocrite
unemployed	....	....	comprehension
violent	....	....	passion

4 Grammar and vocabulary: transformations   10 marks
Rewrite each sentence, using the word underneath in bold and keeping the meaning the same.

1. Most people don't know about it.
   aware

   ....

2. That girl looks like my sister.
   remind

   ....

3. Do you work with people in your job?
   involve

   ....

4. The music was so loud that I couldn't work.
   such

   ....

5. I'm sorry I didn't go.
   wish

   ....

6. I'm afraid I got held up in the traffic.
   stuck

   ....

7. Is the answer connected to transport?
   do

   ....

8. We both disliked the film.
   neither

   ....

9. She can't still be there.
   must

   ....

10. I slept quite well in spite of the noise.
    although

    ....

5 Compound adjectives   10 marks
A Match a word from the left with a word from the right to form five compound adjectives, then use them to complete the phrases below.

short polo shoulder high tight	heeled length sleeved fitting neck

.... shirt	.... hair		
.... shoes	.... sweater		
.... skirt			

B For each word on the left find an opposite on the right.

slim clean–shaven straight tight smart	curly scruffy a beard overweight baggy

6 *Vocabulary and paraphrase*   8 marks

1. It means to take no ....

   Answer: ignore someone

2. It's an illness in which it is difficult to breathe.

   Answer: ....

3. It's what people sometimes suffer from the morning after they drink too much.

   Answer: ....

4. It's when you look at someone or something for a long time with a fixed look.

   Answer: to ....

5. It means you ....

   Answer: blind

6. It's the lines that appear on your face as you get older.

   Answer: ....

7. It's what we call a picture you paint of yourself.

   Answer: a ....

8. Likely to make someone believe something that
   ....

   Answer: misleading

7 *Past simple, past perfect simple and continuous*   8 marks
Underline the correct answer in brackets.

1. When I (*arrived/had arrived*), they (*had painted/had been painting*) for hours.
2. They (*had never visited/had never been visiting*) the museum until they (*went/had gone*) there last week.
3. I (*had looked/had been looking*) for an antique wardrobe for months and then suddenly I (*found/had found*) two within the space of days.
4. When I first (*saw/had seen*) the building, it (*wasn't lived in/hadn't been lived in*) for years.

8 *Common expressions and word partnerships*   8 marks
Complete each sentence with a suitable word.

1. Pollution affects everyone to some ....

2. Law and order is by .... the most important issue.

3. A: What's the answer?

   B: I'm sorry, I haven't the .... idea.

4. I think she got the wrong end of the ....

5. I'm busy, so I won't be able to .... it to the party tomorrow evening.

6. If you see the rest of the class, give them my

   ....

7. She said she'd help, so I was angry when she .... me down.

8. She lives .... the outskirts of Geneva.

9 *Verbs and verb patterns*   6 marks
Choose the best verb to complete each sentence.

1. She .... me but I didn't listen to her.
   a) said   b) ignored   c) warned

2. The referee .... in order to stop the players fighting.
   a) intervened   b) interrupted   c) interfered

3. He .... to hit the younger boys.
   a) promised   b) threatened   c) warned

4. He was .... her, so she told him to go away.
   a) chatting   b) protecting   c) pestering

5. She called you June, so she must've .... your name.
   a) misheard   b) misinterpreted   c) misunderstood

6. The wedding has been ....
   a) turned off   b) called off   c) given up

10 *Writing*   8 marks
On each line of the following letter there is either one word missing or one word too many. If a word is missing, write it at the end of the line and put an arrow to show where it goes (as in the first example); if there is a word too many, put a line through it.

Dear Bob   ↓
I'm just writing to thank you a lovely party   *for*

last week. It was great see you, and we were   ....

very delighted to hear about the new house;   ....

what a fantastic news! As you know, Mary went   ....

into the hospital for a minor operation yesterday, ...

but she came this morning and seems fine despite   ....

of the plaster and bandages. I'll be in touch as   ....

soon as I will get back from Germany, and we   ....

both look forward seeing you after Easter. Until then,
Best wishes

11 Compound nouns and word partnerships   10 marks

Match a word from the left with a word from the right to form ten compound nouns or common word partnerships.

public drug cosmetic jet built-up youth taxi pedestrian shopping snack	hostel precinct bar rank abuse transport lag area centre surgery

12 Types of noun   8 marks

Replace the underlined phrases with a single word. (Include the definite article *the* as well if it is necessary.)

1. There is no access for <u>people in wheelchairs</u>.

   ....

2. We need more houses for <u>people with nowhere to live</u>.

   ....

3. What happened to the <u>people who were hurt</u>?

   ....

4. There is free transport for <u>people over 65</u>.

   ....

5. <u>Everyone in the hall</u> stood up and clapped.

   ....

6. There's a small branch here, but the <u>main offices</u> are in Oslo.

   ....

7. The <u>pool, squash court, gymnasium and cloakrooms</u> are all excellent.

   ....

8. The judge then addressed the <u>twelve men and women</u>.

   ....

Total = 100 marks

1 Tense review   8 marks

Underline the correct verb form in brackets.

1. I (*ring/will ring*) you when I (*get/will get*) back.
2. I expect I (*see/will see*) you later.
3. I (*will arrive/will be arriving*) late, so don't bother to cook a meal for me.
4. I (*stay/am staying*) near you, so it should be easy to meet up.
5. It (*rains/is raining*) constantly at this time of the year.
6. When I went out I suddenly realised I (*left/had left*) my wallet on the counter.
7. I (*lived/have lived*) here for three years and I still love it.

2 Wordbuilding   10 marks

Complete each sentence with the correct form of the word underneath.

1. It's a very .... issue.
   CONTROVERSY
2. He was killed in .... circumstances.
   MYSTERY
3. Who did you vote for in the ....?
   ELECT
4. She's a very powerful ....
   POLITICS
5. It's part of their .... policy.
   ECONOMY
6. Some crimes have increased ....
   DRAMA
7. Did she sign the ....?
   CONFESS
8. I thought it was a .... ending.
   SATISFACTION
9. Is it ever .... to kill someone?
   JUSTIFY
10. You may need to .... the plot.
    SIMPLE

3 Phrasal verbs   10 marks

Complete the sentences below with a verb from the left and a particle from the right. (Remember to put the verbs into the correct form.)

see pick throw sort tell end give calm bring work	out off down up

1. I .... him .... at the airport, then took him to his hotel.

2. She'll have to .... this mess; nobody else can.

3. I tried to .... her ...., but she was so nervous.

4. She .... a career in journalism in order to .... her children.

But now they're grown up, she would like to go back to journalism.

5. I .... the boys .... for being stupid and making too much noise, but they took no notice so in the end we had to .... them ....

6. We went to a number of places and finally .... in a little bar by the harbour.

7. She stayed with me for over a month so I wanted to go to the airport to .... her ....

8. I haven't .... how I am going to organise the new department yet.

4 Synonyms   10 marks

Replace the underlined words in these sentences with a single word that has the same meaning.

1. I find it very <u>irritating</u>.

   ....

2. He was <u>unwilling</u> to help, actually.

   ....

3. It's <u>high</u> time they did something about it.

   ....

4. It was hard work but <u>in the end</u> they got there.

   ....

5. The <u>present</u> situation is very difficult.

   ....

6. I haven't seen them <u>recently</u>.

   ....

7. I was talking to his <u>ex-</u>wife.

   ....

8. The people behind us talked <u>for the whole of</u> the film.

   ....

9. Blue <u>looks good on</u> you.

   ....

10. When you buy an item of clothing, do you buy other items to <u>go with</u> it?

    ....

5 Clothes, patterns and materials   8 marks

For pictures 1–3, identify the item of clothing and the pattern; for 4–8 identify the item of clothing and the material.

1. ....

2. ....

3. ....

4. ....

5. ....

6. ....

7. ....

8. ....

6 Gerund or infinitive?   6 marks

Underline the correct verb form in brackets.

1. I thought it was a waste of time (*to do/doing*) that course.
2. He wants to know if it's worth (*to go/going*).
3. It's important (*to take/taking*) an umbrella.
4. It's pointless (*to try/trying*) to get tickets.
5. Would you be willing (*to vote/voting*) for me?
6. I spend too much time (*to answer/answering*) letters.

7 Verb + noun collocation   10 marks

Match the verbs on the left with the best noun or phrase on the right.

1. start up		a. a job
2. come up with		b. a deadline
3. hand round		c. research
4. tip		d. charges
5. lie down		e. a conversation
6. confirm		f. the waiter
7. do		g. an idea
8. give up		h. on the bed
9. press		i. the booking
10. meet		j. the food

8 Uses of would(n't)   4 marks

Replace *would(n't)* in the first two sentences with a word or phrase with the same meaning; and explain the use of *would* in sentences 3 and 4.

1. When I was younger my parents *would* take us on long walks by the sea.

2. I pushed as hard as I could but the door *wouldn't* open.

3. He said he would ring me.

   Would here is used ....

4. If I had the answers, I *would* tell you.

   Would here is used ....

9 Expressions and word partnerships   10 marks

Fill the gaps with a single word to complete the expressions and word partnerships in bold.

1. **I would be** .... **if you could** return the books to me before the end of the week.

2. This flat is fine .... **the time being**.

3. Can you .... **the difference between** butter and margarine?

4. We **are** .... **to arrive** at midnight, but there is sometimes a delay on this flight.

5. We must take action quickly otherwise the situation could **get out of** ....

6. I think that jacket will .... **well with** your blue trousers.

7. **The** .... **that annoys me is** when people leave lights on.

8. It takes a bit of time **to get into the** .... **of** using dental floss regularly.

9. He's not very good .... **pressure**.

10. You'll have to **make up your** .... soon.

10 Crime vocabulary   8 marks

What word is being defined in each of these?

1. The crime of stealing money from a shop

   ....

2. Giving someone money in return for favours

   ....

3. Money you may have to pay if you commit a minor offence

   ....

4. A person who sees a crime

   ....

5. The crime of driving faster than the legal limit

   ....

6. Obtaining money from someone illegally by clever and complicated methods

   ....

7. Obtaining money from someone by threatening to reveal secrets about them

   ....

8. A substance that can cause death or serious illness if you eat it or drink it

   ....

11 Prepositions   10 marks

Fill the gaps with the correct preposition.

1. What can you see .... the foreground?

2. I'll be .... work .... 5 o'clock; then I'm going for a drink.

3. What is he wearing .... his neck?

4. There was a woman .... a white dress.

5. They were sitting .... the front row.

6. Quite a lot of men suffer .... colour blindness.

7. She worked there .... three years.

8. He was charged .... murder.

9. She was convicted .... manslaughter.

12 Link words and phrases   6 marks

Complete the sentences below with words or phrases from the box.

> surprisingly though   to be honest   naturally
> for instance   in actual fact   luckily

1. I thought it would be expensive, but .... it didn't cost much at all.

2. We didn't know where we were, and it was starting to get dark, so .... we were a bit worried.

3. If you want to buy children's toys, ... dolls, teddy bears or computer games, it is quite expensive.

4. Most of the group enjoyed it, but .... I thought it was too big and far too commercial.

5. I didn't understand a word she said but .... I had my dictionary with me.

6. I didn't do much work and it was a very difficult exam; ...., I passed easily.

Total = 100 marks

1 Pronunciation   8 marks

Look at the underlined letters in the following pairs of words. Is the pronunciation the same or different?

1. pr<u>aw</u>ns   s<u>a</u>lmon
2. p<u>ie</u>   re<u>ci</u>pe
3. p<u>a</u>rsley   r<u>a</u>spberry
4. pot<u>a</u>toes   tom<u>a</u>toes
5. <u>c</u>elery   <u>c</u>ourgettes
6. spin<u>a</u>ch   lett<u>u</u>ce
7. c<u>o</u>llide   c<u>o</u>llapse
8. qui<u>z</u>   enti<u>t</u>led

2 Opposites   8 marks

Write down the opposites of the following.

still water	.... water
a light dessert	a .... dessert
fresh bread	.... bread
sweet apples	.... apples
tough meat	.... meat
bland food	.... food
a slight accent	a .... accent
pick up an accent	.... an accent

3 Verb patterns   10 marks

Rewrite these sentences, starting with the verbs given, and without changing the meaning.

1. I won't do it.

   She refused ....

2. Go on, have a try.

   She persuaded ....

3. He's sorry he didn't finish his degree.

   He regrets not ....

4. You took my pen.

   She accused me ....

5. I didn't take it.

   I denied ....

6. It was kind of you to help me.

   He thanked me ....

7. It's your fault we got lost.

   She blamed me ....

8. I'll send you all home.

   She threatened ....

9. Please don't go.

   He begged me ....

10. Why don't we send him a present?

    She suggested ....

4 Food and cooking vocabulary   10 marks

Label the vegetables on the left and the verbs on the right.

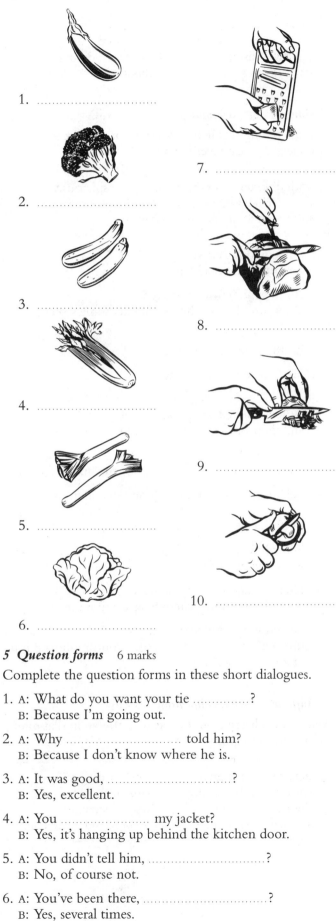

1. ....

2. ....

3. ....

4. ....

5. ....

6. ....

7. ....

8. ....

9. ....

10. ....

5 Question forms   6 marks

Complete the question forms in these short dialogues.

1. A: What do you want your tie ....?
   B: Because I'm going out.

2. A: Why .... told him?
   B: Because I don't know where he is.

3. A: It was good, ...?
   B: Yes, excellent.

4. A: You .... my jacket?
   B: Yes, it's hanging up behind the kitchen door.

5. A: You didn't tell him, ...?
   B: No, of course not.

6. A: You've been there, ...?
   B: Yes, several times.

6 Synonyms 8 marks

Find a synonym in the right-hand box for each of the words in the left-hand box.

dreary adventurous smart row vanish clumsy dismissed back	elegant dull sacked awkward argument reverse daring disappear

7 Adverbs and adverbial phrases 10 marks

Choose the most suitable adverb from the box to complete the sentences below.

with difficulty enthusiastically suspiciously fast irritably in a puzzled way gloomily softly in a silly voice nervously

1. She couldn't run very .... because of her bad leg.

2. All the children volunteered .... when I told them they would get some sweets.

3. He sat down .... in front of his three examiners.

4. He looked out of the window .... when he saw the rain.

5. When I smiled she looked at me ...., and then I realised that she hadn't recognised me.

6. After the operation on his throat, he could only speak .... for the first few weeks.

7. When she comes on the phone she often speaks .... I don't know if it's a joke or if it's her normal way of speaking.

8. She whispered .... in my ear, so no one would hear.

9. He looked at me very .... when I asked him where he kept his money.

10. He answered the phone very ...., then explained that this was the fourth interruption in less than half an hour.

8 Adjective + noun collocation 8 marks

Match the adjective on the left with the noun that often follows it on the right.

deprived disruptive abusive embarrassing physical swollen complete scrambled	egg situation violence behaviour ankle stranger background language

9 Medical vocabulary 8 marks

Fill the gaps with a suitable word.

1. The pain was terrible when I broke my leg. I was in ....

2. I bumped into the table and now I have a large blue .... on my left leg.

3. They told him to use the oxygen mask if he had .... difficulties.

4. The girl needed surgery fast, so they rushed her to the operating ....

5. There was very little in the first aid ....

6. She landed on her head and doctors fear she may have a fractured ....

7. She knew nothing about it because they gave her a general .... before the operation.

8. She had a broken leg and fractured ribs, but their main concern was the danger of internal ....

10 Obligation, prohibition, permission 8 marks

Rewrite these sentences using the word given, and keep the meaning the same.

1. I have to finish by the end of the week.
   got
   ....

2. We should get there soon.
   ought
   ....

3. Can we go into the other room?
   allowed
   ....

4. They made us stay outside.
   forced
   ....

5. You have a right to see your files.
   entitled
   ....

6. You mustn't smoke in there.
   allowed
   ....

7. You have to do military service.
   compulsory
   ....

8. It isn't necessary to stay there.
   have to
   ....

11 Prepositions and particles   10 marks

Fill the gaps with the correct preposition or adverbial particle.

1. She leapt .... the fence.

2. I bumped .... the table.

3. She didn't turn .... for the meeting.

4. I tripped .... running for the bus.

5. I'm afraid I left the electricity ....

6. I collided .... a van coming .... the opposite direction.

7. I fell down and now I'm covered .... bruises.

8. Journalists are always prying .... the private lives of famous people.

9. Business is bad and quite a few people have been laid ....

10. I quickly glanced .... my watch.

12 Expressions   6 marks

Complete the phrase or expression in bold with the correct word.

1. He never stops talking and it's really beginning to **get on my** ....

2. I told him I would **give him a** .... to the station.

3. He's putting on a lot of weight. If he's not careful, he'll need to **go on a** ....

4. When I picked her up she was **light as a** ....

5. I think he **feels** .... **about** the others doing all his work while he does nothing.

6. I **was** .... **to** leave when the phone rang.

Total = 100 marks

1 Number and quantity   8 marks

Complete each sentence with a word from the box. (You don't need all of them.)

> slight   a handful   huge   very   fairly   hardly
> vast   almost   little   quite   few

1. It was great because .... everyone turned up.

2. The .... majority voted against the new proposal.

3. The decision will make very .... difference.

4. .... anyone came to the barbecue.

5. There's only a .... difference between the biggest and the smallest.

6. .... a few people left early.

7. Only .... turned up, so it was disappointing.

8. They had very .... books in the library.

2 Legal and financial vocabulary   8 marks

Match the verbs on the left with the best noun or phrase on the right.

1. settle	a. a charity
2. award	b. a verdict
3. reach	c. for libel
4. sue someone	d. someone's reputation
5. raise	e. damages
6. support	f. in bulk
7. ruin	g. a dispute
8. buy	h. funds

3 Transformations: grammar and vocabulary   10 marks

Rewrite each sentence using the word in capitals underneath, and without changing the meaning.

1. I think military service is a good idea.
   FAVOUR

   ....

2. He's against the new policy.
   OPPOSED

   ....

3. I partly agree with them.
   EXTENT

   ....

4. Generally speaking, we work most weekends.
   TEND

   ....

5. She's done very well when you consider her age.
   GIVEN

   ....

6. Have you any idea where the bank is?
   HAPPEN

   ....

7. Drug taking is on the increase.
   WIDESPREAD

   ....

8. I don't think that's true.
   DOUBT

   ....

9. Would you prefer to stay in?
   RATHER

   ....

10. I lost because I didn't do enough training.
    IF

    ....

4 Wordbuilding   10 marks

Complete each sentence with the correct form of the word underneath.

1. All the staff were very ....
   COURTESY
2. A nation needs an army for its own self- ....
   DEFEND
3. Did he give you an .... ?
   APOLOGISE
4. The company has always been ....
   COMPETE
5. He thinks guns are an effective ....
   DETER
6. I think government .... is the answer.
   SPONSOR
7. I'm sure it was a ....
   THREATEN
8. The army is well-...........................
   EQUIPMENT
9. The scheme is ....
   VOLUNTEER
10. Do they want total ....?
    ABOLISH

5 Conditional sentences   6 marks

Write six different conditional sentences using only words from the box. You can use each word in more than one sentence.

had(n't) work(ed) do hard done if I
even would(n't) well I have will

1. ....
2. ....
3. ....
4. ....
5. ....
6. ....

6 Writing   8 marks

One word is missing from each line of this text. Write it in the space at the end of the line and indicate where it should go on the line.

The aim of the organisation is raise standards   ....

throughout the profession. The idea first put   ....

forward the annual conference three years ago, ...

and then there has been widespread support   ....

for it. We are now looking a guest speaker for   ....

this year's annual conference and we wondering   ....

if you like to give a short talk in support of the   ....

new scheme. We be delighted if you were able to   ....

do it, and we hope that ...

7 Mixed functions   8 marks

Complete these dialogues with a single word in each gap.

1. A: Why on .... are you giving so much money away?
   B: Because I feel like it.

2. A: Would you .... shutting the window?
   B: Sure. No problem.

3. A: I'd be very .... if you could send it to me.
   B: Of course. When do you need it?

4. A: Have you any .... where it is?
   B: No, I'm afraid ....

5. A: Do you know the time of the next train?
   B: No, I'm sorry, I haven't a ....

6. A: Why did you upset her like that?
   B: I'm really sorry. I didn't .... to, but I just said the wrong thing at the wrong time.

7. A: Could you finish the report this afternoon?
   B: I don't know, but I'll do my ....

8 Definitions 8 marks

What word is being defined in each?

1. The name for the holiday that couples go on directly after their wedding ....

2. The place where pedestrians walk ....

3. The piece of paper you receive as proof that you have paid for something ....

4. The name for a vehicle that is so badly damaged it is beyond repair ....

5. Something, usually money, that you give to an organisation or charity in order to help them

....

6. A word used to describe any famous person, but especially someone in the entertainment business

....

7. To use bad language, especially because you are angry

....

8. To behave in a dishonest way, especially to gain an advantage over others in a game or examination

....

9 Compound nouns and word partnerships 10 marks

Match a word from the left with the most suitable word from the right to form ten nouns or common word partnerships.

1. rubbish	a. training
2. mobile	b. warden
3. basic	c. worker
4. nervous	d. ceremony
5. social	e. bin
6. wedding	f. breakdown
7. traffic	g. food
8. market	h. agent
9. travel	i. phone
10. organic	j. stall

10 Tense review 8 marks

Put the verb in brackets into the correct tense and write your answer in the space under each sentence.

1. I (have) dinner when you get back, so don't ring me until after eight.

....

2. Don't ring him at the office at five o'clock – he probably (go) home by then.

....

3. Do you think you (live) in the same town in five years' time?

....

4. We (know) the results by tomorrow.

....

5. I (work) in New York in a week's time, so things (be) very different then.

....

6. We probably (leave) as soon as you get back.

....

7. In a year's time I think I (lose touch) with some of the people in my group.

....

11 Common word partnerships 10 marks

Fill the gaps with a suitable word which forms a strong collocation with the word or words in bold. (There may be more than one correct answer.)

1. Have you ever .... **a crime**?
2. Why did the company .... **bankrupt**?

3. They no longer .... **experiments** on certain animals.

4. That sounds **highly** ...., if you ask me.

5. It's your turn. Come on, ... **the dice**.

6. A: **What are the** .... **of** finishing by 6 o'clock?

   B: Quite good, I'd say.

7. She **left the door** .... **open** – anyone could've walked in.

8. I **look** .... **to hearing from you**.

9. Sadly, unemployment is still **on the** ....

10. I'm afraid there are no **buses** .... after midnight.

12 General grammar 6 marks

Expand the notes below into complete and grammatically correct sentences. You will need to form correct tenses, and add prepositions, articles, pronouns and appropriate link words. (Half a mark for each correct answer.)

Three people/injured/an accident/the rushhour this morning. One man/taken/hospital/he/given emergency surgery. Doctors said his condition/now stable/still remained critical. They planned/issue/further bulletin/the morning.

Total = 100 marks

TEST ANSWER KEYS

1 Sleep vocabulary

1. set   2. nap   3. fell   4. snores/talks   5. lie   6. fast
7. insomnia   8. log

2 Present perfect simple vs. continuous

1. has seen   2. has been working   3. both are possible
4. have been drinking   5. have you known   6. have
finished   7. has been raining   8. have been seeing

3 Wordbuilding

Noun	Adjective
poverty	sincere
corruption	hypocritical
unemployment	comprehensible
violence	passionate

4   Grammar and vocabulary: transformations

1. Most people are not aware of it.
2. That girl reminds me of my sister.
3. Does your job involve working with people?
4. It was such loud music that I couldn't work.
5. I wish I had gone.
6. I'm afraid I got stuck in the traffic.
7. Is the answer to do with transport?
8. Neither of us liked the film.
9. She must've gone.
10. Although it was noisy I slept quite well.

5 Compound adjectives

A
short-sleeved shirt   shoulder-length hair   high-heeled
shoes   polo-neck sweater   tight-fitting skirt

B
slim – overweight; clean-shaven – a beard; straight –
curly; tight – baggy; smart – scruffy

6 Vocabulary and paraphrase

1. notice of someone
2. asthma
3. a hangover
4. stare
5. cannot see
6. wrinkles
7. self-portrait
8. isn't true

7 Past simple, past perfect simple and continuous

1. arrived; had been painting
2. had never visited; went
3. had been looking; found
4. saw; hadn't been lived in

8 Common expressions and word partnerships

1. to some extent   2. by far   3. haven't the faintest idea
4. got the wrong end of the stick   5. make it
6. give them my regards (or love)   7. let me down
8. on the outskirts of

9 Verbs and verb patterns

1. c   2. a   3. b   4. c   5. a   6. b

10 Writing

Example: thank you <u>for</u> a
line 2: great <u>to</u> see
line 3: omit *very*
line 4: omit *a*
line 5: omit *the*
line 6: came <u>back</u> this
line 7: omit *of*
line 8: omit *will*
line 9: forward <u>to</u> seeing

11 Compound nouns and word partnerships

public transport   drug abuse   cosmetic surgery
jet lag   built-up area   youth hostel   taxi rank
pedestrian precinct   shopping centre   snack bar

12 Types of noun

1. the disabled   2. the homeless   3. injured   4. the retired
5. the audience   6. headquarters   7. facilities   8. jury

1 Tense review

1. will ring; get   2. will see   3. will be arriving
4. am staying   5. rains   6. had left   7. have lived

2 Wordbuilding

1. controversial   2. mysterious   3. election
4. politician   5. economic   6. dramatically
7. confession   8. satisfactory   9. justified/justifiable
10. simplify

3 Phrasal verbs

1. picked him up 2. sort out 3. calm her down
4. gave up; bring up 5. told the boys off; throw them
out 6. ended up 7. see her off   8. worked out

4 Synonyms

1. annoying 2. reluctant 3. about 4. eventually (also
finally) 5. current 6. lately 7. former
8. throughout 9. suits 10. match

5 Clothes, patterns and material

1. a checked shirt 2. a tartan tie 3. a plain white
blouse 4. denim/cotton jeans 5. corduroy trousers
6. a fur coat 7. a woollen sweater 8. a leather jacket

6 Gerund or infinitive?

1. doing 2. going 3. to take 4. trying 5. to vote
6. answering

7 Verb + noun collocation

1. start up a conversation 2. come up with an idea
3. hand round the food 4. tip the waiter 5. lie down
on the bed 6. confirm the booking 7. do research
8. give up a job 9. press charges 10. meet a deadline

8 Uses of would(n't)

1. used to 2. refused to 3. as the past of *will* in
reported speech 4. as part of a conditional sentence

9 Expressions and word partnerships

1. I would be grateful if you could 2. for the time
being 3. tell the difference between 4. are due to
arrive 5. get out of control 6. go well with 7. the
thing that annoys me is 8. to get into the habit of
9. under pressure 10. make up your mind

10 Crime vocabulary

1. shoplifting 2. bribery 3. a fine 4. a witness
5. speeding 6. fraud 7. blackmail 8. poison

11 Prepositions

1. in 2. at; until 3. round 4. in 5. in 6. from
7. for 8. with 9. of

12 Link words and phrases

1. in actual fact 2. naturally 3. for instance 4. to be
honest 5. luckily 6. surprisingly though

1 Pronunciation

1. different 2. different 3. same 4. different (same in
US English) 5. different 6. same 7. same
8. different

2 Opposites

1. fizzy 2. heavy 3. stale 4. sour 5. tender
6. tasty 7. strong 8. lose

3 Verb patterns

1. She refused to do it.
2. She persuaded him/her to have a try.
3. He regrets not finishing his degree.
4. She accused me of taking her pen.
5. I denied taking it.
6. He thanked me for helping him.
7. She blamed me for getting lost.
8. She threatened to send us all home.
9. He begged me not to go.
10. She suggested sending him a present. (or *that they
should send him a present* or *that they sent him a present*)

4 Food and cooking vocabulary

1 aubergine 2 broccoli 3 courgettes 4 celery
5 leeks 6 lettuce (or cabbage) 7 grate 8 carve
9 chop 10 peel

5 Question forms

1. for 2. haven't you 3. wasn't it 4. seen 5. did you
6. haven't you

6 Synonyms

dreary/dull
adventurous/daring
smart/elegant
row/argument
vanish/disappear
clumsy/awkward
dismissed/sacked
back/reverse

7 Adverbs and adverbial phrases

1. fast 2. enthusiastically 3. nervously 4. gloomily
5. in a puzzled way 6. with difficulty 7. in a silly
voice 8. softly 9. suspiciously 10. irritably

8 Adjective + noun collocation

deprived background
disruptive behaviour
abusive language
embarrassing situation
physical violence
swollen ankle
complete stranger
scrambled egg

9 Medical vocabulary

1. agony   2. bruise   3. breathing   4. theatre   5. kit
6. skull   7. anaesthetic   8. bleeding (*damage* would also be possible)

10 Obligation, prohibition, permission

1. I have got to finish by the end of the week.
2. We ought to get there soon.
3. Are we allowed to go into the other room?
4. They forced us to stay outside.
5. You are entitled to see your files.
6. You aren't allowed to smoke in there.
7. Military service is compulsory.
8. You don't have to stay there.

11 Prepositions and particles

1. over   2. into   3. up   4. over   5. on   6. with; in
7. in   8. into   9. off   10. at

12 Expressions

1. nerves   2. lift   3. diet   4. feather   5. guilty
6. about

TEST 4

1 Number and quantity

1. almost   2. vast   3. little   4. hardly   5. slight
6. quite   7. a handful   8. few

2 Legal and financial vocabulary

1. g   2. e   3. b   4. c   5. h   6. a   7. d   8. f

3 Transformations: grammar and vocabulary

1. I'm in favour of military service.
2. He's opposed to the new policy.
3. I agree with them to some extent.
4. We tend to work most weekends.
5. She's done very well given her age.
6. Do you happen to know where the bank is?
7. Drug taking is becoming more widespread.
8. I doubt if that's true.
9. Would you rather stay in?
10. If I had done more training, I wouldn't've lost / would've won.

4 Wordbuilding

1. courteous   2. defence   3. apology   4. competitive
5. deterrent   6. sponsorship   7. threat   8. equipped
9. voluntary   10. abolition

5 Conditional sentences

1. If I work hard, I will do well.
2. If I worked hard, I would do well.
3. Even if I worked hard, I wouldn't do well.
4. If I had worked hard, I would have done well.
5. If I hadn't worked hard, I wouldn't have done well.
6. Even if I had worked hard, I wouldn't have done well.

6 Writing

line 1: is to raise
line 2: idea was first
line 3: forward at the
line 4: and since then
line 5: looking for a
line 6: we were wondering
line 7: you would like
line 8: we would be

7 Mixed functions

1. earth   2. mind   3. grateful   4. idea; not   5. clue
6. mean   7. best

8 Definitions

1. honeymoon   2. pavement   3. receipt   4. a write-off
5. donation   6. celebrity   7. swear   8. cheat

9 Compound nouns and word partnerships

1. e   2. i   3. a   4. f   5. c   6. d   7. b   8. j   9. h
10. g

10 Tense review

1. will be having   2. will probably have gone   3. will be living   4. will know   5. will be working; will be
6. will probably leave (or *will probably be leaving*)   7. will have lost touch

11 Common word partnerships

1. committed   2. go   3. carry out/conduct/do
4. unlikely   5. throw   6. chances   7. wide   8. forward
9. increase   10. running (or *operating*)

12 General grammar

Three people were injured in an accident in/during the rushhour this morning. One man was taken to hospital where he was given emergency surgery. Doctors said his condition was/is now stable but still remained critical. They planned to issue a further bulletin in the morning.

ACKNOWLEDGEMENTS

Authors' acknowledgements

We would like to thank Joanne Collie and Stephen Slater for their original inspiration in the development of *True to Life*.

We are genuinely indebted to our friends and colleagues at International House, London, and the London School of English for their support and encouragement; and for specific feedback, ideas and activities we would like to thank: Frances Eales, Kristina Teasdale, Robin Wileman, Jane Hann, Mark Hind and Lin Coleman.

There are numerous authors whose work has influenced and inspired us, among them Michael Swan, Ros Aitken, Jill Hadfield, Andrew Littlejohn, Penny Ur, Mike McCarthy and Ruth Wajnryb.

At Cambridge University Press we would like to express our very sincere thanks to Kate Boyce for her immense commitment and excellent management of the project. We also wish to thank Helena Gomm, a consummate professional with a great sense of humour. We would also like to thank all those, past and present, who contributed to the design and production of the work.

Particular thanks go to Martin Williamson, who produced and shaped the listening material, and Andy Tayler, the staff at AVP and all the actors who shared their stories with us.

Finally, our thanks go to the commissioning editor, Peter Donovan, who set the project in motion, and to all the staff at CUP.

The authors and publishers would like to thank the following individuals and institutions for their help in testing the material and for the invaluable feedback which they provided:

Mary Anne Ansell; Tess Goodliffe; Gillian Lazar; Liz Munro; Silvia Rettaroli; Julia Sawyer, Australian International College of Language, Southport, Australia; Andrew Thomas, Sydney English Language Centre, Bondi Junction, Australia; Anikó Szilágyi, London Studio, Budapest, Hungary; Zsuzsa Vidra, Globus 2000, Budapest, Hungary; Maggie Baigent, British Council, Bologna, Italy; Carmel Fullam, Buckingham School, Rome, Italy; Ann Travers, Oxford institutes italiani, Vicenza, Italy; Guy Perring and Andrew Hill, Language Education Center, Hiroshima, Japan; James Boyd, ECC Gaigo Gakuin, Osaka, Japan; Jackie Halsal, Karya Yabanci Dil Kursu, Istanbul, Turkey; Bahar Darn, Dokuz Eylül University, Izmir, Turkey; Christopher Hart, Saxoncourt, London, UK; Robin Wileman, International House, London, UK.

The authors and publishers are grateful to the following copyright holders for permission to reproduce copyright material. While every endeavour has been made, it has not been possible to identify the sources of all material used and in such cases the publishers would welcome information from copyright sources. Apologies are expressed for any omissions.

p. 39: Newspaper Publishing plc for the recording based on the article 'Colour blindness' (*The Independent on Sunday*, 18 July 1993); p. 58: Scott Meredith Literary Agency, New York, on behalf of Fred Brown for the story 'Hobbyist' published in *Playboy Magazine*, 1961. Copyright © by HMH Publishing Corporation; pp. 67–9: Faber and Faber Ltd and Grove/Atlantic Inc for an extract from the play *A Night Out* by Harold Pinter, and Judy Daish Associates Ltd for the recording of Act 1, Scene 1 from the play; pp. 78–9: Newspaper Publishing plc for the recording based on the article 'Enough, Already' (*The Independent Magazine*, April 1996); pp. 94–5: University of Cambridge Local Examinations Syndicate for questions from past examination papers.

The authors and publishers are grateful to the following illustrators:
Kathy Baxendale: pp. 61, 133, 135; Hilary Evans (handwriting): p.116.

Design and production by Gecko Ltd, Bicester, Oxon.
Sound recordings by Martin Williamson, Prolingua Productions, at Studio AVP, London.